Banking and Financial Systems

Center for Financial Training

THOMSON
—★—™
SOUTH-WESTERN

Australia · Canada · Mexico · Singapore · Spain · United Kingdom · United States

THOMSON

SOUTH-WESTERN

Banking and Financial Systems
by Center for Financial Training

Vice President/
Executive Publisher
Dave Shaut

Team Leader
Karen Schmohe

Executive Editor
Eve Lewis

Project Manager
Enid Nagel

Production Manager
Patricia Matthews Boies

Production Editor
Todd McCoy

Executive Marketing Manager
Carol Volz

Channel Manager
Nancy A. Long

Marketing Coordinator
Yvonne Patton-Beard

Manufacturing Coordinator
Kevin Kluck

Design Project Manager
Tippy McIntosh

Cover Design
Paul Neff

Editorial Assistant
Linda Keith

Production Assistant
Nancy Stamper

Compositor
Argosy Publishing

Printer
Quebecor World
Dubuque, IA

About CFT

Center for Financial Training (CFT) is a network of more than 25 centers throughout the country that provide career-enhancing training solutions to the financial services industry. Through innovative educational formats, CFT is the training partner for financial institutions that helps improve performance to meet the needs of tomorrow's challenging business environment.

Copyright © 2003 South-Western, a division of Thomson Learning, Inc. Thomson Learning™ is a trademark used herein under license.

ISBN: 0-538-43241-1

Printed in the United States of America
2 3 4 5 6 07 06 05 04 03 02

ALL RIGHTS RESERVED. No part of this work covered by the copyright hereon may be reproduced or used in any form or by any means—graphic, electronic, or mechanical, including photocopying, recording, taping, Web distribution or information storage and retrieval systems—without the written permission of the publisher.

For permission to use material from this text or product, contact us by

Tel: 800-730-2214
Fax: 800-730-2215
Web: www.thomsonrights.com

For more information, contact South-Western, 5191 Natorp Boulevard, Mason, OH, 45040. Or you can visit our Internet site at www.swep.com.

International Divisions List

Asia (including India)
Thomson Learning
60 Albert Street, #15-01
Albert Complex
Singapore 189969
Tel 65 336-6411
Fax 65 336-7411

Australia/New Zealand
Nelson
102 Dobbs Street
South Melbourne
Victoria 3205
Australia
Tel 61 (0)3 9685-4111
Fax 61 (0)3 9685-4199

Canada
Nelson
1120 Birchmount Road
Toronto, Ontario
Canada M1K 5G4
Tel (416) 752-9100
Fax (416) 752-8102

Latin America
Thomson Learning
Seneca 53
Colonia Polanco
11560 Mexico, D.F. Mexico
Tel (525) 281-2906
Fax (525) 281-2656

Spain (including Portugal)
Paraninfo
Calle Magallanes 25
28015 Madrid
Espana
Tel 34 (0)91 446-3350
Fax 34 (0)91 445-6218

UK/Europe/Middle East/Africa
Thomson Learning
Berkshire House
168-173 High Holborn
London WC 1V 7AA
United Kingdom
Tel 44 (0)20 497-1422
Fax 44 (0)20 497-1426

YOUR COURSE PLANNING JUST GOT EASIER!

★ *Economic Education for Consumers*
by Miller and Stafford
Make your students "super-informed" consumers! This text has exciting features, engaging lessons, and multimedia ancillaries to help economic, consumer, and personal finance concepts come to life.

Student Text	0-538-68686-3
Student Workbook	0-538-68687-1
Data CD	0-538-68692-8
Interactive Study Guide CD	0-538-69302-9

Instructor Support Material Available

★ *NEW! Managing Your Personal Finances*
by Ryan
Discover new ways to maximize earning potential, develop strategies for managing resources, explore skills for the wise use of credit, and gain insight into the different ways of investing money. This text will inform your students of their financial responsibilities as citizens, students, family members, consumers, and active participants in the business world.

Student Text	0-538-69958-2
Student Activity Guide	0-538-69961-2
Planning Tools CD	0-538-43448-1
Data CD	0-538-69963-9

Instructor Support Material Available

★ *NEW! Fundamentals of Insurance*
by Crews
While opening the door for new career opportunities, this text will give your students a full understanding of health and property insurance, insurance rates, claims procedures, careers in insurance, and annuities. The extensive use of hands-on activities helps your students understand the importance of insurance and how it affects them today and through their retirement years.

Student Text	0-538-43201-2

Instructor Support Material Available

★ *Investing in Your Future*
by NAIC
This text and software package teaches how the stock market works and how sound principles of saving and investing focus on the long term. Every book comes with the Stock Selection Guide CD!

Student Text/CD Package	0-538-68607-3

Instructor Support Material Available

★ *NEW! Security First Bank*
by Sargent and Ward
This ever-popular simulation empowers students by providing a sound foundation in banking procedures from a consumer standpoint. Students learn by doing!

Simulation (one per student)	0-538-43187-3

Instructor Support Material Available

THOMSON
SOUTH-WESTERN

Join us on the Internet at www.swep.com

CONTENTS

REVIEWERS

Project Coordinator

Deborah S. Sefcik
Executive Director
Center for Financial Training
South Central States
Little Rock, AR

Banking Consultants

Phyllis Perry Brents
Bank Consultant
Little Rock, AR

David L. Conrad
President and CEO
The Citizens National Bank
Putnam, CT

Timothy W. Grooms
Attorney, Quattlebaum, Grooms, Tull
and Burrow PLLC
Little Rock, AR

Tiffany Guynes
Supervisor, Human Resources
Federal Reserve Bank of St. Louis
Little Rock, AR

Loyd Hoskins
Educational Consultant – Banking
Loyd Hoskins and Associates
Lakewood, CO

B. Mott Jones
First Tennessee Bank
Memphis, TN

Paul Keller
Asset Manager
Fleet National Bank
Buffalo, NY

Barbara T. Kriesel
Training Manager
First Community Credit Union
Houston, TX

L. Douglas LaPlante
Vice President
Sovereign Bank
Springfield, MA

Michael K. Meakem
President
CFT, Southern New England
Norwich, CT

Frantz Neptune
Human Resources Officer
Thomaston Savings Bank
Thomaston, CT

William L. Oliver, Jr.
Sr. Vice President
First National Bank
Paragould, AR

Barry W. Pearson
Sr. Vice President
Training Officer
Enterprise Bank and Trust Company
Lowell, MA

Lisa Phillips
Executive Director
CFT, Southeast Regional
Jacksonville, FL

David Ridley, Jr.
Executive Vice President & Cash
American Bank, N.A.
Waco, TX

Stephen G. San Paolo
President
Springfield Catholic Credit Unio
Springfield, MO

Kathy K. Smith
Executive Advisor
Education and Training
CFT, Western States
Denver, CO

Joyce Tyler
Vice President
Frost Bank
Houston, TX

Karen Vanderwerken
Executive Director
CFT, Texas
Fort Worth, TX

Educational Consultants

Michelle Brown
Little Rock, AR

Andrew B. Cole
Houston, TX

Patricia Deike
Riverside, CA

Cheryl A. Dunkley
Weatherford, TX

Crystal Force
Jacksonville, FL

Rhonda Hatter
Reston, VA

Margaret M. Hoffman
Inverness, FL

Tammy Mathews
Anderson, SC

Ronda M. Matthews
Gonzales, LA

Cynthia Maynard
Riverside, CA

Jeannie Moore
Conway, AR

Eileen Tims
Houston, TX

······HOW TO USE THIS BOOK ·········

ENGAGE STUDENT INTEREST

CAREERS IN BANKING
Highlights a real-world bank and the careers it offers to demonstrate various career possibilities.

······ Careers in Banking

THE ARLINGTON BANK

The Arlington Bank in Upper Arlington, Ohio, is an example of one new trend in banking. As competition and mergers among banks have created giant corporations, niche markets have opened for small banks specializing in customer service with a personal touch.

The Arlington Bank opened in 1999. Its six founders are all former employees of a thrift institution that had been acquired by a larger bank. The bank has 15 employees and assets of $95 million—tiny compared to the multi-state giants. The bank offers a full menu of checking and savings accounts and provides financing for a large share of local construction and remodeling projects. Using knowledge of the community, the Arlington Bank tailors its services to the needs of local people and businesses.

Employee compensation is competitive with larger banks in the area. Working in a small bank offers employees the opportunity to experience all facets of the banking business, rather than having to specialize in one area or skill. Such an environment allows people to stay connected to each other and the community.

THINK CRITICALLY

1. Why might small banks have an advantage in certain markets?
2. What would be some of the advantages and disadvantages of working for a small bank?

· · · · · · ·

banking.swep.com

Dedicated web site **banking.swep.com** that provides activities with links and crossword puzzles for each chapter.

PROJECT
Group or individual activity that has activities for each lesson.

·········· PROJECT ·········

BANK ACCOUNTS and YOU

PROJECT OBJECTIVES

● Learn more about specific accounts offered in your community
● Compare local account offerings to each other in terms of interest and features
● Categorize local account offerings in terms of industry criteria
● Recognize variations in deposit requirements and regulations as they apply to accounts in your area

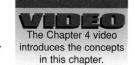

The Chapter 4 video introduces the concepts in this chapter.

CNN Banking Video contains clips that can be used to introduce concepts in each chapter.

GOALS
Begin each lesson and offer an overview.

DEFINE the term
mortgage

IDENTIFY
several types of mortgages

BANKING SCENE
Lesson opening scenario that provides motivation.

Rosa Lopez is preparing to open a checking account at a local bank on which she has not yet decided. She knows that there is a wide variety of checking accounts, and that similar accounts may have different names at different banks. She has decided to collect information from various banks in an effort to find an account that will best suit her needs. To do so, she plans to make a list of questions about how she expects to use the account. Using answers to her questions, Rosa hopes to be able to match her requirements to account features offered by banks. What kind of questions about her own needs should Rosa include in her list?

SPECIAL FEATURES ENHANCE LEARNING

In small groups, make a list of checks that affect your daily life. Make a log to show the maker of the check, the type of check, and its purpose. Compare your list to those of other groups.

BANKING MATH CONNECTION
Worked example that reinforces and reviews math concepts.

BANKING MATH CONNECTION

Calculate the simple interest earned on a savings account in nine months that begins with a deposit of $2,200 and pays $4\frac{1}{2}$ percent interest.

SOLUTION
The formula for calculating interest is

$$\text{Principal} \times \text{Rate} \times \text{Time} = \text{Interest}$$
$$\$2{,}200 \times 0.045 \times 0.75 = \$74.25$$

If you had such an account, you would have earned $74.25 in interest, giving you a balance of $2,274.25. This example assumes no compounding and that the interest is paid at the end of the nine months, which might not reflect conditions of an actual account.

WORKSHOP
Provides activities to use in class.

Credit card use is growing among college students. In 2000, 78 percent of undergraduate college students had at least one credit card, up from 67 percent in 1998. The average balance in 2000 was $2,748, up from $1,879 two years earlier.

TECH TALK
Provides information about new technology that is being used in banking.

TECH TALK

EDI IMPLEMENTATION
Computers "talk" to each other by means of conventions, called protocols, for information exchange. EDI is an acronym for electronic data interchange, a set of standards for business-to-business exchange of information. As technology improves and extends further into the banking business, implementation of EDI becomes more critical to run such applications as online banking, smart card applications, and other forms of electronic commerce.

THINK CRITICALLY
Research more information on EDI systems. What sort of challenges do you think might be involved with implementing EDI?

DID YOU KNOW?
Provides an interesting fact about the **topic.**

Write a sample letter to a credit reporting agency disputing an inaccurate entry on your report.

COMMUNICATE
Provides activities to reinforce, review, and practice communication skills.

WORLD VIEW
Provides international banking connections relevant to today's current events.

ETHICS IN ACTION
Provides a real-world situation where students decide an ethical action.

ETHICS IN ACTION

Former Senator Phil Gramm of Texas commented on the difficulty of writing banking legislation that protects consumers without harming banks by saying that it is impossible to regulate something that cannot be defined. He was referring to predatory lending practices, which numerous acts and amendments have attempted to prohibit.

THINK CRITICALLY
Where is the line between strict business practices and taking advantage of someone? What, in your opinion, is predatory lending? How would you recognize it in contract terms, in advertising, and in discussions with a customer?

CONSUMER LENDING IN JAPAN
The Japanese economic system, the most westernized of Asian economies, also depends on credit. From the first store card issued by Marui Department Store in 1960 to the present, the use of credit has grown dramatically in Japan. Japanese consumers face issues similar to Americans with their use of credit. Japanese bankruptcies are on the rise, especially as Japan has faced several waves of recession.

There are three primary consumer reporting agencies in Japan, one for banks, one for companies doing their own financing, and one for credit-granting companies. Although there are no laws limiting credit reporting in Japan, agencies abide by voluntary guidelines. According to *Credit and Collections World Magazine*, the guidelines do not allow reports to be used for employment screening or any purpose other than credit evaluation.

THINK CRITICALLY
What factors in a nation's economy would lead to a sophisticated system of credit reporting? What would likely be the result if the voluntary guidelines were not followed?

ASSESSMENT AND REVIEW

CHECKPOINT   Short questions within lesson to assist with reading and to assure students are grasping concepts.

THINK CRITICALLY ●●●●●●●●●●●●●●●●●●●●●●●●●

1. Why is it important for consumers to compare interest rates on bank accounts and other interest-bearing instruments?

2. How does the frequency at which interest is compounded change the effect of compounded interest rates?

3. Why is APY a more useful measure for comparing interest rates than APR?

MAKE CONNECTIONS ●●●●●●●●●●●●●●●●●●●●●●

4. **BANKING MATH** Marie Broussard puts $10 a week in a savings account. At the end of two years, how much more would Marie have in savings if she found an account that paid interest of 5.5 percent instead of 4.5 percent per year, assuming both accounts compound annually?

5. **HISTORY** The practice of paying and charging interest has been around a long time. Do research on interest, and write a one-page report on the earliest beginnings of the practice.

6. **TECHNOLOGY** Online financial calculators are becoming increasingly useful tools, performing complex calculations quickly. Find three such calculators on the Internet, and describe the particular features, advantages, and disadvantages of each.

CHAPTER REVIEW   Contains Chapter Summary, Vocabulary Builder, Review Concepts, Apply What You Learned, and Make Connections.

APPLY WHAT YOU LEARNED

23. Should FICO scores be released to consumers? Why or why not?

25. What factors should a person consider before obtaining a loan?

27. Why is having many credit card accounts a risky practice?

28. What kinds of abuses are consumer protection laws intended to eliminate?

REVIEW CONCEPTS

12. Give three examples of installment loans.

18. List six steps in the credit-granting process.

20. What is a credit-scoring system?

22. What five items appear in most credit reports?

MAKE CONNECTIONS ●●●●●●●●●●●●●●●●●●●●●

30. **SOCIAL STUDIES** Using the Internet, research one of the laws discussed in Lesson 6.4. Prepare a detailed report on its history, its provisions, and its effect on the lending industry. Write a three-page report on what you learn.

31. **ECONOMICS** Analyze the impact of credit on the banking system as a whole.

32. **ART/DESIGN** Prepare a brochure for consumer education that highlights effective and safe ways to choose and use credit. Include information on government agencies that consumers can contact for more information.

33. **COMMUNICATION** Interview an executive or loan officer of a local bank on the subject of consumer lending. Gain insight into the officer's daily life, changes in the business in the last few years, and the effects of regulation. Present your findings to the class in an oral report.

CHECK**POINT**

What is underwriting?

END-OF-LESSON ACTIVITIES
Think Critically   Provides opportunities to apply concepts.
Make Connections   Provides connections to other disciplines.

Internet icon indicates opportunity to research on the Web.

CHAPTER 6 ··············· REVIEW

CHAPTER SUMMARY

LESSON 6.1 Consumer Loans
A. Installment loans are the most common form of consumer lending. They may be secured or unsecured. The principal, interest, fees, finance charge, total payments, and schedule of payments must be fully explained by law.
B. The amount owed on an open-end loan is flexible, as is the term. Open-end loans include credit cards and lines of credit.

LESSON 6.2 Granting and Analyzing Credit
A. A lender must determine whether extending credit is a sound decision.
B. Many lenders base credit decisions on reports from consumer reporting agencies (CRAs). CRAs and lenders often use credit-scoring systems.

LESSON 6.3 Cost of Credit
A. The cost of credit varies with annual percentage rate and term and depends on the method of calculation. Minimum payments reduce balances slowly.
B. Consumers should pay close attention to their credit standing because poor credit can result in numerous long-running financial problems.

LESSON 6.4 Credit and the Law
A. Four main laws (TILA, ECOA, FCRA, and FDCPA) provide the foundation for consumer protection in lending. Other federal and state laws apply as well.
B. Banks must document their compliance with all applicable state and federal regulations and spend considerable resources doing so.

VOCABULARY BUILDER

Choose the term that best fits the definition. Write the letter of the answer in the space provided. Some terms may not be used.

a. collateral
b. consumer reporting agency (CRA)
c. Equal Credit Opportunity Act
d. Fair Credit Reporting Act
e. Fair Debt Collection Practices Act
f. FICO score
g. grace period
h. installment loan
i. lien
j. open-end loan
k. secured loan
l. subprime rate
m. Truth in Lending Act
n. underwriting
o. unsecured loan

_____ 1. Period for which no interest charges accrue if balance is paid in full by due date

_____ 2. Guarantees that all information about costs of a loan is provided in writing

_____ 3. Loan with fixed amount of payments, rate of interest, and length of term

_____ 4. Loan backed by some item of value in case the borrower defaults

_____ 5. Dominant credit-scoring system

_____ 6. Loan backed by only the reputation and creditworthiness of the borrower

_____ 7. Company that compiles and sells credit records

_____ 8. Item used to secure a loan

_____ 9. Reviewing a loan for soundness

_____ 10. Loan with flexible principal and term

_____ 11. Protects consumers from unfair collection techniques

CHAPTER 1

THE BUSINESS OF BANKING

1.1 INTRODUCTION TO BANKING

1.2 ROLE OF BANKS IN THE ECONOMY

1.3 HOW THE BANKING SYSTEM WORKS

1.4 OTHER FINANCIAL INSTITUTIONS

Careers in Banking

NATIONAL CITY BANK

Founded in 1845 and now headquartered in Cleveland, Ohio, National City Corporation operates banks and other financial service companies. Through mergers and acquisitions, it has become a multi-state operation, with offices in Ohio, Michigan, Pennsylvania, Indiana, Kentucky, and Illinois. National City offers a wide range of financial services including personal banking, corporate and small business banking, trust and investment services, mortgage lending, insurance, and accounting and transaction processing services for businesses. National City's assets total almost $90 billion.

National City actively recruits qualified employees and tries to attract them with a full range of benefits. Along with a variety of insurance and pension plans, the corporation offers such things as flexible scheduling, employee discounts on financial services, stock purchase plans, tuition reimbursement for employees furthering their education, and even child-care discounts at some centers. National City tries to promote from within and supports diversity in its work-force. The corporation is one of the sponsors of DiversityInc.com, a news and resource center on workplace diversity issues.

THINK CRITICALLY

1. Which employee benefits seem most attractive to you? Why?
2. Why are companies such as National City willing to spend considerable money on employee benefits?

PROJECT

BANKING in YOUR LIFE

PROJECT OBJECTIVES

- Become aware of the way the business of banking touches your life
- Consider the impact of banks in your local community
- Note bank offerings of specific financial services
- Make distinctions between banks and other types of financial service businesses

VIDEO
The Chapter 1 video introduces the concepts in this chapter.

GETTING STARTED

Read through the Project Process below. Make a list of any materials you will need. Decide how you will get the needed materials or information.

- Keep an ongoing list of all businesses you discover that offer financial services in your community. List potential sources of information.
- As you make your list, take notes about each company, including the products and services it offers.
- Make a chart placing each institution you list under one of the categories of financial institutions you learn about in this chapter.

PROJECT PROCESS

Part 1 LESSON 1.1 Discuss in class your personal experience with banks and other financial institutions. What do you know from your own life?

Part 2 LESSON 1.2 Expand your awareness of banks in your community. Bring in newspaper articles about banks. Find out about community activities they participate in or sponsor.

Part 3 LESSON 1.3 Collect print advertisements for specific financial services. Compare the offerings and terms shown in the ads. Determine which checking account services are available only at the bank and which ones are available online.

Part 4 LESSON 1.4 Compare banks with other firms offering financial services in your community. Use the chapter content and what you learn locally to describe similarities and differences.

CHAPTER REVIEW

Project Wrap-up Hold a class discussion about banking in your life. Make a list of things you learned about banking that you did not know before studying the chapter and completing the project.

Lesson 1.1
INTRODUCTION TO BANKING ••••••••••••

GOALS

DEFINE the business of banking

IDENTIFY trends in modern banking

WHAT IS A BANK?

When you think of a bank, what image comes to mind? Do you see a near-by building where people deposit their paychecks? Maybe you visualize the automated teller machine (ATM) where people use a card to get cash fast, or you recall the bank statements that many people still get in the mail. Perhaps you see a tall tower with a logo or name you recognize. If you're technologically savvy, you may imagine someone going over personal finances while on the Internet.

However you think of banks, and they include all these ideas and more, don't lose track of one basic idea. A bank is a business. Banks sell their

Edouard Ramirez has taken his first full-time job working as a summer lifeguard at a local pool. After receiving his first paycheck, Edouard has decisions to make about how to handle that money. Along with choices about budgeting and spending, Edouard must decide what to do with that check, such as how to cash it, where to put his money, how to gain access to it, how to use it effectively, and how to take advantage of the range of services available to modern consumers. Writing checks, using ATMs, learning about debit and credit cards, and investigating forms of saving and investment are all things Edouard wants to consider. How can he get this information?

services to earn money, and they market and manage those services in a competitive field. In many ways, banks are like other businesses that must earn a profit to survive. Understanding this fundamental idea helps explain how banks work, and helps you understand many modern trends in banking and finance.

A Unique Business

Banks, of course, don't manufacture cellphones or repair automobiles. The services banks offer to customers have to do almost entirely with handling money for other people. Money is a **medium of exchange**, an agreed-upon system for measuring value of goods and services. Once, and still in some places today, precious stones, animal products, or other goods of value might be used as a medium of exchange. Roman soldiers were sometimes paid in salt, because it was critical to life and not easy to get. The word *salary* and the expression *not worth his salt* come from that practice. Anything with an agreed-upon value might be a medium of exchange. Today, many forms of money are used. Money simply shows how much something is worth, whether it is a new stereo or two hours of your labor. When you have money, a bank can act as your agent for using or protecting that money. A bank is a **financial intermediary** for the safeguarding, transferring, exchanging, or lending of money. Banks distribute the medium of exchange.

Because banks and money are essential to maintaining not only economies but entire societies, they are closely regulated and must operate by strict procedures and principles. In the United States, banks may be chartered by federal or state government agencies. Banks are usually corporations and may be owned by groups of individuals, corporations, or some combination of the two. In the United States, all federally chartered banks have been required to be corporations since 1863. A few states permit noncorporate banks, which are owned by partnerships or individuals. Around the world, however, banks are supervised by governments to guarantee the safety and stability of the money supply and of the country as much as possible.

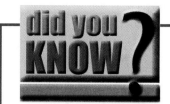

did you KNOW?

The first automated teller machine (ATM) appeared at a Chemical Bank branch in Rockville Center, New York, in 1969.

As a class, make a list of all the banks or financial institutions that you can think of in your area. Based on what you know, try to rank these banks from largest to smallest.

Types of Banks

Actually, many businesses are involved in financial services. If you consider the definition of a bank to be a business that safeguards, transfers, exchanges, and lends money, many firms might qualify. Certainly, banks perform these roles, but so do trust companies, insurance companies, stockbrokers, investment bankers, and other companies. Especially since U.S. banks were deregulated in the 1980s, the line between "pure" banking and other providers of financial and investment services has grown fuzzy. Banks provide a multitude of financial services of many types beyond the traditional practices of holding deposits and lending money. As a consequence, not only has banking changed considerably, so have the people who work in the banking world.

- **Commercial banks** are the institutions commonly thought of as banks. Commercial banks do about 60 percent of the deposit and loan business in the United States, and provide familiar services such as checking and savings accounts, credit cards, investment services, and others. Commercial banks are so called because, at one time, they offered their services only to businesses. Today, commercial banks seek the business of any worthy customer.

- **Retail banks** and other thrift institutions such as mutual savings banks, savings and loans, and credit unions developed to help individuals not served by commercial banks save money, acquire loans, and invest. Over time, their services expanded, and they too now offer a wide range of financial services to a broad customer base.

- **Central banks** are the governmental banks that manage, regulate, and protect both the money supply and the banks themselves. Central banks serve as the government's banker. Central banks issue currency and conduct monetary policy. In the United States, the Federal Reserve System performs the central banking function. Although the Federal Reserve is technically owned by the banks themselves, the Board of Governors is appointed by the President with the consent of the Senate. The President also selects the powerful chairman of the Federal Reserve.

Edouard Ramirez has a number of options for what he might do with that paycheck. He'll need to know more about banking to make wise decisions that fit his needs.

List four functions that define a bank.

_____

_____

BANKING TODAY

Banking used to be thought of as a solid and slow-moving industry. Banking today is an exciting, fast-moving, around-the-clock, around-the-world activity. Changes in regulation, changes in technology, and changes in competition have pushed banking, like most other businesses, to become organizations that must respond rapidly to changing business conditions in order to survive.

Mergers

One of the most significant changes in banking in the last twenty years has been the number of mergers. A *merger* occurs when one or more banks join or acquire another bank or banks. Mergers increase the size of banks, giving them more resources. Mergers also decrease the number of banks.

The effects of mergers have been mixed. Banks are larger, and fewer and fewer banks control more and more of the nation's money. About 25 large

TOP TEN LARGEST BANKS WORLDWIDE
(Ranked by size of assets)

Bank	Country
Mizuho Financial Group	Japan
Citigroup	United States
Deutsche Bank	Germany
JP Morgan Chase Co.	United States
Bank of Tokyo-Mitsubishi	Japan
HSBC Holdings	United Kingdom
Hypo Vereinsbank	Germany
UBS	Switzerland
BNP Paribas	France
Bank of America Corp.	United States

banks control 45 percent of U.S. assets, and the number of commercial banks has dropped to around 8,000 from more than 14,000 in the 1980s. Some consumers face higher fees and find less community involvement and lending in local areas. People like to feel that their money is staying close to home. Mergers also created an opening, though, for a new wave of small local banks. Small banks have doubled the amount loaned to businesses in the last decade.

Banking is an international business as well, and becoming more so all the time. Technology has allowed instant communication as well as transfer of funds, so barriers of geography apply less than ever. U.S. commercial banks actively seek international business, putting together huge investment transactions overseas and engaging in investment banking prohibited in the United States.

Technology

As with many industries, technology has changed everything. Perhaps no business has been more affected by the growth of computers and telecommunications than banking. Not only have accounting, auditing, and examining functions been taken over by fast and efficient technology, funds transfer, record keeping, and financial analyses have become instantaneous because of the powerful tools now available.

Interview someone from a local bank and learn more about its history. Find out when and where it was founded and how it has changed over the years. Write a one- to two-page report on what you learn, and present your report to the class. Be sure to identify your sources.

Technology's changes are not limited to bankers either. Consumers' relationships with their banks have changed also. Gone are the banker's hours of 9:00 to 3:00, for consumers want services just as they do from other businesses, and they want access to their money at any time. Automated teller machines (ATMs), networked computers that allow access from around the world, "smart" cards with embedded microchips, and online banking via the Internet are some of the technological innovations changing the face of banking.

Competition

Banking is a business, and as with any business, competition is the heart of the matter. As government regulations have changed, competition between banks has become fiercer. This fact has resulted in mergers and decreasing numbers of banks, but it has also made more services available to consumers, as banks compete to earn customers' financial business. Banks compete not only with other banks, but with other businesses that sell financial services, such as credit unions. Banks are more sales oriented than ever, with emphasis on service, innovation, and marketing that could scarcely have been imagined 30 years ago.

CHECK**POINT**

What three factors in modern banking have changed the industry?

_____

_____

_____

THINK CRITICALLY ●●●●●●●●●●●●●●●●●●●●●●

1. In what ways is a bank like any other business? In what ways is it different from other businesses?

_____

_____

_____

2. Name three ways you interact with your own bank. For each, explain how technology has changed the interaction between the bank and the customer.

_____

_____

_____

_____

3. Why do governments regulate banks?

_____

_____

4. What challenges do you think the trend toward mergers poses toward banks? What skills will these challenges require of those making careers in banking?

_____

_____

_____

_____

_____

MAKE CONNECTIONS ●●●●●●●●●●●●●●●●●●●●●

5. COMMUNICATION Banking has changed over the years. Interview a member of a previous generation to find out more. Prepare a list of questions that will generate memories about banking in earlier days. What were banks and banking like? In what specific ways have banks changed? Which of those changes were for the better? Which, in the opinion of your interviewee, were for the worse? Compare the results of your interview with those of classmates. Compile a class list or table showing the composite results.

6. BANKING MATH In international banking, exchange rates are used to compute the value of currencies between different countries. Locate the current exchange rates in a newspaper or on the Internet. Using these exchange rates, compute the value of $20,000 $US expressed in Canadian dollars, Mexican pesos, and Japanese yen.

_____

_____

_____

_____

_____

ROLE OF BANKS IN THE ECONOMY ......

GOALS

LIST banking activities that contribute to economic stability

EXPLAIN how banking expands the economy

BANKS AND ECONOMICS

Money is a medium of exchange and the basis of the modern economy. Banks play a huge role in the distribution of funds throughout society. Although there are many institutions involved in the movement of money today, banks remain fundamental to the motion of money that maintains local, national, and global economies.

Banks and other institutions play this critical role by performing services essential to the functioning of an economy. Safeguarding, transferring, lending, and exchanging money in various forms, along with evaluating creditworthiness of customers, are the main activities that banks perform. Each of these roles has a ripple effect in the economy at large that helps keep money moving.

BANKING *Scene*

As Edouard Ramirez thinks about how to use his paycheck, he begins to notice money and banking in the world around him. On the radio and television, he hears ads mentioning automobile deals and interest rates, and financing or refinancing plans for houses. He sees people using checks, debit cards, and credit cards as well as cash at the grocery store. Some even use an ATM in the store. When Edouard notices a clerk examining a twenty-dollar bill at a fast-food place, he begins to wonder about the nature of money itself. What other ways do banking functions play a role in Edouard's life?

Keeping Your Money Safe

Safeguarding the holdings of people may be the oldest bank function. Long before banks existed, people looked for ways to secure their valuables, whatever the medium of exchange. Many of these you may easily imagine. In some societies, such as Babylonia about 2000 B.C., people began to store money in temples, perhaps because they thought others would be less likely to steal from houses of gods. Ancient records indicate that about 4,000 years ago the temples were in the business of lending and exchanging money, and were thus acting as banks.

You may think of a bank vault or a safe-deposit box when you think of safeguarding money, and those on-site measures are certainly ways of protecting valuable assets. Yet there is much more to safeguarding money than simply storing it in a secure place.

- *Record keeping is an important part of securing your money.* Banks devote much time and attention to both the practice and technology of maintaining and storing accurate records. If banks expect you to let them hold and use your money, they know you expect them to keep careful track of it. The same principle applies to large transactions between banks and industry, and banking institutions and the government as well.

- *Identification is an important security function of banking, too.* Obviously, you don't want unauthorized people walking in and taking money from your account, but the issue of security and identification goes far beyond the local branch. Identifying theft is a growing concern in the economy, and bank officials work closely with technology experts and law enforcement agencies to prevent various forms of identity fraud involving conventional checking accounts to online banking or shopping.

- *Enforcement is a part of safeguarding money that involves catching those who attempt to take it.* Not only does this function involve physical security, but it also includes tracking down fraud, making collections, and pursuing legal actions against those who inflict losses on the bank, whether they be robbers, white-collar embezzlers, or people who default on loans.

- *Transfer security is important to banks, too.* Although cash is still an important part of bank transactions, most money moves merely on computer screens. High-tech security measures are increasingly more critical to banking operations between banks and customers, between banks and banks, and between banks and the government. As all financial intermediaries move closer to fully electronic banking, technology takes a greater and greater role.

Work in small groups to identify specific examples that you have encountered of each of the five ways that banks safeguard your money.

• ***Sound business practices also safeguard your money.*** Most of these involve good judgment and management of day-to-day bank operations. Banks invest time and money in training employees in procedures and practices, to ensure accuracy, and also to make good decisions about when and to whom to extend credit and how to make sound financial decisions. Federal or state bank examiners closely review the records of banks to protect consumers, and their examinations include not only the accuracy of records but the prudence of banks' policies. These thorough examinations may take a week or more for a small bank, and a much longer time for a larger institution.

You can see how these various ways of safeguarding your money work together within the local bank and the banking community at large to create a more secure financial environment. That stability is important to the economy and society as a whole.

CHECK**POINT**

Name five ways banks safeguard your money.

_____

_____

SPREADING THE WEALTH

Banks are critical to the economy. Although there are many ways that money moves around the economy, banks play a central role in establishing the financial environment. Transferring money to provide growth and stabilizing the monetary supply are important functions in which banks play a key part. Bank lending makes money available to consumers and businesses to make purchases they might not otherwise be able to make, or at least not for a very long time. In addition, banks help determine creditworthiness so that good money is not lost on bad loans.

Transferring

Banks move money. They move it between banks, between banks and individual customers, between banks and industry, between banks and governments, and sometimes between governments. Sometimes the sums involved may be huge. This motion of money throughout the nation and the world allows businesses to have access to capital. With capital to invest, businesses can expand, jobs are created, products get manufactured, services are performed, and the economy grows. This large-scale transfer of assets is a feature of the modern economy, ever more so in an age of fierce competition and globalization.

Industries seek out financing wherever they can find it, and banks seek out investment opportunities wherever they may be. In international banking, exchange rates measure the relative strength of one form of currency against another, and these variable rates are often indications of the strength of a nation's economic position.

The ability to transfer sums of money between financial institutions safely and effectively depends on the stability of the institutions and the security of the money supply itself.

Lending

Need a new car? Reach into your wallet and pull out $25,000. How about a new home? Do you have $150,000 in your piggy bank? Most people don't, of course, and bank lending is the main reason that people are able to own homes and cars without waiting forever to buy them.

Lending is a big part of a bank's business. Many bank deals are more complex than automobile or home loans. In fact, banks lend money to businesses and governments in a wide variety of ways, with lengths of loans ranging from a single day to decades. These many types of loans are a primary way banks transfer money in the economy, and in the far-ranging and fast-shifting world of banking, real management skill and a thorough understanding of finance are required.

Credit cards issued by banks are another form of lending, and they are not only good business for the bank, they help the economy. People buy things with credit, and keep merchandise moving and jobs producing at a more rapid rate than if transactions had to take place in cash. Although there is risk in unwise use of credit cards by consumers, the judicious use of credit stimulates the economy.

Home loans constitute an important part of the banking business. People want to own their own homes and will work hard to do so. Home ownership, in turn, provides jobs for people who construct, furnish, and repair homes, and those workers want homes built, furnished, and repaired for themselves, and so the cycle of economic activity expands. Without bank lending, the cycle would be far smaller and slower. The automobile and housing industries have grown hand in hand with a solid banking industry, and the American economy has grown with it.

THE EUROPEAN UNION AND THE EURO

In Europe, banking has changed dramatically in the past decade. European nations have been working since 1958 to provide a single market and single banking structure. The European Union (EU) consists of 15 nations, essentially all of western Europe except Norway and Sweden. Eleven of the fifteen agreed to use a single currency (Greece, Denmark, Sweden, and the United Kingdom were the exceptions). On January 4, 1999, these nations began using the euro, an agreed-upon currency with stable values among the nations. For example, a euro is always worth 6.55957 French francs, the same way a dollar is always worth ten dimes, regardless of the overseas value of a dollar. On January 1, 2002, the euro became the official currency of the European Union.

The implications for banking were huge. Although recognizing the primacy of a host country's banking laws, member nations accepted common rules and a common central bank, the European Central Bank (ECB), for the euro. All government debt, stock quotes, prices, and monetary policies were referenced in euro. Results have been mixed so far, as differing laws in countries have affected the flow of capital, but with the pressures of technology and globalization increasing, the EU may eventually bring about price stability, increased banking efficiency, and more services for western Europe's 400 million people. Eleven central and eastern European nations are now considering membership in the EU.

THINK CRITICALLY

What advantages for member nations are there in using a common currency? Why might some nations be reluctant to do so? Do you think there will ever be a world currency? Why or why not?

Creditworthiness

Evaluating the creditworthiness of customers, whether large industries or governments or individual consumers, is another banking function that affects the economy at large. It is a good business practice for banks to evaluate loan applications carefully because their profits, and in some cases their survival, depend upon being repaid the principal and interest from loans. If banks were to overextend themselves with uncollected loans, they could begin to fail, and if they fail, the economy at large is at risk. Bank failures played a role in the Great Depression. Banking policies and regulations regarding creditworthiness and the ratio of loans to deposits help guarantee a secure financial environment. These policies also assure that businesses get paid for the things that consumers buy with bank funds.

Guaranteeing the Money

So what makes that piece of green paper that Edouard handed the cashier worth twenty dollars? The government guarantees that it is, and the banks back up the guarantee. In the United States, banks and the government work together to form the banking system and to make sure the money supply is adequate, appropriate, and trustworthy. Much of this guarantee is backed through the central banking function of the Federal Reserve. Individual banks also work with the government to implement monetary policy, perform exchange functions for citizens, and defeat counterfeiters of currency.

In addition, banks guarantee their own policies. Networks of banks agree to honor credit cards. If you write a check or use a debit card, you can be sure that the recipient will receive his or her money from your bank, providing you have money there to cover it. These actions make the transfer of money between citizens and business easy, helping to keep the economy going.

The Substance of Society

The functions that banking institutions perform do more than move money through the economy. They also provide a common system. A great part of an economic system is psychological. It is your belief and trust in the financial system that makes you willing to borrow and pay later for a car, to invest money in businesses you've never seen, to deposit money in banks that is in turn loaned to people you don't know, or to take on a mortgage for 30 years. Banks are at the heart of this financial system, and their effect on your life cannot be calculated.

How does lending stimulate the economy?

_____

_____

THINK CRITICALLY ●●●●●●●●●●●●●●●●●●●●●●●●●

1. How do banks contribute to the stability of the society at large while safeguarding the funds of their own customers?

_____

_____

_____

2. Governments don't routinely examine the books of many businesses. Poor business practices just put them out of business. Why should banks be treated any differently?

_____

_____

_____

3. In what ways have security issues for banks changed in the last 30 years?

_____

_____

_____

MAKE CONNECTIONS ●●●●●●●●●●●●●●●●●●●●●●

4. TECHNOLOGY Banks have been using computer networks to transfer funds for some time. Customers can now get in on the act with online banking. Use the Internet or other reference materials to find out what a secure server is. Summarize ways that Internet providers attempt to guarantee security and privacy.

_____

_____

_____

_____

_____

5. HISTORY One banking function is guaranteeing the worth of money. One big historical change was the growth of paper money, which depended upon people believing that the paper was worth something. Research the history of paper currency. Choose an interesting example, and write a one-page report explaining the case.

6. COMMUNICATION With a classmate, make a list of the most important services you want from a bank. Rank these services in order of importance. Compile a class list from the results of all pairs, and come to a consensus on the most important services customers want.

_____

_____

_____

_____

_____

LESSON 1.3
HOW THE BANKING SYSTEM WORKS ......

MONEY AT WORK

Despite their central role in the economy at large, banks are businesses too. For their services, banks earn money in various ways. Banks also have income from other sources, but most of their money comes from lending— or, to be more precise, the interest that people or businesses pay as they repay a loan.

When banks lend money, they put it to work. The money that people borrow goes to buy and build things or to start businesses that sell things to people who buy and build things. In this way, the money that banks lend works to keep the economy going.

BANKING *Scene*

As he considers places to deposit his paycheck, Edouard Ramirez sees a bewildering array of offers from banks and other financial institutions. He recognizes that banks want his business, no differently from the electronics store where he bought a CD player or the grocery where his mother shops. Unlike those stores, however, banks are selling services. He knows that banks are big businesses, but he wonders where they get their funds. He knows they make money on services, but how exactly does the bank earn its profit? What sources of information might Edouard use to find answers to these questions?

The Spread

People who put money into banks are called **depositors**. Banks encourage them to do so by protecting the money and by paying *interest*, a percentage earned over a period of time, to the depositor. The depositor thus earns some money from the deposits. Using the accumulated funds of many depositors, the bank makes loans to those it considers likely to repay. The bank charges more interest on the money it lends, so when the money is repaid, more comes in than went out. Banks charge higher interest rates for loans than they pay to depositors in order to make money. The difference between what a bank pays in interest and what it receives in interest is called the **spread**, or *net interest income*.

The spread is not pure profit. The spread is income, or *revenue*, but costs have yet to be considered. It costs the bank something to maintain the security of your money and to pay the tellers, the accountants, the computer technicians, the electricity bill, and so forth. **Profit** is what's left of revenue after costs are deducted. What happens if the homeowner can't repay the loan? The bank still must pay the interest expense, so in such a case, the bank incurs a *loss*.

What happens if after two months a tree falls on your roof and you need to withdraw your $10,000? The bank has loaned it to the other homeowner. The bank must have reserves to meet the obligation. It's not really the same money. The bank also has other depositors, not all of whom, the bank hopes, need their money at once. Even if they did, the bank has a backup, the Federal Reserve System.

> Revenue
> − Cost
> = **Profit**

Other Funds

Banks have other sources of income, too. In addition to loan income, including credit card interest, they also charge for various services. Charges are incurred for everything from rental of safe-deposit boxes to account maintenance fees for checking accounts, online bill payment, ATM transactions, and other services. It is important to note that banks do not earn

Calculate the spread for one year for a bank that receives a deposit of $10,000 from a customer and lends it out to a homeowner who needs to make some repairs. Assume the bank pays a straight 6% per year interest to the customer and charges 12% per year for the loan.

SOLUTION

The formula for calculating the spread is

Income from interest − Interest paid to depositors = Spread

Income from interest: 12% × $10,000 = $1,200
Interest to depositor: 6% × $10,000 = ___600
Spread = $ 600

The spread is $600. This is a simplified example and does not take into account compounding, declining balances, or other factors that affect depositing and lending in the real world.

interest on money kept on hand for services such as ATM transactions. Thus, banks charge fees to offset the loss of interest. Fees for services have grown in both number and amount in recent years to keep pace with the rising cost of servicing accounts. These charges can be a substantial source of revenue for banks.

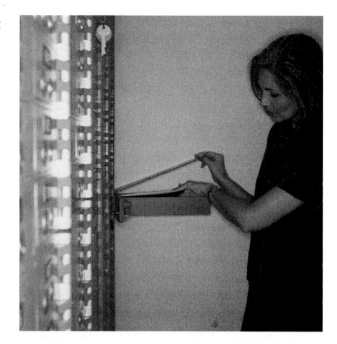

Banks also make money on investments, just as people or other corporations do. Especially since the early 1980s, banks have become large and careful investors in some types of securities and government bonds. Because banks can sometimes put together large amounts of money to invest, they can do well, but they face the same risks as other investors. Because of the speed of modern communication, banks can move their investments quickly if they need to do so. Even a day or two of investment can yield a good return if the investment itself is large enough. Professional investment staffs work hard to make every dollar return a profit in the financial market.

In addition, because most banks are corporations, banks may have funds at their disposal from stockholder investments. Shareholders actually buy a piece of the bank, hoping for a return on their investment. They also get a say in how the bank does business.

Assets and Liabilities

Why aren't deposits themselves a form of bank income? The answer is because the money doesn't really belong to the bank. You may not like to think of your savings account as a problem for the bank, but it is a potential one in theory. If everyone wanted all their money from their accounts all at once, banks would be in trouble.

An **asset** is anything of value. In financial terms, that usually means money. A **liquid asset** is anything that can readily be exchanged, like cash. A **liability**, in financial terms, is a cash obligation. If you borrowed $5 from a friend for lunch, you have a liability of $5 and your friend has an asset of $5. How liquid the asset is depends upon how quickly you've agreed to repay the sum and how reliable you are.

For banks, deposits are liabilities. A depositor has the right to request his or her funds, and the bank is obligated to pay them. Whenever a bank calculates its liabilities, the sum of its deposits goes into the liabilities column. Money the bank may have borrowed is also a liability, for it represents an obligation that must be paid.

A bank's assets are the loans and investments it has made. These assets may be less liquid by contract than an obligation imposed by a deposit. A deposit may have to be returned any time, while an asset could arrive in small amounts over a long period.

WORKSHOP

Work as a class to make a chart that shows the type of assets and liabilities that a family might have in its personal economy. Which of these assets and obligations might be considered fairly liquid?

Because banks have more money out working than they keep on hand, two principles of the banking business come into play.

- *A bank's liabilities exceed its reserves.* The money is loaned out, and the reserves don't match the total of deposits (liabilities). On the positive side, the money is out working, financing businesses and expanding the economy.

- *A bank's liabilities are more liquid than its assets.* The bank is obligated to give depositors their money if they request it. The bank's assets, however, may be less liquid because they are tied up in longer-term loans, so the bank can't get them as quickly. If many depositors need their money at once, the bank must either break its promise to depositors or pay until its reserves are gone. If the bank fails, unpaid depositors lose their money. In the United States, deposit insurance, backed by the government since 1934, has kept people from fearing the loss of their deposits. Thus, a "run on the banks," when people call for their money all at once, is rare.

A problem for banks has been faulty investment strategies. Especially in international banking, some banks have sometimes invested substantial amounts of money in questionable businesses. If those businesses fail, the banks simply don't get their assets. A crisis in the Asian economy in the late 1990s nearly destroyed the Asian banking system, which was neither carefully funded nor controlled.

So today's banking is not as simple as earning more interest than is paid out. Rapidly changing conditions, a wide variety of complex factors, and a twenty-four-hour-a-day global economy determine the banking climate.

Name three sources of bank revenue. What is a bank's spread?

_____

_____

BANKS WORKING FOR YOU

The word *bank* comes from the Italian word *banco*, or bench, from which money changers in medieval Italy carried on their business in the marketplace.

Like any business, a bank must attract customers in order to make money. Banking has changed radically in the last 20 years, and it is now one of the most competitive businesses in the world. Today, large regional banks may have huge resources, and when these giants compete, consumers can sometimes be the winners. Smaller banks that target particular consumers work in **niche markets**, targeting particular customers in defined locations or by particular services. They use the flexibility that sometimes comes with smaller size to their advantage.

Although there are fewer commercial banks than there were ten years ago, there is an ever-wider array of services. It was not always so. One consequence of the Great Depression of the 1930s was heavy regulation of banking. Banks could make good profits simply on the spread, for there were fewer financial options for consumers.

In the early 1980s, however, interest rates rose for all types of debts and investments. Banks were still paying only $5^1/2$ to $5^3/4$ percent, as prescribed by law. Consumers, who could get 10 to 14 percent on other investments such as mutual funds, began removing their money from banks or depositing it elsewhere. Some banks (primarily savings and loans associations) had trouble, and with their problems the American economy was at risk. A series of laws passed in the early 1980s loosened the restrictions on bankers and let them compete in the open market like other financial businesses. This loosening of government control, called **deregulation**, changed the banking environment in the United States completely.

Changes in Traditional Services

One of the most obvious changes in banking was a new focus on consumers. Banks were not as customer-oriented as they are now and advertising was far different. They often kept the so-called "banker's hours" of 9:00 to 3:00, closed on Saturdays, and sometimes closed Wednesdays. That way of doing business is a fading memory, as banks keep doors and windows open longer hours and have branches in more places than ever. Innovations such as drive-up windows with extended hours took on more importance as banks scrambled to attract customers. Many banks are now open six days a week, and bank operations at most banks run twenty-four hours a day, seven days a week. Also, many banks have opened branches in retail stores and shopping centers, making it more convenient for consumers to access their services.

In addition, changes in traditional services help keep customers. These are the promotions you may often see in banking advertisements today. Several types of checking accounts, for example, are typically available at a single institution, as banks tailor their offerings to match consumer needs. No-cost checking above a minimum balance, overdraft protection, interest-bearing accounts, no-frills checking accounts, or a custom-tailored mix of features let customers pick an account to suit their wishes and balances.

Traditional savings accounts still exist too, but so do other savings options. A variety of ways to compound interest maximize the money customers can earn, or they may place funds in special accounts, such as money-market accounts that may offer higher interest rates.

Marketing is an ever more important matter to banks in today's environment. Bank personnel often become experts in certain services, and selling is now an important part of any banker's job. Small community banks often offer excellent personal service, important to survival in a niche market, on such personalized traditional services as loans, trust accounts, and safe-deposit boxes.

New Services

One of the biggest effects of deregulation was that banks moved into new areas of business. Banks began offering more financial services such as credit cards, innovative lending options, and technology-related services.

Credit Cards Banks (or their holding companies) are facilitators in the credit card business in a big way. This profitable field is a form of lending that has become larger than ever in the last few years. Some economists worry that the growth in this business comes at the expense of saving, perhaps a recipe for long-term trouble. Still, banks compete fiercely for this business and offer varying forms and types of credit card accounts. Many banks change or negotiate rates with consumers, and special low-rate promotions are a daily fact of credit card life.

Innovative Lending New types of lending are also available to consumers. A recent boom in second-mortgage loans has brought a wave of new business. These loans, called home-equity loans, are secured by the difference between the value of a home and the amount the homeowner still owes on it. The loans may take the form of a special credit card, a line of credit, or a single disbursement. They have become a popular form of credit because the interest on them is tax-deductible for the consumer.

Technology Tools Probably the flashiest new services banks offer involve technology. The revolution in computers and telecommunications affected banks dramatically. New and expanded services based on the blend of technologies are now available.

- *Automated teller machines (ATMs)* were the first of the high-tech revolutions for consumers. First appearing as novelties in the late 1960s, ATMs have made "banker's hours" irrelevant. Customers can now perform almost any banking function from an ATM and have access to their accounts day or night. Networked ATMs have made it possible to do business with one's bank at any time from almost anywhere in the world. ATMs cost banks less per transaction in  processing, encourage frequent use of the bank, and earn income from fees. Using an ATM, which often intimidated early customers, is today a common and casual act that most people take for granted.

- *Smart cards* are credit, debit, or other types of cards that have embedded microchips. Smart cards are useful for a wide variety of "electronic purse" applications, which allow the card to store a value. When the card is used, the stored value decreases. You may have used these already in grocery or video-rental stores. Gift cards, security cards, and customer loyalty reward

INTRANET

You know about the Internet, of course, but do you know what an *intra*net is? An intranet is a private network that uses Internet tools and software to store forms, data, and programs for internal use by a company. Essentially, an intranet is a collection of web sites to which only specified users can gain access. Passwords, software security measures, and data encryption protect the intranets from unauthorized use. Intranets make it possible for employees to use the resources on them with standard Internet browsers on their desktop PCs without a special network or special software. Banks and other companies are experimenting with the use of intranets for employees and customers, including online banking applications.

THINK CRITICALLY

Why might intranets, if carefully secured, help overcome consumer concerns about banking over the Internet?

cards are also examples of smart cards. Although smart cards caught on more slowly in the United States than in Europe, the potential for a single smart card to replace many pieces of plastic in consumers' wallets makes them a potentially powerful addition to banking technology.

- *Online banking* takes advantage of growing Internet use. Whether called Internet banking, electronic banking, home banking, or PC banking, online banking allows customers to perform banking transactions from their home computers. Everything from balance checking to bill paying to applying for a loan may be available online at any time. Some banks use Internet technology in intranets, and others simply provide a dial-in service to their mainframe computer. Online services can be complicated and costly to set up, and some consumers are not comfortable using computers for private matters such as banking. The future is bright for online banking, though, as security systems improve, software applications become more sophisticated, and a new generation of customers comfortable with the technology matures.

The new services and the new environment for banking offer both challenges and rewards to consumers and bankers alike. Opportunities to handle money more efficiently and effectively for both are increasing, and they offer possibilities unimagined just a few years ago. They also require thorough understanding of how the system and its tools work, and how money moves in an increasingly complex economy.

What changes have deregulation and competition brought to modern banking?

_____

_____

1. How does the fact that consumers have many choices for places to put their money affect the banking industry?

_____

_____

2. Savings deposits today are smaller by percentage than they once were. Why do you think some economists feel that this is a risk to the economy?

_____

_____

_____

_____

_____

3. What reasons might some people have for not taking full advantage of today's banking services and technology?

_____

_____

4. How might smart card technology reduce the number of cards in a consumer's wallet or purse?

_____

_____

MAKE CONNECTIONS ●●●●●●●●●●●●●●●●●●●●●●

5. BANKING MATH If you had $8,400 placed in an account that earned 5$\frac{1}{2}$ percent interest, paid just once a year, how much money would be in the account at the end of four years, assuming you made no withdrawals of any kind from the account?

_____

_____

_____

_____

6. TECHNOLOGY Explain online or electronic banking. Find out more about online banking. Visit the online site of three banks of your choice. Many online banking sites offer a demonstration of how the system works. List the services available on the sites you choose, and identify what you need to enroll in online banking.

_____

_____

_____

_____

_____

_____

LESSON 1.4
OTHER FINANCIAL INSTITUTIONS ......

GOALS

EXPLAIN depository financial institutions

EXPLAIN nondepository financial institutions

DEPOSITORY INTERMEDIARIES

A bank is a financial intermediary for the safeguarding, transferring, exchanging, or lending of money. There are two primary types of financial institutions. **Depository intermediaries** are those that obtain funds from the public and use them to finance their business. **Non-depository intermediaries** are those that do not take or hold deposits. They earn their money selling specific services or policies.

Depository intermediaries receive deposits from customers and use the money to run their businesses. These institutions may have other sources of income, but the bread and butter of their business is handling deposits, paying interest on them, and lending money based on those deposits. There are four main types of depository institutions. Although there are fewer differences today than in the past, some important distinctions remain.

BANKING *Scene*

Deciding how to manage his earnings, Edouard Ramirez has investigated various local banks and learned about their services. An uncle who works at a nearby college is a member of a credit union. He mentions to Edouard that credit unions can perform many of the same functions of a bank, although some of the terms may be different. Edouard wants to learn more about credit unions. What other types of financial institutions act as intermediaries to help people handle money?

Banks are required by law to offer their products and services on an equal opportunity basis. According to the Federal Trade Commission, the Equal Credit Opportunity Act (ECOA) ensures that all consumers are given an equal chance to obtain credit. This doesn't mean all consumers who apply for credit get it. Factors such as income, expenses, debt, and credit history are considerations for creditworthiness.

What the law guarantees is that all applicants be treated fairly. Applications for credit cannot be evaluated on the basis of sex, race, marital status, national origin, or religion.

THINK CRITICALLY

Banks want to attract and keep customers. Why do you think a law like ECOA might have become necessary?

Commercial Banks

You have been working with concepts and services based mostly on commercial banks throughout this chapter. One of the big distinctions between commercial banks and other depository institutions is that commercial banks are owned by stockholders who expect a profit on their investments. Today commercial banks may work with both businesses and individuals. Commercial banks that specialize only in business banking are sometimes called *wholesale banks*.

Savings and Loan Associations

Savings and loan associations (S&Ls) may go by various names. Building and loan associations, homestead banks, and cooperative banks are all names for savings and loan associations. Savings and loan associations receive most of their deposits from individuals. Chartered by either state or federal government, these institutions grew by focusing on real estate lending for people. Today, they offer most of the same services as commercial banks. Savings and loan associations are owned not by outside investors, but by depositors themselves, who receive shares of the company.

Mutual Savings Banks

Mutual savings banks are similar to savings and loan associations. They receive deposits primarily from individuals and concentrate also on private real estate mortgages. Mutual savings banks are owned by depositors as well. These state-chartered banks are sometimes granted greater powers with regard to assets and liabilities than S&Ls, but usually not as much as those of commercial banks.

Mutual savings banks and savings and loan associations are sometimes called *thrift institutions*. Few remain as a result of a crisis in the industry in the 1980s. These institutions are regulated and protected by the state or federal government, which is not necessarily true of non-depository intermediaries.

Credit Unions

Credit unions also are owned by depositors, but there are a couple of key differences. First, users of credit unions must be members. Membership is usually based on some type of association, such as a common employer, a certain line of work, a geographic region, or even a social or religious association. Second, credit unions are *not-for-profit* financial institutions that exist to benefit the members. Any money beyond costs is returned to the members in the form of dividends on savings, reduced fees for services, or lower rates for loans.

What is a wholesale bank? What is the primary difference between credit unions and other depositor-owned financial institutions?

_____

_____

NON-DEPOSITORY INTERMEDIARIES

As the name suggests, non-depository intermediaries don't take deposits. Instead, they perform other financial services and collect fees for them as their primary means of business. In many cases, these institutions are private companies. Although they may be regulated by the government, they are usually not backed or protected by the government.

Insurance Companies

You might not think of insurance companies as financial institutions, but they are. Insurance companies make money on the policies they sell, which protect against financial loss and/or build income for later use. The policies are not tangible and the protection they offer is financial, so the companies are performing a financial service. Some types of insurance policies have a cash value that can be redeemed at any time, and some policies let customers remove cash gradually. Insurance companies do not typically make loans, although the cash value of a policy may be used to secure a loan from elsewhere in some cases. Insurance premiums (costs) are not deposits. Private insurance companies try to earn a profit from the premiums beyond the cost of insurance payouts. Many professional money managers regard insurance as essential financial protection, but not a good investment.

Using a telephone book, find local examples of each type of depository and non-depository financial intermediary discussed in this chapter. Which type has the most offices?

Trust Companies/Pension Funds

Companies that administer pension or retirement funds also perform financial services. These companies manage money for a fee and promise in return to provide future income. Some pension funds are closely regulated, but others may not be. Growth for the contributor comes not from interest on deposits, but investments made by the administrator. These investments may yield a profit, but there is a risk of loss as well.

Brokerage Houses

Brokers are people who execute orders to buy and sell stocks and other securities. They are paid commissions. Their service is to help investors do as well as possible with their investments. Brokerage houses may offer advice or guidance, but are private companies who make a profit on the transactions.

Loan Companies

Loan companies, sometimes called finance companies, are not banks. They do not receive deposits, and they should not be confused with banks, savings and loan associations, or credit unions. They are private companies who lend money and make a profit on the interest. Loan companies sometimes make loans to customers when other institutions will not, but they charge higher interest rates to offset the risk. A new form of loan company sometimes makes extremely short-term loans against a soon-coming paycheck or other check at high interest rates. These companies also may perform some of the same services as currency exchanges.

Currency Exchanges

Currency exchanges do not make loans or receive deposits. Currency exchanges are private companies that cash checks, sell money orders, or perform other exchange services. They charge a fee, usually a percentage of the amount exchanged. Because their business depends on these fees, rates are usually higher than at banks or other financial institutions. Currency exchanges often locate in areas where no other financial intermediaries exist, and they offer the only financial services available to people in those areas.

A wide range of financial services is available from both depository and non-depository intermediaries. Most of the non-depository institutions are private companies earning money by performing specific services. You don't make deposits, earn interest, or have checking or savings accounts with them. Non-depository institutions are a part of the financial world and help move money through the economy. However, they are not part of the banking system and may not really be considered to be in the business of banking.

CHECK**POINT**

Why is an insurance company considered a financial intermediary? What is the primary difference between depository institutions and most non-depository institutions?

_____

_____

THINK CRITICALLY ●●●●●●●●●●●●●●●●●●●●●●●●

1. Services from depository institutions have become similar since deregulation. Why is there any need for different forms of depository institutions?

_____

_____

_____

2. Credit unions are not-for-profit institutions. They return profits to members. Why wouldn't everyone place their money only in credit unions?

_____

_____

_____

_____

_____

3. Do you think currency exchanges take advantage of those who do not have access to other forms of financial services? Why or why not?

_____

_____

_____

4. How does the fact that the government backs many forms of depository institutions affect the confidence of consumers about their deposits?

_____

_____

_____

MAKE CONNECTIONS ●●●●●●●●●●●●●●●●●●●●

5. SOCIAL SCIENCE Until late in the twentieth century, the financial world was male territory. Contact a large bank and learn what policies they have in place to guarantee and encourage equal opportunity careers in the banking profession. List some of those policies.

_____

_____

_____

_____

_____

_____

6. HISTORY Although services offered seem similar today, there was once a great difference between thrift institutions and banks. Find out more about the way these institutions arose to meet a particular social need. Write a one-page report about the beginnings of savings and loans, credit unions, and mutual savings banks.

CHAPTER 1 •••••••••••••••••••••••••••• REVIEW

CHAPTER SUMMARY

LESSON 1.1 Introduction to Banking
A. Banks are financial intermediaries that safeguard, transfer, exchange, and lend money. Central, commercial, and savings banks are three main types.
B. Mergers, competition, and new technology have reshaped banking.

LESSON 1.2 Role of Banks in the Economy
A. Banks safeguard our money through various business practices that protect, record, and evaluate banking transactions and businesses.
B. Banks expand the economy by transferring and lending funds to credit-worthy borrowers, thus creating markets and jobs.

LESSON 1.3 How the Banking System Works
A. Banks make money on the spread between interest paid and received. Bank assets include earnings and investments, but deposits are liabilities.
B. Bank deregulation brought expansion of customer services. New services banks offer to stay competitive include credit cards, new types of loans, and new technologies.

LESSON 1.4 Other Financial Institutions
A. Depository intermediaries include banks, savings and loan associations, mutual savings banks, and credit unions. Most of these are backed by the government.
B. Non-depository institutions include insurance companies, trust companies, loan companies, and currency exchanges. Most of these are private firms that are not part of the national banking system.

VOCABULARY BUILDER

Choose the term that best fits the definition. Write the letter of the answer in the space provided. Some terms may not be used.

a. asset
b. central banks
c. commercial banks
d. depositors
e. depository intermediary
f. deregulation
g. financial intermediary
h. liability
i. liquid asset
j. medium of exchange
k. niche market
l. non-depository intermediary
m. profit
n. retail banks
o. spread

_____ **1.** The difference between interest paid and interest received

_____ **2.** A private company that does not receive deposits but sells financial services

_____ **3.** Government banks that regulate and manage money supply

_____ **4.** A targeted smaller group of customers

_____ **5.** Most common form of government-backed corporate bank

_____ **6.** To banks, deposits represent this type of obligation

_____ **7.** The loosening of government control

_____ **8.** Holds funds for the public and uses the funds to finance their business

_____ **9.** Anything of value that can be readily exchanged

_____ **10.** Revenue minus cost

_____ **11.** An agreed-upon system for measuring value of goods and services

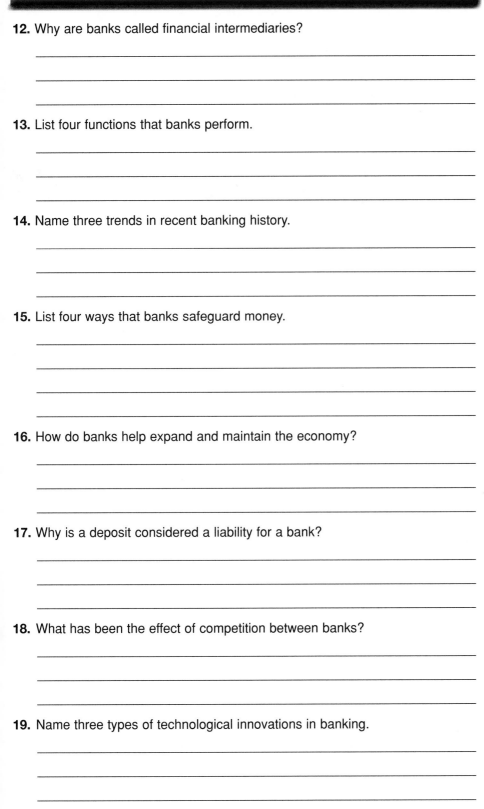

REVIEW CONCEPTS

12. Why are banks called financial intermediaries?

_____

_____

_____

13. List four functions that banks perform.

_____

_____

_____

14. Name three trends in recent banking history.

_____

_____

_____

15. List four ways that banks safeguard money.

_____

_____

_____

_____

16. How do banks help expand and maintain the economy?

_____

_____

_____

17. Why is a deposit considered a liability for a bank?

_____

_____

_____

18. What has been the effect of competition between banks?

_____

_____

_____

19. Name three types of technological innovations in banking.

_____

_____

_____

POINT YOUR BROWSER

banking.swep.com

20. Name two types of thrift institutions.

_____

_____

21. What is a non-depository financial institution?

_____

_____

_____

APPLY WHAT YOU LEARNED

22. Why are banks regulated and protected by government?

_____

_____

23. What are advantages and disadvantages of the trend toward mergers in banking?

_____

_____

_____

_____

_____

_____

24. How did deregulation ultimately result in more banking services for consumers?

_____

_____

_____

25. Would consumers be better off if all public utilities, including electric and gas companies, were deregulated so that the marketplace could set prices?

_____

_____

_____

_____

26. Consumer debt is higher than ever in the United States. What would happen if people suddenly stopped borrowing from banks?

_____

_____

_____

27. If private, non-depository loan companies charge higher interest than depository institutions backed by government, how do they stay in business?

_____

_____

_____

_____

MAKE CONNECTIONS •

28. PROBLEM SOLVING Most insurance is bought to protect against the possibility of loss, except life insurance. Everybody who buys life insurance eventually dies. Can you explain how life insurance works?

_____

_____

_____

29. ADVERTISING Analyze five bank advertisements from a variety of media, such as newspapers, magazines, radio, television, billboards, and the Internet. What do banks do to get your business? Keep a journal for one week, noting each advertiser, the services being advertised, and a basic description of each ad. Make a chart that shows your analysis.

30. BANKING LAW _Usury_ is the practice of charging extreme interest rates. From your library or the Internet, find out more about usury limits, what they are, how they work, and what the usury limits are in various states. Write a one-page report summarizing what you learn.

31. ETHICS ATM fees are a source of revenue for banks. If you use an ATM from a bank different from your own, you may be charged a fee for the transaction both by the bank that owns the machine and by your own bank for processing the transaction. Does this seem fair to you? Why or why not?

_____

_____

_____

_____

_____

_____

_____

32. CAREERS Visit the web site of a large regional bank. Find out what opportunities the bank offers to prospective employees. Make a list of some of the positions available and the training and experience required.

_____

_____

_____

_____

CHAPTER 2

DEVELOPMENT OF U.S. BANKING

2.1 CREATION OF A NATIONAL CURRENCY
2.2 BANKING BEFORE 1913
2.3 BANKING IN THE TWENTIETH CENTURY
2.4 THE FEDERAL RESERVE SYSTEM

Careers in Banking

THE FEDERAL RESERVE

The Federal Reserve is the central banking system of the United States. Established by an act of Congress in 1913, the Federal Reserve operates 12 District Reserve Banks around the country to distribute funds, process payments, and implement monetary policy. There is also a Board of Governors site in Washington D.C.

The Federal Reserve offers employment to a wide range of qualified personnel. Positions range from clerical to professional, including everything from check processors to bank examiners to research economists to mainframe programmers. Requirements for employment vary with each position, but professional positions require degrees, and most positions require some specialized training.

The Federal Reserve offers excellent benefits. Included are a variety of insurance programs, and savings and retirement plans that include employer contribution. "The Fed," as it is often called, also offers liberal vacation, paid holidays, casual dress, and flexible schedules.

THINK CRITICALLY

1. Why might the Federal Reserve be a surprising source of banking career possibilities?
2. What differences and similarities might exist between working for the Federal Reserve and for a large commercial bank?

BANKING HISTORY and YOU

PROJECT OBJECTIVES

- Consider the connections between bank history and modern banking
- Identify traces of early U.S. banking that survive today
- Link banking system reforms to modern banking practice
- Increase awareness of Federal Reserve activities

VIDEO

The Chapter 2 video introduces the concepts in this chapter.

GETTING STARTED

Read through the Project Process below. Make a list of any materials you will need. Decide how you will get the needed materials or information.

- Make a list of state and national banks in your area. You might want to use materials you compiled for the project in Chapter 1.
- Identify banks for which you will create a history. These may be entire corporations or specific buildings or branches. Identify sources of information.
- Make a timeline that shows important developments in the history of U.S. banking.

PROJECT PROCESS

Part 1 LESSON 2.1 Discuss in class how you use currency. Compare its use with other forms of exchange media, such as checks or credit and debit cards. What are its advantages and disadvantages?

Part 2 LESSON 2.2 Compile histories of several local banks. Focus on changes in structure, ownership, and services.

Part 3 LESSON 2.3 Learn more about the effect of the Great Depression in your community. Use the library or newspaper archives to find out how it affected the local financial community and how the community responded both to the crisis and to governmental reforms.

Part 4 LESSON 2.4 Find out about the Federal Reserve District Bank for your region. Visit the web site of your regional bank for information. Find out who its officers are and who serves as its directors. Learn as much as you can about these people. Study career possibilities.

CHAPTER REVIEW

Project Wrap-up Hold a class discussion about the structure of the banking system. Make a list of things about the Federal Reserve that you did not know before studying the chapter and completing the project. Make another list of things about which you would like to know more or that you still don't understand.

CREATION OF A NATIONAL CURRENCY··

GOALS

IDENTIFY different types of currency

EXPLAIN how currency evolved through the early days of the United States to what it is today

WHAT IS CURRENCY?

Money is a *medium of exchange* for people to use to trade things of value. Anything from fur to grain to metal can fill that role. In most places of the world, some form of money is the agreed-upon medium of exchange. So what is meant by the term "currency"?

Most people associate the word with paper money, and they're mostly right. Strictly speaking, **currency** is all media of exchange circulating in a country. This definition includes coins as well as paper money, and in today's society it also includes credit instruments, such as bonds, checks, and even some types of loan papers.

BANKING *Scene*

When Katie Conlon finished high school, an aunt gave her a $100 bill as a graduation gift. As she wrote her thank you note to her aunt, Katie took a good look at the bill. As much a part of life as cash is daily, she had never given it much thought. How and why did currency start circulating in the United States? What part of the government prints money? Katie started checking the Internet to find out. What web sites would be good places to start looking?

Classifying Currency

To keep terms straight, most economists make some other distinctions, dividing the term currency between coins, called *metallic currency*, and paper money or credit instruments, called *paper currency*. There are further terms for paper currency, depending upon who issued it. *Government currency* is money printed by a government. In some countries, banks issue notes against their reserves called bank notes, which are referred to as *bank currency*. Checks are also a form of currency, and they are called *deposit currency*, because that is how their value is redeemed.

Shifting Meanings

As with many financial concepts, the idea of currency has changed. Before World War I (1914–1918), many countries had governments that did not issue paper money. Paper currency meant only notes issued by large banks. In the United States, however, paper currency meant the money that the government printed, and nothing else. Following the war, the idea of currency began to take on the broader sense in use today. In part, this broader sense was the result of changes in banking and economics that circulated many more forms of valuable paper, including the various credit instruments comprising the concept of currency today.

What is currency?

_____

_____

_____

THE GROWTH OF AMERICAN CURRENCY

An account of the earliest days of American currency is generally a history of a mixture of types of money—not unlike the mixture of people who came to populate the country. In the early days, some settlers used shells and nails to trade for what they needed, making them a kind of coinage. Quickly thereafter, various types of money, both coins and paper, started circulating among the settlements that would one day rise up and create a nation.

Colonial Cash

Coins were the most common medium of exchange. Some British-type coins were minted on American soil as early as the 1650s, but few colonists trusted them much. Foreign money was much more common. Though the colonies did use English pounds and shillings, a Spanish dollar called the *real* was the most popular. Higher in silver content than other coins, the real was the most trusted form of currency in America. Early American coins were imitations of reals.

There was always some form of paper money in the colonies, too. Much of it consisted of English or other foreign bank notes. Most of this paper money could be redeemed for coins, which were trusted far more than paper certificates.

U.S. GOVERNMENT PAPER CURRENCY TODAY

Amount	Portrait on Front
One dollar note	George Washington
Two dollar note	Thomas Jefferson
Five dollar note	Abraham Lincoln
Ten dollar note	Alexander Hamilton
Twenty dollar note	Andrew Jackson
Fifty dollar note	Ulysses S. Grant
One hundred dollar note	Benjamin Franklin

Five hundred, one thousand, five thousand, and ten thousand dollar notes have been unavailable from the Treasury since 1969. Last printed in 1945, these large denominations are still legal tender, although most are in the hands of collectors.

During the Revolutionary War, the Continental Congress issued paper money to buy desperately needed supplies. Few people had any confidence in this currency. In fact, the scornful phrase "not worth a continental" referred for many years to any worthless item.

Currency in the United States

After the Revolutionary War, the new United States decided to replace the many colonial coins then circulating. The Mint Act of April 1792 authorized $10, $5, and $2.50 gold coins; $1, 50¢, 25¢, 10¢, and 5¢ silver coins; and 1¢ and 1/2¢ copper coins. The U.S. mint began operation in 1794, but many of the foreign coins remained in common circulation well into the 1830s.

The U.S. government did not print paper money itself until 1861. Before then, bank notes from two chartered Banks of the United States and from many different state banks were the only paper currency.

The many types of currency often caused problems. During the crisis of the Civil War, people became so concerned about the value of money that some stores even issued their own currency. The National Currency Act of 1863, later rewritten as the National Banking Act of 1864, established standards for currency. It also taxed state bank notes, making them unprofitable. State banks gradually got out of the business of issuing currency, and a system of national currency came into being. Problems with the money supply still persisted, though, and in 1913 the Federal Reserve Act established the basic banking system in use today.

CHECK**POINT**

WORKSHOP

In a group, keep a record for one week of all types of currency that pass through your hands. Record the denomination and number of each type of currency with which you come in contact. Include both coins and paper currency. Compare your results with those of other groups.

What was the most common medium of exchange in Colonial America? When did the U.S. government begin to issue paper currency?

_____

_____

THINK CRITICALLY ●●●●●●●●●●●●●●●●●●●●●●●

1. Why was early American currency a mixture of forms of money?

_____

_____

_____

2. Outline the early history of money in the U.S. economy.

_____

_____

_____

_____

_____

_____

3. Why might people have distrusted the value of paper currency issued by the Continental Congress during the Revolutionary War?

_____

_____

_____

_____

4. Why might currencies issued by the many state banks have caused confusion before the Civil War?

_____

_____

_____

_____

MAKE CONNECTIONS ●●●●●●●●●●●●●●●●●●●●●

5. HISTORY Another form of currency that didn't hold its value was currency issued by the Confederate States of America during its rebellion from the Union in the Civil War. Use the library, the Internet, or other research sources to learn more about Confederate currency. Write a one-page report that explains the problems that the Confederate States had with its currency and why it couldn't hold its value. What are specimens of Confederate currency worth today?

6. SOCIAL STUDIES The U.S. Bureau of Engraving and Printing is responsible for printing currency for the U.S. government. Incorporated in the design of each note are symbols that represent ideas from American philosophy and identifying features of the particular note. Visit the Bureau's web site at www.bep.treas.gov to learn more about some of these features. Choose a note of some denomination, and create a chart or graphical representation that interprets and explains the symbols and features and what they mean.

7. TECHNOLOGY Both metallic and paper currency are so common in society that hardly anyone gives them a second glance. Did you ever wonder how they are produced? Research sources of your choosing and create a written, oral, or computer presentation that explains the process used to make either paper or metallic currency.

IDENTIFY the reasons for the establishment and expiration of both the first and second Banks of the United States

DESCRIBE the continuing problems that led to the Federal Reserve Act

BANKS IN THE YOUNG UNITED STATES

In many ways, democracy in the new United States of America was an experiment. Never before had a country attempted such an enterprise. The young nation had to work its way through many problems of government, trying to find the right balance between the role of the government and the freedom of individuals. In a similar way, banking in the early United States also had an experimental quality. Some of the history of U.S. banking was a process of trial and error, and some of the issues were the result of struggles between competing ideas—just as in the nation at large.

The First Bank of the United States

George Washington's Secretary of the Treasury, Alexander Hamilton, believed that without a strong central government and a strong bank, the new nation would eventually fail. Hamilton encouraged the new

When Katie Conlon moved from her home in New Jersey to attend college in Bloomington, Indiana, she wanted to set up a bank account in town. She saw advertisements for many banks, but two banks caught her eye. BankOne, a national bank, and Peoples State Bank both offered services that looked more or less the same. What was the difference between a state bank and a national bank? How could she find out?

government to not only accept and pay with interest the debts of the Revolutionary War, but also to assume responsibility for debts of individual states incurred in the struggle. In this way, the Federal government established itself as the final authority for the economic security of the new nation.

Hamilton also urged the creation of a Bank of the United States. Thomas Jefferson, who believed creating such an institution gave too much power to too few people, fiercely opposed him in this idea. Over Jefferson's objections, the bank was chartered in 1791.

The first Bank of the United States was not an institution of government. The bank was privately held. Although the government owned about 20 percent of the bank, the rest was in the hands of private investors and foreign governments, to the continuing unhappiness of those who opposed it.

As the chief depository of the U.S. government, the bank gained power. By 1805, the bank had eight branches. Its bank notes became the most common form of currency circulating in the United States. It also exercised control on state-chartered banks, not by law but by demanding that state banks redeem their bank notes with gold or silver when they were deposited in the first Bank of the United States. Thus, the bank almost accidentally performed the role of a central bank. As the nation grew westward, more people resented the control of powerful Eastern bankers. When the bank's charter expired in 1811, there was not enough political support to renew it.

The Second Bank of the United States

Within five years, conflicting state bank policies and changing economic conditions caused Congress to reconsider. In 1816, Congress granted the second Bank of the United States a twenty-year charter. After a slow start, the bank began to do well under its president, Nicholas Biddle.

Biddle deliberately improved upon the central banking functions of regulating credit and the money supply, but had to do so by restraining state banks, who then saw the U.S. bank as an enemy. A new class of entrepreneurs and developers who thought regulation of money and credit supply was not in their interest was gaining power. Rising resentment of what people saw as an aristocracy again spelled trouble for the bank.

President Andrew Jackson took office in 1828 and was an unyielding opponent of the bank. Jackson's chief rival, Senator Henry Clay, tried to renew the bank's charter four years early in 1832, hoping to make the renewal an election issue. Jackson vetoed the bill, arguing that the bank represented "the advancement of the few at the expense of the many." The bank did indeed become a campaign issue, but Jackson trounced Clay in the election.

The bank's charter still had four years to run. Determined to kill the bank that he saw as unconstitutional, Jackson forced the withdrawal of government funds from it, moving money instead to a number of state banks, which came to be called his "pet banks." The second Bank of the United States weakened and died when its charter expired in 1836.

In small groups, collect images of as many types of old currencies as you can. You may include certificates, notes, coins, Confederate money, and even legal tender that has been recently updated but remains in circulation. Visit the Bureau of Engraving and Printing's web site at www.bep.treas.gov for more information on these currencies.

CHECK**POINT**

Why did the two first U.S. National banks fail?

_____

_____

THE BANK OF ENGLAND

The Bank of England, one of the oldest central banks, was nationalized in 1946. The bank advises the government on monetary issues, but its freedom to act independently is limited. The bank implements the chosen monetary policy and performs other central banking functions, such as funding public borrowing, issuing bank notes, and managing reserves. It also deals with international banking issues on behalf of the government.

THINK CRITICALLY

What are the advantages of a central banking system entirely under the control of the government? What are the disadvantages?

STEPS TOWARD CENTRAL BANKING

In the absence of a national banking system, state banks grew in number and influence. Private banks sprang up, each with its own policies and currency. This fragmented system supplied money for the economy, but without some overriding control, chaos with credit and the money supply reigned. The Independent Treasury System, a network of federal offices that handled U.S. government money, could not manage the banking system adequately.

The National Banking Act of 1864

The Civil War brought monetary issues to a head. Rampant inflation threatened the entire economic system. The National Banking Act of 1864 was enacted to stabilize the banking system. The law established the office of the Comptroller of the Currency to issue charters to national banks. These banks were authorized to issue national bank notes. A high tax on state bank notes made the currency business unprofitable, so state bank currencies died out. State banks continued to survive by expanding their deposit functions and other services. The dual federal and state banking system survives today.

Continuing Issues Although the National Banking Act helped by establishing a national currency, it still did not provide for ongoing monitoring and regulation of the credit and money supply, nor did it guarantee the safety of banks. Money supply problems occurred time and again in the expanding industrial economy after the Civil War. Serious crises and bank failures occurred in 1873, 1883, 1893, and 1907. Finally, in 1913, the Federal Reserve Act created a system to stabilize the banking system, and a formal central banking system for the United States came into being.

What was the purpose of the National Banking Act of 1864?

_____

_____

THINK CRITICALLY ●●●●●●●●●●●●●●●●●●●●●●●●

1. Do you agree with Hamilton or Jefferson about the creation of a private bank to handle government banking? Explain your reasoning.

_____

_____

_____

2. How did conflicting political views ultimately cause the demise of the first two Banks of the United States?

_____

_____

_____

3. Prior to the Federal Reserve Act of 1913, what factors made the banking system and the economy unstable?

_____

_____

_____

MAKE CONNECTIONS ●●●●●●●●●●●●●●●●●●●●●●

4. TECHNOLOGY Counterfeiting is an ongoing problem associated with paper currency since the government first began printing it. Visit the U.S. Bureau of Engraving and Printing's web site at www.bep.treas.gov to learn about anti-counterfeiting measures. What challenges does modern technology present and what steps does the Bureau take to meet them?

_____

_____

_____

_____

_____

_____

5. HISTORY The battle between Hamilton and Jefferson over the Bank of the United States led to the formation of political parties. Find out how. In what way did the disagreement between Hamilton and Jefferson over the bank reflect two fundamentally different views of the union of states? How did this tension affect the growing economy of the United States?

_____

_____

_____

_____

_____

6. COMMUNICATION In some ways, the argument over power and influence of monetary policy that raged in the early 1800s is still with us. Conduct a poll of classmates, friends, relatives, or your community to find out who the public thinks controls the economy. Compile your results as a class, interviewing at least 50 total subjects.

BANKING IN THE TWENTIETH CENTURY

GOALS

EXPLAIN why Congress estabished the Federal Reserve System

IDENTIFY challenges that the banking system of the United States faced in the twentieth century

A TRUE NATIONAL BANKING SYSTEM

In the half century before the Federal Reserve Act of 1913, America transformed itself into an industrial powerhouse. This massive industrialization sometimes caused problems with the banking system as the demand for credit and money was high. The National Banking Act of 1864 put a reserve system in place, with small banks able to borrow reserves from city banks, which could in turn borrow from central reserve city banks. However, this structure was not flexible. Sudden economic downturns could cause a chain reaction, with a few banks causing stress on the entire system because there was not enough *reserve liquidity*, or ways to convert the reserves readily to cash.

Before she left for college, Katie Conlon visited her grandmother, who had given her a check toward her education and told her to put it in a "good, safe bank." Then her grandmother told Katie stories of her own childhood during the Depression, including how her father had lost his savings when a bank went out of business. "Could that happen today?" Katie wondered. What are good resources to learn about the Great Depression?

The Federal Reserve Act of 1913

After a severe economic panic in 1907, Congress formed a bipartisan group (made up of members from both political parties) to study the problem. The Federal Reserve Act in 1913 founded a system of central banking that was both adaptable and flexible. A board of directors controlled district reserve banks from which member banks could borrow money to meet demand. The original Federal Reserve Board consisted of presidential appointees, the Secretary of the Treasury, and the Comptroller of the Currency. Ten-year terms for appointed members removed the responsibilities of the board from partisan politics.

The Federal Reserve handled the government's central banking function, conducted bank examinations, and decided whether banks could borrow money from the Federal Reserve, based on whether the banks were being run responsibly and whether extending the loan would put stress on the banking system at large. In this way, banks came under the control of an organization whose job it was to monitor and protect the entire banking system. It was also in the interest of member banks to conduct their own operations in such a way as to satisfy the Reserve Board. Thus, the United States at last had a federal institution to manage monetary policy.

The Federal Reserve has changed since its beginning in 1913, both in structure and in operation, largely as a result of the crisis of the Great Depression. Today, the Federal Reserve plays a key role in the economy.

Banks in Crisis

The **Great Depression**, which began in 1929 and extended worldwide until about 1939, was the worst and longest economic crisis in the history of Western industrialized nations. The stock market crash in October of 1929 brought about near-collapse of the economic system in the United States and other nations. Many banks and their customers were its victims.

Ironically, the failure was caused in part by success. The economy was roaring in the 1920s, and the stock market was booming. The market was so attractive, in fact, that everyone wanted in, whether they had the money available or not. People and companies borrowed money to buy stocks or bought them on credit. Many stocks were bought on **margin**, or for a fraction of their price, then resold at a profit, without the full purchase price of the stock ever having been paid. This practice led to risky investments and speculation. When the market began to fall in September 1929, nervous

Interview someone who experienced the Great Depression firsthand. Find out ways that people coped with the economic crisis. Focus as much as possible on the lack of cash and financial services. Write a short report on what you learn and what your interviewee thinks should be learned from that era.

ETHICS IN ACTION

At the time of its founding, the Federal Reserve was hotly criticized by many who felt that its makeup was dominated by bankers, who would act only in their own interests and ignore the "common man." The final structure of the Reserve represented a compromise on these issues.

THINK CRITICALLY

If you were a member of the Federal Reserve Board, how would you separate your own interests from the good of the country's economy?

investors began to sell their stocks. In October, the panic spread, everyone tried to dump stocks, and the market collapsed. There was no money to pay what was owed on margin or on anything else.

In addition, many banks had also invested in the stock market. Those banks that did not fail outright were pressed to their limits and had no money for further loans or investments. Businesses failed, and people were forced out of work. They could not pay back loans from banks, further worsening the position of financial institutions. Hence, the entire economy spiraled rapidly downward. American ties to Europe and continuing economic problems after World War I spread the depression worldwide.

People rushed to their banks to withdraw what money they could. Deposits are liabilities, and no bank keeps enough reserves to cover all liabilities. When many people try to withdraw their money at once, a **bank run** takes place, and many such runs occurred.

Bank failures threatened the entire nation and depositors in most failed banks completely lost their money. On March 6, 1933, after a series of major bank failures, newly elected President Franklin D. Roosevelt closed all banks by proclamation. He declared a *bank holiday* in order to save the remaining assets of banks still in business and to let people calm down, as he tried to assure them that the government could help.

The Banking Acts of 1933 and 1935

Within four days after President Roosevelt declared the bank holiday, Congress passed the Emergency Banking Act of 1933. This law, also called the Glass-Steagall Act, massively reformed the nation's banking system. Among other things, it separated commercial banking from investment banking to protect assets, and it required bank holding companies to be examined by the Federal Reserve. Perhaps most importantly, it established the **Federal Deposit Insurance Corporation** (FDIC), which guarantees deposits against bank failures up to specified limits, currently $100,000. These actions restored public confidence in the nation's banking system. Banks reopened, and three quarters of them survived.

The Banking Act of 1935 made further refinements by expanding the monetary controls of the Federal Reserve and changing the structure of the Federal Reserve Board. The Secretary of the Treasury and the Comptroller of the Currency were removed, and board member terms were lengthened. These two acts, with some modifications made later, have prevented the massive banking failures of the 1930s from recurring.

The scope of the banking problem during the Great Depression was massive. More than 10,000 of the approximately 24,000 banks in the United States went out of business.

What brought about the creation of the Federal Reserve in 1913? What is a bank run?

_____

_____

MODERN BANKING

The basic banking system remained unchanged for the rest of the twentieth century. Changes in the way the Federal Reserve deals with Congress and in the way it prices its services to member banks fine-tuned the system. The Reserve and its chairmen became more independent of government. Its primary goal is to promote general economic health more than any particular policy. Challenges posed by inflation, recession, and modernization have changed banking dramatically from the business it was in Roosevelt's time.

Inflation and Banking

Banks changed in the 1970s and 1980s in part because of the pressure of inflation. **Inflation** is a collective rise in the supply of money, incomes, and prices. You might think that an increase in money supply and incomes is a good thing, but what tends to happen is that prices go up as well. A sustained increase in costs and supply of money leads to money having less purchasing power. For example, in 1932 a wool sweater cost $1.00 and a gas stove cost $19.95. A factory worker earned about $17.00 per week and an accountant earned $45.00. The problem is that in periods of severe inflation, prices tend to rise faster than earnings. When earnings catch up, the general level has risen, and so it becomes true that "a dollar isn't what it used to be." How well could that accountant live on $45.00 per week today?

Although there are many theories about what causes inflation, economic problems usually go with it. In periods of runaway inflation, no one can keep up, because the value of money does not match the value of goods. It takes more and more money to buy fewer and fewer things. In addition, money put aside earlier no longer has the buying power it had when it was saved.

Just such a cycle occurred in the 1970s and 1980s. Prices, wages, and interest rose rapidly, partly because of an excess of easy credit and money supply. During this same period, banks struggled because the law limited the amount of interest they could pay. Faced with more attractive options, depositors put their money elsewhere, and banks again began to have trouble. Although inflation was rising, the economy as a whole was not doing especially well, producing an unusual circumstance called **stagflation**, a combination of a stagnant economy and high inflation, almost 13 percent per year.

To combat inflation, the Federal Reserve tightened the money supply and allowed interest rates to rise. A severe recession followed, but inflation fell and has remained low. The 1990s saw the longest period of sustained growth in U.S. history.

Work as a class to make a chart that shows the prices of a list of typical goods and services thirty years ago as compared to today.

BANKING MATH CONNECTION

Did you get a 13% raise this year? Most people didn't. If inflation is running at 13%, you need a raise of that rate just to break even. If inflation continues to rise for a few years, it can have a ruinous effect. Calculate the cost of 13% inflation for five years on the cost of a $15,000 car.

SOLUTION

The formula for calculating one year's rise is

(Original cost × Inflation rate) + Original cost = Year one cost
($15,000 × 0.13) + $15,000 = $16,950.00

To calculate for five years, you can't just multiply 13% by five (65%) and use that as the rate, because the original cost changes (compounds) every year. The calculation must be repeated five times, using the year one cost in place of the original cost for year two, and so forth.

($16,950.00 × 0.13) + $16,950.00 = $19,153.50   Year two cost
($19,153.50 × 0.13) + $19,153.50 = $21,643.46   Year three cost
($21,643.46 × 0.13) + $21,643.46 = $24,457.11   Year four cost
($24,457.11 × 0.13) + $24,457.11 = $27,636.53   Year five cost

Deregulation

Laws were passed in the early 1980s to let banks compete more freely with other financial firms, opening the doors to the services available today. Not all of the effects of deregulation were good, however. Some financial institutions were allowed to make unwise loans and investments. Many savings and loan institutions (S&Ls) took advantage of new regulations to invest in commercial real estate and speculative loans. When the recession of the mid-1980s struck, these S&Ls failed. Because the Federal Savings and Loan Insurance Corporation (FSLIC), similar to the FDIC for banks, could not cover all the losses, the government stepped in. U.S. taxpayers had to pay for the policies of both the government and the officers of the failed S&Ls.

The Revolution Continues As the twenty-first century began, an economic downturn prompted the Federal Reserve to drop interest rates several times in hopes of stimulating the economy. Additionally, evolving technology combined with competition and mergers to change the banking industry constantly. Although the basic structure of the banking system remains essentially as it was in 1913, the business of banking, with its rapid communication, its global information exchange, and its marketing focus, little resembles the banking industry of an earlier age.

CHECKPOINT

Why is inflation a potentially serious economic threat? Why were banks deregulated in the early 1980s?

_____

_____

THINK CRITICALLY ••••••••••••••••••••••••

1. Why couldn't Congress just allow a free market to determine monetary policy?

_____

_____

_____

2. Why do you think the Federal Reserve Act attempted to remove the members of its board from the pressures of partisan politics?

_____

_____

_____

_____

3. How did consumer fear help cause the bank failures of the Great Depression?

_____

_____

_____

4. Why is inflation particularly hard on those who save money well?

_____

_____

_____

MAKE CONNECTIONS ••••••••••••••••••••••

5. BANKING MATH Inflation is still with us, although the rates are far lower than they were 30 years ago. Anticipating inflation is part of financial planning. If this year's inflation rate is 2.7%, and you placed $2,000 in a savings account at the beginning of the year earning 2% interest, how much must you deposit in the account at the end of the year to hold the same purchasing value?

_____

_____

_____

_____

6. POLITICAL SCIENCE Find out more about how Roosevelt reshaped society during the Great Depression. Although controversial, Roosevelt's efforts brought about the government you recognize today. Choose research materials to write a paragraph about how Roosevelt transformed the nation, listing some of the reforms.

_____

_____

_____

_____

_____

Lesson 2.4
THE FEDERAL RESERVE SYSTEM • • • • • • • • • • •

IDENTIFY the organization of the Federal Reserve System

EXPLAIN how the Federal Reserve influences banks and the economy

STRUCTURE OF THE FED

The Federal Reserve was created to respond to problems with the nation's changing money supply. Now you will look more closely at the modern Federal Reserve System, learn who makes it up, what the system does, and how it does it. The "Fed," as it is often called, functions as the government's banker, providing a range of financial services both to the government and to all financial institutions. It also supervises banks, conducting examinations to identify risk or bookkeeping problems. The Federal Reserve manages monetary policy as well, hoping to benefit not only banks but also the economy at large.

The Federal Reserve is a uniquely American approach to central banking. It is a combination of public and private policymakers working together to control the nation's monetary policy, supervise banks, and provide financial services to the government and banks. The Federal Reserve is set up like a

After opening an account at Peoples State Bank, Katie Conlon stopped at a fast food drive-thru for a soft drink. Waiting to pay, she happened to glance at the bill in her hand. At the top of the bill, she saw the words "Federal Reserve Note." Why, she wondered, are these bills called Federal Reserve notes? Katie resolved to find out more about the Federal Reserve System. Where might she start?

private corporation, with member banks holding stock in their district reserve bank, but the President appoints the Board of Governors. Congress compromised on a mix of private and public interests for the Federal Reserve, and that mix is intended to serve the interest of the nation at large. The Federal government appropriates no money for the Federal Reserve. Its income is derived from financial services and interest on loans to its member banks. Any money made above the cost of providing services is turned over to the U.S. Treasury.

Think of the structure of the Federal Reserve as a pyramid, with member banks as the base, District Reserve Banks in the middle, the Board of Governors near the top, and the Chairman at the very peak. Each of these levels depends upon information and action from other parts to hold up the system.

Member Banks

Any bank that is part of the Federal Reserve System is known as a **member bank**. All national banks must be member banks of the Federal Reserve System. They must purchase stock in the District Reserve Banks in their regions. This stock cannot be bought or sold, and it does not offer control of the District Reserve Bank. It does convey voting rights, however, for directors of the District Bank, and it also pays a 6 percent dividend. State-chartered banks are not required to be members of the Federal Reserve System, although they may choose to do so if they meet requirements.

District Reserve Banks

District Reserve Banks carry out banking functions for government offices in their area, examine member banks in the district, decide whether to loan banks funds, recommend interest rates, and implement policy decisions of the Board of Governors. There are twelve regional District Reserve Banks, located in Atlanta, Boston, Chicago, Cleveland, Dallas, Kansas City, Minneapolis, New York, Philadelphia, Richmond, San Francisco, and St. Louis. These banks also have branch offices.

Each district bank is governed by a nine-member board of directors, six of whom are nonbankers elected by member banks. The Board of Governors selects the three other board members. Each board also elects the president of its district bank, subject to approval by the Board of Governors.

Board of Governors

The President selects members of the Board of Governors, subject to consent of the Senate. Each of the seven governors serves a 14-year term, one beginning January 31 of every even-numbered year so that terms are staggered. The Board of Governors is the policy-making arm of the Federal Reserve Board, and its decisions control monetary policy. The Board of Governors oversees the District Reserve Banks and also controls mergers, bank holding companies, U.S. offices of international banks, and the reserves of depository institutions.

The Chairman

The President also selects the Chairman and Vice-Chairman of the Federal Reserve from the membership of the Board of Governors, subject to confirmation of the Senate. The Chairman and Vice-Chairman each serve a four-year term, but no limit is set on the number of terms. The current Chairman, Alan Greenspan, has served since 1987. The Chairman is a visible and powerful symbol and spokesperson of Federal Reserve policies.

The Federal Reserve structure allows for both central control of monetary policy and regional control of district and member banks. Thus, the Federal Reserve, though a central bank, has a decentralized structure that bases policies on both national and regional concerns through close communication.

CHECK**POINT**

What are the four structural elements of the Federal Reserve?

_____

_____

WORKSHOP

In small groups, make a graph that shows the rate of inflation for each of the last 30 years. Divide the research responsibilities for different time segments among group members.

FUNCTIONS OF THE FED

The Federal Reserve acts as the central banking authority of the United States, managing the banking system of the country. The four main functions of the Federal Reserve are to serve as the government's bank, to serve as a bank for other banks, to supervise and regulate bank operations, and to use monetary policy to influence the supply of money and credit.

The Government's Bank

The U.S. government performs many financial actions through the Federal Reserve. Tax payments to the Internal Revenue Service go to accounts in Federal Reserve banks. From these accounts, the government makes payments to employees, to Social Security recipients, to military personnel, and for other expenses associated with the government.

In addition, Federal Reserve banks perform some services for the government that add directly to its income. The Federal Reserve is responsible for selling and redeeming various government securities, such as savings bonds, treasury bills, treasury notes, and treasury bonds.

The Banks' Bank

One of the main reasons the Federal Reserve was created was to serve as a reserve bank for other banks to ease shortages of cash or to credit banks that have an excess. It still performs this role.

The Federal Reserve also processes payments between banks. Originally, this function developed to speed the collection of checks, but the task expanded to processing payments for other large accounts, such as payroll accounts and payments for large manufacturing orders. Today, this role also includes not only paper checks, but also electronic funds transfers, the means by which most large transactions move.

Bank Supervision

The Federal Reserve supervises and regulates all member banks. Agencies such as the Office of the Controller of the Currency and the FDIC participate in regulatory activities as well. State banking authorities also conduct supervisory activities, so that banks, whether member of the Fed or not, are supervised to ensure responsible banking practice.

Conducting Bank Examinations Reviewing a bank's financial condition, its management, and its compliance with banking policies is a key Federal Reserve task. Examiners use the **CAMELS** system to evaluate six criteria of safety and soundness. Each letter stands for one of the criteria: **C**apital adequacy, **A**sset adequacy, **M**anagement, **E**arnings, **L**iquidity, and **S**ensitivity to risk. Risk evaluation measures whether a bank makes good decisions in lending money.

Supervising International Banks Operating in the United States, the Federal Reserve ensures fair competition and communicates with central banking authorities in other countries to promote consistent policies.

Protecting Consumers Consumer protection is another function of the Federal Reserve. Bank examiners monitor whether customers are treated fairly in terms of fees, prices, penalties, and even advertising. Banks must show that they offer and perform their services, including making loans, on an equal opportunity basis.

The Federal Reserve has actually been making electronic funds transfers since the 1920s, when the telegraph was used to "wire" money. The Fed used telegraph technology until the 1970s.

FEDWIRE

Like many businesses and private individuals, the Federal Reserve System uses electronic funds transfer (EFT) to make and receive payments. The Fed has its own system, called Fedwire, with special capabilities. Fedwire connects the Federal Reserve, the Treasury, other government agencies, and more than 9,500 financial institutions.

In 1999, about 102.8 million transfers totaling $343 trillion took place over the Fedwire network. The Federal Reserve by law must charge for its Fedwire services and prices them according to cost.

THINK CRITICALLY

In what ways does Fedwire strengthen the entire Federal Reserve System? Why might the law mandate a charge for this service?

Monetary Policy

The most famous function of the Federal Reserve is conducting monetary policy. The primary goals of the Federal Reserve's monetary policy are to maintain economic growth, to stabilize prices, and to keep international payments flowing smoothly. Federal Reserve actions affect the amount of reserves banks hold, affecting the money supply, which affects the economy.

Open Market Operations The Fed buys and sells securities issued by the Treasury Department or other government agencies. These are called *open market* sales because the Fed does not control with whom it is doing business in the sales, but trades at a profit or loss in order to accomplish monetary control. These transactions affect the *federal funds rate*, the rate at which banks borrow from each other. When the Fed wants to increase reserves, it buys securities. When it wants to decrease reserves, it sells them. These adjustments are short-term, sometimes taking place within a few days or hours.

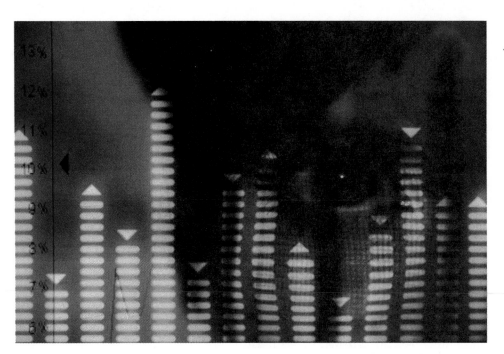

Setting Reserve Requirements The Fed adjusts the portion of total deposits that banks must keep on hand in their vaults or at the Federal Reserve. The higher the reserve requirement, the less money in circulation.

Adjusting the Discount Interest Rate The Fed indirectly affects interest rates at large. The **discount rate** is the rate of interest that the Federal Reserve charges banks for short-term loans. Other interest rates often rise or fall with the discount rate. The **Federal Open Market Committee** (FOMC) makes discount rate decisions. The committee consists of the seven-member Board of Governors (which includes the Chairman of the Federal Reserve), the Chairman of the New York District Reserve Bank, and presidents of four other District Reserve Banks who serve on a rotating basis. The Federal Reserve performs these actions in response to economic conditions and has a staff to compile and analyze large amounts of data for support. Economics is an inexact science, but the Federal Reserve has so far avoided the catastrophes of the 1930s in spite of some uncertain economic times.

CHECK**POINT**

What are the primary functions of the Federal Reserve?

_____

_____

THINK CRITICALLY ●●●●●●●●●●●●●●●●●●●●●●●●

1. Why do you think only national banks are required to be members of the Federal Reserve System?

_____

_____

_____

2. Why are Federal Reserve District Banks distributed across the nation?

_____

_____

_____

3. How does increasing a bank's required reserve result in less money circulating in the economy?

_____

_____

_____

4. Why doesn't the government legislate the value of money and set interest rates by law?

_____

_____

_____

_____

MAKE CONNECTIONS ●●●●●●●●●●●●●●●●●●●●●●

5. EDUCATION Visit the Federal Reserve Board of Governors' web site at www.federalreserve.gov. From the General Information link, find the District Reserve Bank that serves your area. Find and visit that bank's site, and discover what materials it makes available for citizen education. List those resources here.

_____

_____

_____

_____

_____

_____

_____

6. BIOGRAPHY One of the most influencial Federal Reserve chairmen in recent history has been Alan Greenspan. Use resource material of your own choosing, and write a one-page report on the life and career of this powerful figure. Why did presidents of different political parties choose to renominate him?

CHAPTER SUMMARY

LESSON 2.1 Creation of a National Currency

A. Currency includes all circulating media of exchange in a country. It may include metallic currency (coins) and paper currency (government currency, bank currency, deposit currency, and other credit instruments).

B. There were many forms of currency in early American history. After the Revolutionary War, bank notes from many sources circulated. After the Civil War, forms other than U.S.-issued currency were taxed out of existence.

LESSON 2.2 Banking Before 1913

A. Both the first and the second Banks of the United States were private institutions that ultimately died. Banks were largely unregulated until the Civil War.

B. The National Banking Act of 1864 eliminated many forms of currency and moved toward a central banking system. Money supply problems persisted.

LESSON 2.3 Banking in the Twentieth Century

A. Congress established the Federal Reserve in 1913. It was the first official central banking system in U.S. history.

B. The Great Depression brought many bank failures. Banking reform acts saved the industry. Challenges from inflation and changes from technology characterized later twentieth-century banking.

LESSON 2.4 The Federal Reserve System

A. The Chairman oversees the Federal Reserve Board, which oversees the 12 District Reserve Banks, which monitor and serve the member banks.

B. The Federal Reserve is the U.S. government's bank, a bank for banks, a supervisory organization, and the author of monetary policy. Monetary policy adjusts bank reserves and influences interest rates for economic stability.

VOCABULARY BUILDER

a. bank run

b. CAMELS

c. currency

d. discount rate

e. District Reserve Bank

f. Federal Deposit Insurance Corporation

g. Federal Open Market Committee

h. Great Depression

i. inflation

j. margin

k. member bank

l. stagflation

Choose the term that best fits the definition. Write the letter of the answer in the space provided. Some terms may not be used.

_____ **1.** Interest rate charged to banks by the Federal Reserve

_____ **2.** Combination of a stagnate economy and high inflation

_____ **3.** National or state bank that is part of the Federal Reserve System

_____ **4.** Six criteria of safety and soundness used to evaluate banks

_____ **5.** Circumstance when many depositors withdraw money at once

_____ **6.** All media of exchange circulating in a country

_____ **7.** Agency that guarantees bank deposits

_____ **8.** Worst economic crisis in U.S. history

_____ **9.** Regional bank of Federal Reserve System

_____ **10.** Collective rise in money supply, incomes, and prices

REVIEW CONCEPTS

POINT YOUR BROWSER

banking.swep.com

11. Why did Alexander Hamilton urge the founding of the first Bank of the United States?

_____

_____

_____

12. Why did Thomas Jefferson oppose founding the first Bank of the United States?

_____

_____

_____

13. How did the first and second Banks of the United States exert control over other banks?

_____

_____

_____

14. Why did the first and second Banks of the United States fail?

_____

_____

_____

_____

15. How were banks regulated between 1836 and the Civil War?

_____

_____

_____

16. Why did state banks eventually stop issuing their own currency?

_____

_____

_____

17. Why did Congress establish the Federal Reserve System?

_____

_____

18. What caused massive bank failures during the Great Depression?

_____

_____

_____

19. Name the four organizational components of the Federal Reserve System.

_____

_____

_____

20. What four functions does the Federal Reserve perform?

_____

_____

_____

_____

APPLY WHAT YOU LEARNED

21. In what ways does the disagreement between Hamilton and Jefferson about banking policy still exist today?

_____

_____

_____

_____

22. Outline the history of banking in the U.S. ecomony.

_____

_____

_____

_____

_____

_____

23. What is the advantage of distancing the Federal Reserve System from politics?

_____

_____

_____

_____

24. Why is inflation a constant concern of the Federal Reserve Board?

_____

_____

_____

25. How does the Federal Reserve's monetary policy affect the economy?

_____

_____

_____

_____

_____

MAKE CONNECTIONS ●

26. BANKING MATH Calculate the loss of real value in a $10,000 savings account if inflation is 10% a year for 3 years versus the loss of real value if inflation remains around 3%. How much less would that savings account be worth if inflation goes up? (For this exercise, do not consider interest paid.)

_____

_____

_____

_____

_____

_____

_____

27. MEDIA Collect stories about interest rates, the Federal Reserve, inflation, banking, and current economic conditions from various news media. Take notes from stories on electronic media, such as radio, television, and the Internet. Use these notes in a class discussion about economic trends.

28. HISTORY Thomas Jefferson was an American hero, but his opponent on the bank issue was also a fascinating man. Use research materials of your choice to write a two-page character sketch of Alexander Hamilton, focusing not only on biographical facts but on traits that made him both an effective and resented spokesperson for his opinions.

29. POLITICAL SCIENCE If inflation is such a concern, why not just stabilize the economy by imposing wage and price controls? Wages and prices have occasionally been frozen before in emergency situations. Should wage and price controls be permanently established? Write a paragraph that summarizes your opinion.

_____

_____

_____

_____

_____

_____

30. ART Use printouts from the Internet or photocopies of library materials to create a collage of images from the Great Depression. In your collage, try to convey a sense of the economic conditions of the time.

CHAPTER 3

MONEY AND INTEREST

3.1 THE MONEY SUPPLY
3.2 MONEY CREATION AND CIRCULATION
3.3 INTEREST AND INTEREST RATES

Careers in Banking
CITIBANK

Citibank is part of Citigroup Inc., the largest financial services organization in the United States, as ranked by size of assets. Citigroup includes such other famous financial services companies as Travelers Insurance, Salomon Smith Barney Investments, Diners Club, and AT&T Universal Card. Citibank itself has more than 1,100 branches in 42 countries and prides itself on providing and expanding technological resources for its customers. Direct Access, Citibank's PC banking system, is highly rated, and Citibank also offers banking kiosks in some stores, such as Blockbuster and Kinko's.

Citigroup seeks committed employees in its wide range of businesses and offers a full range of benefits and employee programs. Two-thirds of Citigroup employees own stock in the corporation, which believes that employee ownership is a key to employee commitment and customer service. *Working Mother* magazine named Citigroup one of "the 100 best companies for working mothers," and the corporation takes pride in pointing out that it provides more backup childcare for its employees than any corporation in the world.

THINK CRITICALLY

1. Would you prefer to work for a large banking corporation or a small local bank? Why?
2. Why does stock ownership by employees encourage better performance and customer service?

····· PROJECT ·····

THE MONEY SUPPLY and YOU

PROJECT OBJECTIVES

- Become aware of the way the money supply affects your life
- Assess the current condition of the economy
- Note bank offerings of specific financial services
- Make distinctions between banks and other types of financial service businesses

VIDEO
The Chapter 3 video introduces the concepts in this chapter.

GETTING STARTED

Read through the Project Process below. Make a list of any materials you will need. Decide how you will get the needed materials or information.

- Keep an ongoing list of references you encounter in your daily life that might relate to the money supply.
- As you make your list and as you go through the chapter, jot down questions about concepts that confuse you.
- Identify outside resources like magazine articles and web sites that provide more information on topics in the chapter.

PROJECT PROCESS

Part 1 LESSON 3.1 Before studying the chapter, discuss in class your ideas about what the money supply is and what it includes. Try to derive a definition.

Part 2 LESSON 3.2 Look for examples in your community of evidence that money creation is at work. Collect advertisements and news articles about deposits, reserves, and loans. Relate them to concepts in the lesson.

Part 3 LESSON 3.3 Log current interest rates for various types of financial services. Try to assess the current state of the economy based on what you learn from the chapter and the interest rates.

CHAPTER REVIEW

Project Wrap-up Hold a class discussion about things that you learned in this chapter. Which was the most surprising or remarkable to you? How does this knowledge affect your understanding of what banks do?

Lesson 3.1
THE MONEY SUPPLY ● ● ● ● ● ● ● ● ● ● ● ● ● ● ● ● ●

DEFINE money supply, and **EXPLAIN** how it is measured

DESCRIBE two types of money, and **EXPLAIN** the fractional-reserve system

WHAT IS THE MONEY SUPPLY?

As you learned about the creation of a national currency and problems throughout the nineteenth and early twentieth centuries with the money supply, did you wonder where money comes from? Why can't the government just print more money? What would happen if it did?

The Federal Reserve was established to solve currency problems and manage the money supply. Its adjustments are indirect, and because banks are private institutions, it doesn't simply command the money supply. The Federal Reserve influences the conditions under which banks do business and sees that those banks abide by banking regulations. You may be surprised about what money really is in the United States, as well as what isn't. You will get a sense of how much money is out there, what it is doing, and how its movements are measured. You will also learn more about how banks and the Federal Reserve work together to create and manage money.

When Elizabeth Axtell paid for her gasoline fill-up, she received a ten-dollar bill as change. She happened to notice that on the bill someone had written "Happy Birthday, Betty!" This greeting on the bill caused her to think of all the people and places through which this particular bill might have passed. As she put the bill away, she wondered how much money there is circulating out there at any given moment, and she resolved to learn more about it. How might Elizabeth begin to define "out there"?

The Concept of Money Supply

Even after state currencies disappeared and a national monetary system was in place, serious problems with the banking system occurred in 1873, 1883, 1893, and 1907, resulting in bank failures and large-scale economic problems. The crisis in 1907 caused Congress to commission a study group, which ultimately led to the establishment of the Federal Reserve.

The source of these problems was the money supply. The **money supply** is defined as the liquid assets held by banks and individuals. Those assets include all the money in circulation and money held in banks or other financial institutions. This money is moving in the economy from place to place and person to person. The flow of money—and the amount of it flowing—has a direct effect on how the economy performs.

The basic idea is simple: if there is too much money around, prices rise to the point of inducing problematic inflation. If there is too little money around, there is not enough to meet needs and a "credit crunch" slows the economy. If the economy slows too much, commerce spirals down, jobs are lost, less and less money moves, and so forth. The trick is to keep the money supply and economy growing at a stable rate so that wealth spreads, yet without inducing inflation. Unfortunately, there are so many factors in a complex economy that providing steady growth is not easy.

Expanding the Money Supply

Why might extra money in the economy cause inflation? Assume you have an income of $3,000 per month that meets your basic needs. Suddenly, your income jumps 15 percent to $3,450. What would you do with the extra money? Most people would probably buy things. That seems good, doesn't it?

Now assume you own an electronics store. If a large rush of customers came in demanding DVD players, how would you respond?

Consider the following questions: What would happen to prices of DVD players? Why? What would happen to the supply of DVD players? What effect might that have on prices? If prices for all goods and services also went up, what would be the net effect on your 15 percent increase in income compared to what it actually buys?

The supply of DVD players will decrease, thus causing prices to rise. If prices for all goods and services go up, the 15 percent increase in income will actually buy less. If this trend continues for a period of time, it can result in inflation.

Measuring the Money

The definition of the money supply as all the money in circulation and held by banks and individuals may not be detailed enough to track the ebb and flow of money. **Liquidity** is a measure of how quickly things may be converted to something of value like cash. Liquidity is variable, depending on the nature of the asset or liability. Your savings account is not as liquid as coins in your pocket, but more liquid than a certificate of deposit that doesn't mature until next June.

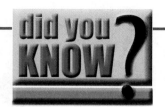

As of June 2001, there was about $555 billion of currency in circulation. About 95 percent of this currency consisted of Federal Reserve notes. The other 5 percent was in the billions of coins moving from place to place.

All the money in all types of accounts is part of the money supply. However, some types of money are more liquid than others. To estimate money's movement, economists and the Federal Reserve use various measures. These measures, called M1, M2, M3, and a relatively new one, MZM, take into account various types of money and various circumstances of liquidity.

Measure	Explanation
M1	Money that can be spent immediately. M1 includes currency (paper and metallic) and various types of checking accounts, including nonbank travelers' checks, standard checking accounts, and NOW (interest-bearing) accounts.
M2	All the money in M1 plus short-term investments, such as small savings accounts (less than $100,000), money market accounts, and money market mutual funds.
M3	All the money in M1 and M2 plus large deposits, such as agreements among banks and institutional money market funds.
MZM	Money at zero maturity. This measure of the annual change in the money supply has become a way of tracking what the money supply is doing year to year.

Taken together, these **aggregate measures** of the money supply are used to estimate its size. M1 is sometimes referred to as the "base" money supply, and M2, M3, and MZM give some indication of potential demand on the money supply. In general, increasing growth of the money supply accompanies a strengthening economy, while decreasing growth of money implies the economy is slowing. None of these measures is a safe predictor of inflation. Other factors such as supply, demand, labor, resources, and political events also play a role in determining the rate of inflation.

TECH TALK

MEASURING NONTRADITIONAL FORMS OF MONEY

How will "electronic money" and automated payment systems affect the money supply and monetary policies? These nontraditional forms may alter the measurement of the money supply, which in turn could shift the way monetary policy is implemented. Most consumer electronic money falls easily into the M1 demand-deposit category, and it has already begun to be measured as such. But as these services grow, they may alter the definition of certain monetary instruments. Already, economists rely less on the M1, M2, and M3 measures than they once did, and some think they are relatively unimportant.

THINK CRITICALLY

Why are the M1, M2, and M3 measures becoming less important? How does changing technology also alter the Federal Reserve's supervisory task?

What makes up the money supply? Why do economists use different measurements to track the money supply?

_____

_____

THE NATURE OF MONEY

To understand where the money supply comes from, how it moves, and how banks and the Federal Reserve influence it, you need to understand what money in the United States really is. Although the monetary system has remnants from long ago, it is also a modern "agreement" dating from the 1930s. Two essential ideas dominate the monetary system. One is the idea of _fiat money_, and the other is the idea of a _fractional-reserve system_.

Two Types of Money

Why does money have value? Money is a medium of exchange—something with an agreed-upon value used for trade. Today that agreed-upon value is strictly a convention of the government and has no necessary relationship to the value of gold, silver, bushels of grain, feathers, or any other commodity. A dollar is worth a dollar because everyone agrees that it is, not because it is backed by an amount of precious metal somewhere. Historically, there are two types of monetary systems.

COMMUNICATE

Interview several people from various walks of life. Ask them what they think makes our money valuable. Write a short report listing the various opinions (right or wrong), and share the ideas with your class.

Commodity money is based on some item of value, for example, gold or precious stones. Coins, the oldest form of currency, had some value because of the metal in them. Bank notes were originally issued to represent holdings of precious metal and became the first paper currency. The notes had value because they could be exchanged for an actual amount of a valuable commodity. Although many of the symbolic ideas and concepts associated with commodity money remain in play, commodity money is not generally in use today.

Fiat money is money that is deemed legal tender by the government, and it is not based on or convertible into a commodity. The word _fiat_ refers to any order issued by legal authority, and in the case of money, the authority is the Federal Reserve as created by Congress. Take a look at a dollar bill. It announces that it is a Federal Reserve note. The cost to make a dollar bill is only a little more than four cents, and you cannot take Federal Reserve notes to the bank and exchange them for gold or silver. What makes Federal Reserve notes valuable is that they are the only kind of money the government will accept for payment of taxes and for payments of debts related to court actions. They are, in short, the official currency of the United States.

Fiat money makes sense as a medium of exchange. If you and some friends agreed to use certificates you made for value between you, and you

WORKSHOP

In a small group, design some fiat money to trade among yourselves, assigning agreed-upon value to common tasks, favors, and objects.

all abided by that convention, your currency system would work. Saran might be willing to trade you a CD for two of the certificates, which you might then give Luisa for an hour of raking leaves. Luisa might use them to buy a basket of flowers from Dawn for Saran, and Dawn might offer you two certificates to care for her dog while she's away. As long as you all agree on the relative values, the system works. In the case of the national system, the government enforces what is acceptable currency, and the Federal Reserve, banks, and market influence its value. In any case, there is no longer silver in a quarter, though everyone agrees that it is worth 25 percent of a dollar.

The Fractional-Reserve System

One of the key concepts in understanding how money is created and manipulated arose almost a thousand years ago. Some people say "modern" banking began in England around 1200. At that time, people began to pay goldsmiths to store precious metals safely. The goldsmiths charged a fee for this service. When people left gold or silver, the goldsmiths gave them receipts, indicating that the holder of the receipt had deposited a certain quantity. Soon, people began to use these receipts as a medium of exchange, because trading them was a lot simpler than going to the goldsmith, getting the gold, and giving it to the person owed. It was easier just to give the receipt. These receipts were the first bank notes in England, and became a form of paper currency.

The goldsmiths quickly got into the business of lending the gold and silver they had on deposit, charging interest for the loans. That business was good, so goldsmiths began to pay interest to attract deposits, and thus spread was born.

The goldsmiths also noticed something else. Not everyone wanted their gold back at the same time. Therefore, the goldsmiths adopted a **fractional-reserve system** whereby they needed to keep back, or reserve, only a fraction of the total gold that had been deposited—just enough to cover those who might want to withdraw their gold. They could also lend notes, thus making more money without actually having gold to back it up. The paper notes in circulation eventually exceeded the reserves of gold that the goldsmiths actually held. In effect, money was "created" without changing the amount of gold.

Although what the goldsmiths noticed was based on a system of commodity money, some of the same principles apply today. First, even though Federal Reserve notes are fiat money, money is created in more or less the same way. Second, a fractional-reserve system is still in use today, and adjusting its requirements is one way that the Federal Reserve controls the money supply.

What is fiat money? What is meant by fractional reserve?

_____

_____

_____

THINK CRITICALLY ●●●●●●●●●●●●●●●●●●●●●●●

1. Why are there more elements to the money supply than just the money that is actively circulating?

_____

_____

_____

2. Why do different parts of the money supply need to be measured differently?

_____

_____

3. Why must the government enforce the value of fiat money by requiring its use for settling private debts in court or for transactions with the government?

_____

_____

_____

4. What would have happened to the English goldsmiths if for some reason everyone had wanted their gold back at the same time? What could the goldsmiths have done?

_____

_____

_____

_____

_____

MAKE CONNECTIONS ●●●●●●●●●●●●●●●●●●●●

5. HISTORY Besides fiat money, the U.S. government has issued other types of money, such as silver certificates. Find out what a silver certificate is, when the last one was issued, and what one is worth today. Record your findings here.

_____

_____

_____

_____

_____

6. BANKING MATH The Federal Reserve requires banks to hold a reserve on customer deposits subject to checking. Required in 1999, for example, was a reserve of 3 percent on the first $44.3 million and 10 percent on all amounts above that. If a bank had $91 million in such deposits, what was the amount of required reserves?

_____

_____

_____

Lesson 3.2
MONEY CREATION AND CIRCULATION •

DESCRIBE how money is created by bank activities

EXPLAIN how money circulates in the United States

HOW MONEY IS CREATED

How money is created and how currency is printed are two different things. The Bureau of Engraving and Printing performs the task of printing currency. No matter how much the Bureau prints, it isn't actually considered part of the money supply until the Federal Reserve System calls for it. Money is actually created by the interaction of the demand for it, banks' use of it, and the Federal Reserve's supply and control of it.

Banks and other financial institutions play a key role in the creation of money by transacting their business. Banks earn much of their profit by lending. The lending function, however, does much more than earn money for the bank and its stockholders. Because of the function of the Federal Reserve and the banking system as a whole, banks actually "create" and circulate money as they do business.

As Elizabeth Axtell pulls away from the gas station, she thinks about how currency circulates. She also begins to wonder more about where money actually originates. She knows the government prints it, of course, but under what circumstances? How does the money supply grow? What would you tell her?

Deposits and Reserves

Your deposits are liabilities for the bank that holds them, because the bank will have to give your money back to you. In order to guarantee that the bank will have money on hand to cover its liabilities, the Federal Reserve requires banks to hold money in reserve. Only a portion of the total amount of deposits is required to be reserved. **Primary reserves** consist of cash on hand, deposits that may be due from other banks, and the percentage required by the Federal Reserve System, either held in the vault or on deposit in the District Reserve Bank for the area. A bank may have other reserves as well, called **secondary reserves**. These include securities the bank purchases from the Federal government, usually in the form of government securities. Those reserves held by a bank beyond its reserve requirement are called **excess reserves**. The excess reserves are the resources a bank uses to create money through its business transactions.

The Multiplier Effect

To understand the role banks play in creating money, consider again the fractional-reserve system. Remember that a bank needs to keep on hand only part of its total liabilities, and that liabilities always exceed reserves. This fractional-reserve system works just as it did for the goldsmiths long ago. Money on deposit, minus the reserve requirement, can be loaned to customers. When it is, it creates new deposits, which also go out to customers as loans and create more deposits, thus expanding the amount of money in the system. This phenomenon is called the **multiplier effect**.

Let's say you deposit $1,000, and the bank has a 10 percent reserve requirement. That leaves $900 that may be loaned out to someone. That $900 may be used to buy something, and the seller will probably end up depositing that $900 in another bank. (It could be the same one, but let's use a different one for the sake of the example.) Of the $900 deposited in the second bank, 10 percent is reserved, leaving $810, which the second

BANKING MATH CONNECTION

Calculate the total amount of money "created" from a deposit of $15,000 as it moves through four cycles of deposit. Assume a reserve rate of 10 percent.

SOLUTION

The formula for calculating the money available from a deposit is

$$\text{Deposit} - \text{Reserve} = \text{New Deposit}$$

Repeat the operation for each deposit, then total the new deposits.

Deposit 1: $15,000 − $1,500.00 = $13,500.00   0.10 × $15,000 = $1,500.00
Deposit 2: $13,500 − $1,350.00 = $12,150.00   0.10 × $13,500 = $1,350.00
Deposit 3: $12,150 − $1,215.00 = $10,935.00   0.10 × $12,150 = $1,215.00
Deposit 4: $10,935 − $1,093.50 = $ 9,841.50   0.10 × $10,935 = $1,093.50
                    Total Deposits = $46,426.50

These four deposits result in the "creation" of more than $46,000 available for use in the money supply.

bank will lend and will thus end up deposited in a third bank. Your original $1,000 deposit has resulted in deposits in three separate banks totaling $2,710. Of this total, $1,710 was "created" by the transactions.

Now, of course, your bank must have enough total reserves to cover the $900 check it wrote for the loan when the second bank presents that check for payment. Your bank must also be prepared to give your original $1,000 back to you if you decide to withdraw it. It may use excess reserves for this money, or money from its cash flow of other business, or it may borrow from the Federal Reserve or other sources. Estimating the amount of reserves needed at a particular point in time is critical to banking, although it is impossible to do so with complete accuracy. The bank can't absolutely know when you will want your money, and it can't absolutely know when someone wants a loan. Banks follow the money supply and the economy as closely as they can in order to anticipate their liabilities and reserve needs. In order for all these transactions to pay off, the bank must be making a solid profit on the money it lends. That $900 loan and others like it must earn enough income to defray the costs of creating money. Banks that make poor judgments about the type and amount of loans they extend may find themselves in trouble. If enough banks get into trouble, the whole system could be in jeopardy. Overseeing sound banking practices is one of the important functions of the Federal Reserve, as shown by this example.

CHECKPOINT

Why must banks keep money on reserve? What is the multiplier effect?

_____

_____

Banks move money. Not only do they move money, they create it by making deposits in other financial institutions so the monetary system as a whole expands.

Transfers and Circulation

As you considered the multiplier effect in the last section, did you get the sense that there's a lot going on as money moves? If you did, you're right. That simplified example showed only one small deposit at work. It did not consider the millions of customer and commercial transactions taking place every day, nor did it consider transactions flowing from banks and the Federal Reserve that make up the reserves any of the banks were holding. It also did not show the effect of the loans themselves on the economy, what products might have been purchased with the borrowed money, or what jobs depended upon them, so that

the people holding those jobs could also make deposits—and thus fuel more expansion. All these transfers and transactions, as well as simpler movements of currency, such as bills passing as change, constitute the circulation of money.

If you look again at the elements of the money supply, M1, M2, and M3 represent so many potential transactions that the circulation of money is a complex phenomenon. Of course, most large transactions do not actually involve the movement of physical currency. Most, including creation of deposits at banks and at the Fed, involve *ledger entries*. A record of the transaction appears, just as you record your deposits and spending in your checking account. Many of these records are now entirely paperless.

The Fed and Fiat Money

It is important to remember what money is and isn't. When banks "create" money with deposits, it comes from somewhere. Where it comes from is the theoretical idea of the money supply, which is possible because of the fiat system. The Federal Reserve manages this fiat system, and it adjusts required deposits in bank accounts at the Federal Reserve to affect the money supply and banking system accordingly. The Fed has the power to contract the

In small groups, list as many possible ways you can think of that money circulates. Include large transfers as well as small ones.

U.S. CURRENCY ABROAD

The Federal Reserve estimates that, in 2000, about $534 billion worth of Federal Reserve notes and coins were in circulation. More than half of that currency, perhaps as much as 60 percent, was held by people from abroad. Though their governments have their own money and may not be part of our fiat system, many people around the world use U.S. Federal Reserve notes and coins as a medium of exchange for both local and international business.

THINK CRITICALLY

Why might U.S. currency be seen as valuable in other countries? Why might people who have no direct business with anyone in the United States value U.S. currency?

money supply by raising reserve requirements if the economy seems to be overheating. If banks must hold more in reserve, there is less available to lend. Similarly, by lowering reserve requirements, the Fed expands the money supply by making more money available to create deposits. The Fed also influences bank activity by control of interest rates.

Money As an IOU

Did you know that you hold an IOU from the government? A dollar bill in your hands represents an obligation of the government to provide something of value to you. Because it is fiat money, the government promises not a quantity of gold, but a pledge that the note will be good in the United States. The thing of value being provided to you is the guarantee that it will be accepted for payment of taxes and settlement of debts.

Because currency is an IOU in this way, it is also a liability on the Federal Reserve's books. When the Federal Reserve creates a deposit in a bank's account at the Reserve, it has "created" more money (and may call for actual paper currency to support it). Required by law to balance the books, the Fed buys and holds *Treasury securities* from the government itself as pledge against the IOUs it has issued. These securities are what back your currency, although they would be paid in Federal Reserve notes. Because the fiat money system is a closed system, the full faith and credit of the U.S. government is what actually backs your bill. As long as the government is operating and able to maintain the system, its IOU to you (its money) will be a valuable medium of exchange.

CHECK**POINT**

What circulates money in the United States? What backs the currency in circulation in the United States?

_____

_____

THINK CRITICALLY ●●●●●●●●●●●●●●●●●●●●●●●

1. Why can't banks and the Federal Reserve just create money at will so that all people will have what they need?

_____

_____

_____

2. Why do some people say that money is "borrowed into existence"?

_____

_____

_____

3. Why is the stability of the U.S. government such a large factor in the monetary system?

_____

_____

_____

MAKE CONNECTIONS ●●●●●●●●●●●●●●●●●●●●●●●

4. BANKING MATH Revisit the Banking Math Connection on page 70. Recalculate the amount of new deposits created as a result of an original deposit of $15,000 and a required reserve rate of 12 percent instead of 10 percent. How much less money does this reserve rate create in deposits? Why would making such a change slow the economy?

_____

_____

_____

_____

_____

_____

5. BIOGRAPHY Other factors influence the money supply as well, including government actions and policies. Two giants in economics, John M. Keynes and Milton Friedman, had differing opinions. Choose one of these men and write a one-page biographical sketch, outlining his principal ideas.

6. COMMUNICATION With a classmate, discuss ways that the information in this chapter has changed your understanding of currency. Summarize your discussion here.

_____

_____

_____

_____

_____

Lesson 3.3
INTEREST AND INTEREST RATES ··········

GOALS

LIST factors that affect interest rates

EXPLAIN which factors the Federal Reserve affects

INTEREST RATES AND BUSINESS

In the discussion of how money is created to expand the economy, little mention of interest rates has appeared. Yet interest rates are the primary way banks make money and the focal point of almost everything they do. Bankers are not creating money purely from the goodness of their hearts. Banks are businesses, and businesses depend on profit to survive. The money supply and the economy are linked closely to interest rates. Generally, when rates are high, money is said to be "tight" and business tends to slow, because it costs more to acquire capital. When rates drop, more credit is accessible, and the economy tends to gather speed. Interest rates play a critical role in determining what the economy is doing.

BANKING *Scene*

When Elizabeth Axtell bought her car, she shopped for a loan as well as a vehicle. Most car dealers finance through a bank or through the carmaker's financial company, and rates, just like car prices, are in competition. Elizabeth finally found a rate she was satisfied with, but the following week, she saw that the rate had jumped. Though she felt satisfied with the deal she got, she wondered what factors influence interest rates.

Factors Affecting Interest Rates

Contrary to what many people believe, the Federal Reserve does not decide interest rates, but its actions influence them. The Fed does indeed attempt to nudge rates up or down in the interest of its monetary policy, but forces that determine interest rates are not completely under the Fed's control.

Market forces determine most interest rates. Banks are free to charge whatever rates they want for most of their transactions with customers (within limits), but it is a balancing act. Setting a higher rate for a loan does bring in more income, but it also tends to drive away business. Banking is more fiercely competitive than ever, and the lower the rate banks can charge, the more customers they are likely to have.

The economic conditions at large help determine interest rates too. If the demand for capital is high, interest rates tend to rise like any other prices. If they rise too far, demand falls off. The inflation outlook influences rates as well, as both savers and investors look for higher rates when they fear that inflation will erode the value of what they earn. Bankers are no different from any other investors in this regard.

The cost of money itself is a factor, and here the Federal Reserve's monetary policy matters. The Federal Reserve does control two rates.

WORKSHOP

Work as a class to make a chart of interest rates advertised for various types of financial services, such as home loans and car loans. Don't forget to include rates adjusted by monetary policy.

- The **federal funds rate** is the amount of interest charged for short-term, interbank loans. Banks are constantly monitoring and adjusting their reserves to make sure they can cover their liabilities, both those required by the Federal Reserve and those that occur in day-to-day banking. They often borrow or lend funds to each other to make those adjustments. The Fed influences the interest rates on these loans through its open market operations with Treasury securities.

- The **discount rate** is the interest rate that the Federal Reserve sets and charges for loans to member banks. This rate is not to be confused with the **prime rate**, which is the rate that banks charge their best and most reliable customers. The prime rate is usually the same among major banks, and movement in it often follows movement of the discount rate, but they are not the same thing.

Changes in these rates affect the amount of money banks are willing to borrow to maintain reserves. If rates rise, it discourages borrowing, so lending activity slows. When rates fall, banks may feel safe to lend more to earn more. The goal of these rates is to implement monetary policy by affecting reserves, which in turn affect the money supply, which affects the economy.

ETHICS IN ACTION

One of the regulatory duties of the Federal Reserve is to monitor banks' compliance with the Community Reinvestment Act (CRA) of 1977. The CRA was a response to *redlining*, a practice by which some banks refused to lend money in low-income areas, although they accepted deposits.

THINK CRITICALLY

Should the Federal Reserve be an agency of social policy? Should a bank be free to choose where and with whom it does business?

CHECKPOINT

What interest rates does the Federal Reserve control or affect?

_____

_____

MONETARY POLICY AND INTEREST RATES

The goals of the Federal Reserve's monetary policy are to maintain economic growth, to stabilize prices, and to help international payments flow. Adjusting reserves, setting the discount rate, and influencing the federal funds rate are its tools for achieving policies.

The Federal Reserve sets the discount rate, but it only influences the federal funds rate. Using open market operations, the Fed buys and sells government securities, paying for them by making a deposit in the selling bank's Federal Reserve account. When it sells the securities to dealer banks, it withdraws their cost from the dealer's account at the Federal Reserve. In this way, reserves are increased or decreased, affecting the rate that banks charge each other for interbank loans. The Federal Reserve may buy or sell securities to yield a higher rate than the federal funds rate in order to achieve its goals, without taking gain or loss into consideration.

CHECKPOINT

How does the Federal Reserve influence the federal funds rate?

_____

_____

THINK CRITICALLY

1. Why do you think so many people believe that the Federal Reserve controls interest rates?

_____

_____

_____

2. Why does the prime rate so often move up or down with the discount rate?

_____

_____

_____

3. Why would it not be a good idea if the government completely controlled the money supply?

_____

_____

_____

4. How does the Fed's use of open market operations reflect a free-enterprise economy?

_____

_____

_____

MAKE CONNECTIONS

5. COMMUNICATION Poll people outside your class to see what they think is the dominant factor affecting interest rates. Make a table that shows what your survey finds. What percentage of the total number of people you poll thinks the government sets them?

_____

_____

_____

_____

6. PROBLEM SOLVING Visit the St. Louis Federal Reserve Bank's web site listing of prime interest rates from 1929 to the present located at www.stls.frb.org/fred/data/irates/prime. Make a graph showing average interest rates for five-year periods. What might you infer about the economy at various times from the data on your graph?

_____

_____

_____

_____

_____

_____

CHAPTER SUMMARY

LESSON 3.1 The Money Supply

A. The money supply consists of liquid assets held by banks and individuals. The supply includes money in circulation and money held by banks and other financial institutions. Various measures track the money supply.

B. The United States uses a fiat system of money in which the value of money is declared and guaranteed by the government. The system still operates on a fractional-reserve system, left over from commodity money systems.

LESSON 3.2 Money Creation and Circulation

A. Banks use their excess reserves to create money. By loaning the money not required to be reserved, new deposits are created. The multiplier effect expands the amount of money in the money supply.

B. Money circulates by means of the millions of transfers associated with the various elements of the money supply that occur daily, including consumer transfers, interbank transfers, and Federal Reserve to bank transfers.

LESSON 3.3 Interest and Interest Rates

A. Market factors control interest rates, although the Federal Reserve influences them.

B. Federal reserve activities affect the cost of money to banks, thus affecting the size of reserves and the money supply.

VOCABULARY BUILDER

a. aggregate measures
b. commodity money
c. discount rate
d. excess reserves
e. federal funds rate
f. fiat money
g. fractional-reserve system
h. liquidity
i. money supply
j. multiplier effect
k. primary reserves
l. prime rate
m. secondary reserves

Choose the term that best fits the definition. Write the letter of the answer in the space provided. Some terms may not be used.

_____ 1. Liquid assets held by banks and individuals

_____ 2. Interest rate that the Fed charges for loans to member banks

_____ 3. Currency based on some item of value, such as gold or precious stones

_____ 4. Tools used to estimate the size of the money supply

_____ 5. Interest rate banks charge their best and most reliable customers

_____ 6. Cash on hand, deposits due from banks, and the percentage required by the Federal Reserve System

_____ 7. Phenomenon that creates new deposits from lending

_____ 8. Interest charged for short-term, interbank loans

_____ 9. Practice of reserving only part of a deposited quantity

_____ 10. Money deemed legal tender by the government, but not based on or convertible into a commodity

_____ 11. Measure of how quickly things may be converted to something of value like cash

REVIEW CONCEPTS

POINT YOUR BROWSER

banking.swep.com

12. What are the components of the money supply?

_____

_____

13. Identify and define two types of money.

_____

_____

_____

14. List four measures of the money supply and describe them.

_____

_____

_____

_____

15. List and define three types of bank reserves.

_____

_____

_____

_____

_____

16. How does the multiplier effect create new deposits?

_____

_____

_____

_____

17. Why might Federal Reserve notes be thought of as IOUs?

_____

_____

_____

18. What actually backs the currency of the United States?

_____

_____

19. What is the difference between the discount rate and the prime rate?

_____

_____

_____

20. What factors determine interest rates?

21. How do interest rates influence the quantity of money available in the economy?

APPLY WHAT YOU LEARNED

22. Why is an expanding money supply generally a good thing?

23. What are the dangers of a money supply that expands too rapidly?

24. Under what circumstances is it a good idea to contract the money supply?

25. What are the dangers of contracting the money supply too much?

26. How does adjusting the reserve requirements cause the money supply to expand or contract?

27. Why would a booming economy affect the demand for money?

_____

_____

_____

_____

28. Why do banks want interest rates to remain low?

_____

_____

_____

_____

MAKE CONNECTIONS •

29. BANKING MATH Calculate the total amount of money "created" from a deposit of $10,000 as it moves through three cycles of deposit. Assume a reserve rate of 8 percent.

_____

_____

_____

_____

30. HISTORY Many people objected strongly when the United States adopted a fiat money system (and some still object today). Learn more about the gold standard and how it established currency values. Write a one-page summary of what you learn.

31. COMMUNICATION If economics is a science, and economic data are measurable, why is there so much disagreement about the best way to handle the economy? Collect statements from ten people about the best thing that could be done to help the economy and why their ideas would help. Which of them seem to make the most sense to you and why?

_____

_____

_____

_____

_____

32. ECONOMICS Find current information about the money supply at www.federalreserve.gov/releases/H6/Current. Examine this data and draw conclusions about the growth of the money supply. Do your conclusions seem to match the current economic conditions and interest rates?

_____

_____

_____

_____

_____

CHAPTER 4

DEPOSITS IN BANKS

4.1 DEPOSIT ACCOUNTS
4.2 INTEREST-BEARING ACCOUNTS
4.3 FLOW OF DEPOSITS
4.4 DEPOSIT REGULATIONS

Careers in Banking

THE ARLINGTON BANK

The Arlington Bank in Upper Arlington, Ohio, is an example of one new trend in banking. As competition and mergers among banks have created giant corporations, niche markets have opened for small banks specializing in customer service with a personal touch.

The Arlington Bank opened in 1999. Its six founders are all former employees of a thrift institution that had been acquired by a larger bank. The bank has 15 employees and assets of $95 million—tiny compared to the multi-state giants. The bank offers a full menu of checking and savings accounts and provides financing for a large share of local construction and remodeling projects. Using knowledge of the community, the Arlington Bank tailors its services to the needs of local people and businesses.

Employee compensation is competitive with larger banks in the area. Working in a small bank offers employees the opportunity to experience all facets of the banking business, rather than having to specialize in one area or skill. Such an environment allows people to stay connected to each other and the community.

THINK CRITICALLY

1. Why might small banks have an advantage in certain markets?
2. What would be some of the advantages and disadvantages of working for a small bank?

BANK ACCOUNTS and YOU

PROJECT OBJECTIVES

- Learn more about specific accounts offered in your community
- Compare local account offerings to each other in terms of interest and features
- Categorize local account offerings in terms of industry criteria
- Recognize variations in deposit requirements and regulations as they apply to accounts in your area

VIDEO
The Chapter 4 video introduces the concepts in this chapter.

GETTING STARTED

Read through the Project Process below. Make a list of any materials you will need. Decide how you will get the needed materials or information.

- Make a list of financial institutions from whom you will acquire information.
- For each institution, note the type of institution, size, number of branch offices, ATM locations, online banking services, and so forth.
- As you collect information, think about how it compares to information in the content of this chapter. Translate marketing names for accounts into common industry names by analyzing the features of the accounts. Categorize local accounts by comparing them to chapter content.

PROJECT PROCESS

Part 1 LESSON 4.1 Discuss in class your personal experience with various types of accounts. What accounts do you have firsthand knowledge of, and what do you know about their features and requirements?

Part 2 LESSON 4.2 Expand your awareness of account services in your area. Begin with a list of local institutions, and find out about the specific accounts and account names offered by each. Divide the class into areas of responsibility for acquiring information about the accounts.

Part 3 LESSON 4.3 Organize the data collected in Part 2 into broad, general categories of accounts, using information from this chapter.

Part 4 LESSON 4.4 Make a chart showing general types of accounts, their marketing names, features, and requirements for each. Include summary information about requirements and regulations.

CHAPTER REVIEW

Project Wrap-up Hold a class discussion about what you have learned regarding local deposit accounts. What information and terminology would you recommend consumers know as they make choices about deposit accounts? How could the information on the chart you made for this project be used for consumer education?

Lesson 4.1
DEPOSIT ACCOUNTS •

GOALS

DEFINE the term *transaction accounts*, and **IDENTIFY** major types of checking accounts

DEFINE the term *time deposits*, and **IDENTIFY** major types of savings accounts

MAKING YOUR DEPOSIT

You have studied the big picture of how the national banking system works to keep money circulating. Now you will walk through the local bank doors and look more closely at the various types of accounts available to individual consumers. You may see a bewildering array of accounts to choose from, but things are really not as complicated as they seem. Although each bank may use different names for the various accounts offered, most banks offer essentially the same types of accounts. A bank may assign "marketing names" to its accounts as a way of distinguishing itself from its competitors. Features and fees may vary, but the essential services are the same with a few exceptions. Banks are required to provide explanations of their fees and policies—a requirement enforced by federal and state regulations.

Rosa Lopez is preparing to open a checking account at a local bank on which she has not yet decided. She knows that there is a wide variety of checking accounts, and that similar accounts may have different names at different banks. She has decided to collect information from various banks in an effort to find an account that will best suit her needs. To do so, she plans to make a list of questions about how she expects to use the account. Using answers to her questions, Rosa hopes to be able to match her requirements to account features offered by banks. What kind of questions about her own needs should Rosa include in her list?

Transaction Accounts

Deposit accounts fall generally into one of two categories: *transaction accounts* and *time deposits*. A **transaction account** is an account that allows transactions to occur at any time and in any number. These accounts are **demand deposits**, as they are payable on demand whenever the depositor chooses. The most common form of a transaction account is a *checking account*. You withdraw money from the account by means of a check, which is a written notice to the bank to pay a named person a specified amount from your account. Checking accounts offer customers quick access to their money and a convenient way to pay bills or transfer funds to other institutions, provided the customer has deposited funds in the bank equal to the amount of checks written and fees deducted. Most checking accounts also allow access to deposits via ATMs and debit cards. Debit card transactions function like check transactions, except that no check is written. Because there are many kinds of checking accounts from which to choose, consumers can find accounts that best meet their needs.

Checking Accounts

Basic checking accounts offer a few simple services for minimal cost. These accounts may vary considerably in set fees and services. Some are free, some may be free if a minimum balance is maintained, and many have a basic fee and price extra services per item. For example, you may have a set number of checks or deposits allowed per month, and all transactions beyond these incur an extra charge. Extra charges may also be incurred for ATM and debit card transactions. The return of canceled checks may cost you, or may not be an option at all. There are numerous forms of basic checking accounts with many names, but the same fee-for-service principle applies.

Interest-bearing checking accounts also vary widely. They do pay interest on the balance deposited in the account, but usually only if the deposited balance is maintained at or above a required level. Generally, the higher the interest offered, the higher the minimum balance required. Minimum balance may be calculated based upon the average balance in your account each day of the month, or it may be a preset level. If your balance falls below the level on any day of the month, higher service charges apply.

It pays consumers to look closely at fees charged and services offered for their checking accounts. A basic account may actually cost more money to operate than another type of account if there are many transactions raising the fees. In the same way, the interest earned on an interest-bearing account may not be enough to offset the higher cost of fees if the balance maintained is fairly low, especially if it falls below the minimum balance requirement. Consumers should read carefully the account regulations for each account and consider how they will really use their accounts.

In small groups, make a poster that illustrates and explains all the parts of a check. You will need to research this information in other books or on the Internet. Design the poster so that you could use it to teach others what a check is, what its features are, and how to write one.

Certain other transactions are also categorized as demand deposit transactions, such as traveler's checks and ATS (automatic transfer service) transactions that make automatic withdrawals or transfers to pay bills without writing checks. All deposits to cover these transactions are called *checkable deposits*, as are the funds deposited in checking accounts. The total funds in transaction accounts affect the money supply because of their high liquidity. If you recall the definition of the M1 category of the money supply, you will recognize that transaction accounts and M1 are the same. These demand deposits require banks to hold reserve funds, because the money could be moved instantaneously.

What is a transaction account? Why are transaction accounts considered demand deposits?

_____

_____

TIME DEPOSITS

Time deposits, as the name implies, are deposits that are held for or mature at a specified time. Generally, time deposits include savings accounts, are less liquid than checkable deposits and money market deposit accounts, certificates of deposit (CDs), and various bonds. Time deposits, including savings accounts, are less liquid than checkable deposits and are not currently subject to the Fed's reserve requirements.

Savings Accounts

Savings accounts are the time deposits with which most people are familiar. For time deposits, banks may require up to a seven-day notice from a depositor who wants to withdraw money. Demand deposits require no notice. As a practical matter, most banks don't impose this requirement for savings accounts, but reserve the right to do so.

Passbook savings accounts helped build the banking industry. **Passbook savings accounts** provided a ledger of activity that the teller updated when the customer made deposits or withdrawals. This traditional type of savings account has all but disappeared, replaced by statement savings accounts. Both types of accounts allow you to make deposits in person, by mail, electronically, or by direct deposit.

Statement savings accounts, now the industry standard, provide a monthly or quarterly computerized statement detailing all account activity, including interest additions and fees charged. Often, statements are combined with those of other accounts you have at the bank, providing a complete and clear picture of all banking activity.

Savings accounts are among the safest places to put money. Accounts are insured by the Federal Deposit Insurance Corporation (FDIC) up to $100,000 per depositor. Interest income on savings accounts is relatively low, however. You can get your money at any time, so liquidity is high, but the low rate of interest makes other time deposits more attractive if you intend to keep the money deposited for an extended period of time.

Money Market Deposit Accounts

Money market deposit accounts (MMDAs) offer a higher rate of interest than savings accounts, but they usually require a higher initial deposit to open an account. In addition, minimum balance requirements to avoid the imposition of fees are also higher. The FDIC insures MMDAs for amounts up to $100,000 per depositor. The bank invests money market deposits in a variety of savings instruments. Similar accounts, called *money market mutual fund accounts*, invest the money in mutual funds. Although they are not insured, banks make most of these investments in safe, short-term savings instruments with high credit ratings.

Liquidity of these accounts is not as high as a savings account. You may be restricted to six transactions per month. Only three of them may be checks, and you may have to wait up to seven days to get your money.

Certificates of Deposit

A **Certificate of Deposit (CD)** is a certificate offered by a bank that guarantees payment of a specified interest rate until a designated date in the future. That date is called the *maturity date*. Banks offer CDs with maturity dates from seven days to ten years. Generally, the larger the amount of the CD and the longer the term, the greater the interest rate. Some CDs offer variable rates. Usually, the rate for CDs is higher than the rates offered by money market or savings accounts. For the vast majority of CDs, the maturity date is fewer than eighteen months. You can get your money before the maturity date if you need to, but you will pay an interest penalty, anywhere from three to six months' worth of interest, if you withdraw the money early.

To qualify as a time deposit and thus be exempt from reserve requirements, an account must have no more than six withdrawals or transfers per month. It is up to the bank to ensure that holders of the account comply with the rules.

CASH OR CHEQUE?

The Canadian banking system differs from that in the United States in that it follows a branch-banking system. Unlike the United States, which has a large number of commercial banks, there are relatively few Canadian banks. There are only 13 domestic banks in Canada, varying in size but each with many branches. The Canadian government is directly responsible for regulating these banks, and the Bank of Canada serves as the central banking authority.

Competition, market forces, and technology have changed Canadian banking. Canadians have enthusiastically embraced innovations such as debit cards and lead the world in electronic transactions per capita. Still, most banking services offered by Canadian banks, including chequing and savings accounts, would seem familiar to American customers.

THINK CRITICALLY

How might the competitive environment for banks in Canada differ from that in the United States? Search the Internet for information on Canadian banking. Write a one-page comparison of the Canadian banking system to the U.S. banking system.

Certificates of Deposit are quite safe, as the FDIC insures them for amounts up to $100,000 per depositor, but they are not very liquid. Consumers should consider carefully the maturity date when investing in CDs, because the interest rate remains the same no matter what. If interest rates rise, the CD rate will not earn as much as other forms of time deposits. But if interest rates fall, locked-in CD rates can be an advantage. Depositors must also decide how long they are willing and able to tie up their money.

Credit unions offer transaction accounts and time deposits, too, although these holdings really represent shares in the credit union rather than deposits. A *share-draft account* functions like a checking account, a *share account* works essentially like a savings account, and a *share certificate* is equivalent to a Certificate of Deposit.

List three types of time deposits. Which of these are exempt from reserve requirements?

_____

_____

THINK CRITICALLY ●●●●●●●●●●●●●●●●●●●●●●●

1. Why does the Federal Reserve require reserves for demand deposits but not for time deposits?

_____

_____

_____

2. How might competitive pressures have led to different types of checking accounts?

_____

_____

_____

3. Why do you think passbook savings accounts have disappeared?

_____

_____

_____

4. What factors should be considered when contemplating a Certificate of Deposit?

_____

_____

_____

MAKE CONNECTIONS ●●●●●●●●●●●●●●●●●●●●●●●

5. **COMMUNICATION** With a partner, make a list of questions you need to ask to help determine your checking account needs. Compare various types of checking accounts and focus your questions on what you now know about differences in checking accounts. Come up with at least four questions, and then compare lists with those of other pairs.

_____

_____

_____

6. **BANKING MATH** According to the American Banking Association, Americans write 61 billion checks per year. The population of the United States is about 250 million. Using those figures, how many checks are written per capita in a year in the United States?

_____

_____

_____

_____

_____

_____

INTEREST-BEARING ACCOUNTS ··········

GOALS

EXPLAIN how interest is calculated

DISCUSS why compound interest is such a powerful savings tool

IN YOUR INTEREST

It might not always be good to be called a "calculating person," but when it comes to your finances, you had better be. Banks offer interest on many deposit accounts, and they charge interest on loans they make. Understanding these calculations is absolutely necessary to analyzing your own finances. Whether it's money coming to you or money you're paying to borrow, interest will likely determine how well you fare.

Interest is the price paid for the use of money. The bank is using your money when you deposit funds there and in some cases pays you for the use of it. If you borrow from a bank or other financial institution, you pay to use that money, and interest is the amount you pay. Interest is almost always expressed as a rate or percentage of the total amount of money in use, and it is calculated over time.

BANKING Scene

As she considered what type of checking account to open, Rosa Lopez felt it would be a good idea to open a savings account as well. She looked for advertisements for interest rates on accounts and certificates of deposit, and began to consider how those rates would affect her savings over time. She wanted to design a chart or table to compare rates and intervals at which interest would be paid, and then fill it with some example numbers. How would Rosa design such a chart?

Calculating Interest

To calculate simple interest, you must know the amount of money that is being used. This beginning amount is called the *principal*. The basic formula for calculating interest is $P \times R \times T = I$, where P is principal, R is rate, T is time, and I is interest. To find the interest amount, multiply the principal by the rate, expressed as a percentage, by the time, usually expressed in years or parts of years. In cases of parts of years, time is expressed as a decimal value. Six months is 0.5 years, nine months is 0.75 years, a year and a half is 1.5 years, and so forth.

$$P \times R \times T = I$$

Interest in the Real World

Calculating simple interest gives you an idea of the process, but in the real world there are some complexities. Banks calculate the interest they pay on some fixed interval. Interest may be paid once a year (annually), every six months (semi-annually), every three months (quarterly), or any other interval as defined in the account regulations. If the bank paid 4.5 percent interest on a $2,200 account semi-annually, at the end of six months $49.50 would be added to your account. For the next six-month interval, you would begin with a principal not of $2,200 but of $2,249.50, and you would earn interest on that higher amount. Adding interest to the principal and paying interest on the new total is called paying **compound interest**, and it is the most powerful tool in savings.

In small groups, practice using the interest calculation formula with varying principal amounts, varying rates, and varying times.

What do the terms in the formula $P \times R \times T = I$ stand for?

_____

_____

Calculate the simple interest earned on a savings account in nine months that begins with a deposit of $2,200 and pays $4\frac{1}{2}$ percent interest.

SOLUTION

The formula for calculating interest is

Principal $\times$ Rate $\times$ Time $=$ Interest
$2,200 $\times$ 0.045 $\times$ 0.75 $=$ $74.25

If you had such an account, you would have earned $74.25 in interest, giving you an account balance of $2,274.25. This example assumes no compounding and that the interest is paid at the end of the nine months, which might not reflect conditions of an actual account.

did you KNOW?

For the purposes of computing interest compounded daily, a year is generally considered to be 360 days or twelve 30-day months. Using this figure actually increases the effective rate of interest compared to a 365-day year.

THE POWER OF COMPOUNDING

Compound interest "starts over" with a new principal every time interest is paid, adding the paid interest to create a higher principal on which interest is paid in the next interval. For example, assume you loaned $1,000 to your cousin for three years, who agreed to pay you 5 percent simple interest per year. You'd make $50 in interest the first year, $50 in interest the second, and $50 the third, for a total of $1,150 returned. Assume you put the same $1,000 in a bank account paying 5 percent interest compounded semi-annually. You'd get back $1,159.71. In effect, that's a rate of 5.3 percent per year.

Time	Simple Interest 5%		Compound Interest 5%	
	Interest	Principal	Interest	Principal
Six months	$25	$1,000	$25.00	$1,025.00
1 year	25	1,000	25.63	1,050.63
1½ years	25	1,000	26.27	1,076.90
2 years	25	1,000	26.92	1,103.82
2½ years	25	1,000	27.60	1,131.42
3 years	25	1,000	28.29	1,159.71
Total	**$150**		**$159.71**	

The algebraic formula for calculating compound interest is $F = P(1 + R)^n$, where F stands for future value, P is principal, R is rate, and n is the number of intervals. There are many online calculators that will compute compound interest for you, so memorizing the formula is less important than understanding the idea behind compound interest.

With a larger principal and longer terms, the effect can become dramatic, especially if regular additions are made to the principal, as on a regular savings plan. For example, if you put $20 a week in a savings account earning 5 percent interest compounded annually, at the end of five years you would have deposited $5,200, but your balance would be $6,033.99.

APR and APY

Two terms you may encounter when evaluating interest are APR and APY. Both allow you to compare interest. APR stands for **annual percentage rate**, the nominal rate on which interest is calculated per year. In the example above, both investments have an APR of 5 percent. Another measure gives a better comparison. APY stands for **annual percentage yield** and represents the effect of compounding. In the example above, the APY of the simple interest is 5 percent, and of the compounded interest, 5.3 percent. APY varies according to the APR and the frequency of compounding.

CHECK**POINT**

Why is compound interest such a powerful savings tool?

_____

_____

THINK CRITICALLY ●●●●●●●●●●●●●●●●●●●●●●●●●

1. Why is it important for consumers to compare interest rates on bank accounts and other interest-bearing instruments?

_____

_____

_____

2. How does the frequency at which interest is compounded change the effect of compounded interest rates?

_____

_____

_____

3. Why is APY a more useful measure for comparing interest rates than APR?

_____

_____

_____

MAKE CONNECTIONS ●●●●●●●●●●●●●●●●●●●●●

4. BANKING MATH Marie Broussard puts $10 a week in a savings account. At the end of two years, how much more would Marie's account balance be if she found an account that paid interest of 5.5 percent instead of 4.5 percent per year, assuming both accounts compound annually?

_____

_____

_____

_____

_____

5. HISTORY The practice of paying and charging interest has been around a long time. Do research on interest, and write a one-page report on the earliest beginnings of the practice.

6. TECHNOLOGY Online financial calculators are becoming increasingly useful tools, performing complex calculations quickly. Find three such calculators on the Internet, and describe the particular features, advantages, and disadvantages of each.

_____

_____

_____

_____

_____

_____

_____

GOALS

EXPLAIN the complexity of forces that influence the flow of deposits

IDENTIFY limitations of the Federal Reserve's influence on the flow of deposits

A COMPLEX PATTERN

You go to work, get your check, and deposit it in the bank. Of course, your employer wrote that check against funds deposited in the company's bank, and the money for those deposits came from somewhere too. The next time you are in a bank or waiting in a drive-thru, look around and multiply the process by everyone you see. Then multiply the process by the millions of people at work in the United States, using thousands of banks. If you are starting to get a picture of a complex flow of deposits rocketing around the nation, you are getting the idea.

BANKING *Scene*

Rosa Lopez has made her decisions about what services she needs in checking and savings accounts. Now her task is to choose accounts that match her needs. With so many banks, so many accounts, and so many similar but not identical names, collecting information of specific offerings could be complicated and time consuming. How would you recommend Rosa pursue this task most efficiently?

The Federal Reserve, or Fed, came into being to serve as the nation's central bank. The money supply is sometimes adjusted by the actions of the Fed. Because banking is so important, it may be easy to assume that the government is running everything, but that is not really how it works. In addition to new money and the easing or tightening of credit, the flow of deposits also includes all the money already circulating in the day-to-day business of economic life. Money doesn't just mean currency, but includes checks, ledger transfers, and even credit.

The Economic Engine

The engine that drives the flow of deposits is the economy itself. Basic economic principles of supply and demand for goods and services push money

through banks. In a way, the movement of money is like the movement of communication through phone lines and cellular phones. Individual transmissions may not be very complicated, but there are a lot going on at once, and they may be going in many different directions. At the same moment you deposit your check at the teller window, someone else cashes his or hers at the drive-thru. In addition to these small transactions, banks themselves, just like you, may have changes in cash-flow needs. Maybe revenues are down, or expenses are up, or maybe even business is so good they need more money to support it. In such cases, banks make and receive deposits to each other in *interbank transactions*, and to and from the Federal Reserve.

It is not always easy to predict the results of these transactions, but the best predictor is the past. That is why economists, banks, and the Federal Reserve pay close attention to recording and analyzing economic statistics.

In fact, the economy at large plays a far greater role in determining how money is moving than does the government. Market forces largely determine even interest rates, depending on the need for capital, whether people are saving or spending, and the effects and likelihood of inflation.

WORKSHOP

Working in small groups, ask group members to determine the amount of cash they currently have on hand. Make a list of all the deposits that could possibly result from this source of cash. Come up with as many as you can. The group with the largest chain wins.

CHECKPOINT

What is the greatest factor in the flow of deposits? Why do economists track and analyze so much data?

_____

_____

COMMUNICATE

Conduct a survey among 20 friends, family members, and classmates to examine consumer attitudes. Ask these questions: 1. How much do you consider the economy at large when making purchase and loan decisions? 2. What do you think is the current state of the economy at large, and what are its prospects for the next year? Based on responses to your survey, write a two-page report describing the economic mood of the country.

DEPOSITS AND THE FED

Whether the money supply is expanding through the creation of new money or contracting as credit tightens, supply and demand for money have effects on deposits. The Federal Reserve also has an effect on deposits. For example, the Federal Reserve sets reserve requirements. If reserve requirements are high, banks must keep back more money and consequently have less to lend. If reserve requirements are low, more money may be available for loans. Still, there are reasons not to overestimate the power of this capability.

- Reserve requirements do not change that often and are not as much a factor in bank lending as general economic conditions.

- Reserve requirements only apply to the M1 money supply (the checkable deposits which are already moving freely). Other parts of the money supply are operating entirely by means of market forces, and though less volatile, are not under the Fed's control.

- The Fed does not control other forms of commerce. Much wealth today is generated by nonbank financial institutions, such as stockbrokers and the securities and other instruments they trade, which are a form of money themselves. These instruments, the institutions that sell them, and the policies they have are not controlled by the Federal Reserve, though they affect the economy at large.

In general, the money supply is determined by the supply and demand for credit, and although the Federal Reserve responds to these conditions, it does not necessarily create them.

Adjusting the Money Supply

It is true that the Fed does have an influence on the money supply and the flow of deposits, most frequently through its open market operations.

- ***The Federal Reserve can put more money into the economy.*** To do so, it buys U.S. government securities on the open market. The Fed buys these securities by creating new money, or *raw money*, which the sellers of the securities deposit in financial institutions. Thus, deposits flow from the Fed's pool of raw money directly into bank accounts. Banks then have more money to lend, and the money supply expands as a consequence of the multiplier effect.

- ***The Federal Reserve can effectively take money out of the economy.*** If the Fed feels it needs to slow the economy, it sells the Treasury securities it holds. There is a market for them because of their security. When it sells the securities, the money comes from bank deposits, thus leaving less in the system at large. The money the Fed receives for the securities is removed from the economy, as it does not go into a bank account of any kind. It effectively disappears.

In addition, the Fed can adjust the discount rate, which is the rate it charges banks for loans. If the discount rate is low, banks are more likely to borrow money to use to make money. If the discount rate is high, just like consumers, banks are less likely to borrow.

CUP OF JAVA?

Many banks offer interactive tools on the Internet, such as interest calculators of various types. Have you ever wondered how they work? Many of them run by means of Java, a programming language specially designed to run small applications, called "applets," over the Internet. Advantages of Java are that it works with any operating system, such as Windows, Macintosh, or OS/2, and that it allows for distributed processing, so the software need not all be resident on your computer.

THINK CRITICALLY

Why do you think interactive tools on bank Internet sites have become so popular? Search the Internet for bank sites that offer interactive tools. List at least five useful tools you find.

The Banking Business

Governmental measures influence but do not entirely control the flow of deposits. Banks are businesses and do what they can to make a profit. Deposit flow is determined by the needs of all businesses, bank and non-bank, moving money around in the banking system. Banks move money from themselves to consumers, back and forth among themselves as a function of normal business or borrowing funds from each other, and back and forth from the Federal Reserve, in a constant flow of deposits. They function just as you do but on a larger scale, moving and using or even borrowing money to acquire things they need.

CHECK**POINT**

How does the Federal Reserve influence the flow of deposits?

_____

_____

THINK CRITICALLY ●●●●●●●●●●●●●●●●●●●●●●●●

1. Why is it sometimes hard to predict the flow of deposits in the banking system?

_____

_____

_____

2. How might political or national events affect the flow of deposits in the banking system?

_____

_____

_____

3. Do you think the government should have more direct control of the economy and thus the flow of deposits? Why or why not?

_____

_____

_____

4. Give examples of daily economic activities that are more likely to have predictable effects on the flow of deposits.

_____

_____

_____

MAKE CONNECTIONS ●●●●●●●●●●●●●●●●●●●●

5. GRAPHICS Make a graphical representation or flow chart of how money is added or removed from the economy by the Federal Reserve. What activities should be included in the representation?

_____

_____

_____

_____

_____

_____

6. SOCIAL STUDIES How do current economic conditions affect social conditions in our country? Explore the effect of the economy on daily life in the United States. Write a one-page personal essay about ways that you think the state of the economy affects how we live, the values we hold, the ways we spend our time, our political opinions, our career choices, and any other aspects of our lives that you find interesting. These ideas may be personal opinions, but try to express them clearly and be sure to give reasons for your thinking.

LESSON 4.4
DEPOSIT REGULATIONS ••••••••••••••••••••

GOALS

DESCRIBE several deposit account documents

IDENTIFY basic deposit account rules and what they cover

DEPOSIT ACCOUNT DOCUMENTS

The relationship between a financial institution and its customers is more than a business relationship. It is also a legal relationship that offers rights and imposes responsibilities on each party. Banks document these rights and responsibilities and provide customers copies of these documents when they open any account.

Banks are required by state and Federal governments to provide this documentation to customers so that questions about policies and procedures related to their accounts have clear answers. These documents protect both the consumer and the bank from misunderstanding and loss.

BANKING Scene

When Rosa Lopez opens her checking and savings accounts, she is given a variety of brochures explaining the features and benefits of the accounts. She is also given sheets that list rules and regulations pertaining to each of her deposit accounts. They are detailed documents that include legal language and are printed in small type without graphics. Why should Rosa read these documents carefully, even though she has a clear picture of account features, charges, and interest?

ETHICS IN ACTION

Some consumer advocates believe that many governing documents are made deliberately hard to read so that consumers won't read them. Banks argue that precise legal language is necessary to protect both themselves and consumers.

THINK CRITICALLY

Would you support legislation that required account rules to be written in "plain English"? Why or why not?

The Federal Reserve in its regulatory capacity, along with state and sometimes local governments, checks to see that deposit account documents are specific, complete, clear, and followed by the banks as they do business. Banks must comply with various state and federal consumer laws, including laws about fairness and full disclosure. Several documents are typically included in this document package.

- *Account rules* explain characteristics of each type of account. They include definitions, requirements, restrictions, and other information associated with each account.
- *Deposit rate schedules* list interest rates in effect at the time for various types of accounts.
- *Fee schedules* show all charges that apply to each specific type of deposit account.
- *Check hold policies* explain when deposited funds will be available for use by the consumer. Usually, deposited funds are credited provisionally, until full and final payment is received. In most cases, funds are available for use immediately, but the bank may charge back to the account any amount that turns out to be uncollectible.
- *Disclosure statements* provide full information about bank policies, such as electronic funds transfer policies, lending policies, interest crediting, and compliance with banking regulations. These statements are required by law.

Deposit account documents are sometimes collectively called *governing documents*. Banks are free to change them, but they must give customers written notice of changes.

Why are governing documents necessary?

_____

_____

ACCOUNT RULES

The statement of account rules supplied for each account provides a detailed explanation of the policies, procedures, requirements, and agreements that apply to that account. They are usually extremely specific, spelling out what is expected of both the customer and the bank.

Reference to Governing Documents Account holders agree to abide by the rules as set forth in the rest of the governing documents. Here the bank also notes that it may change the rules from time to time, acknowledging its responsibility to provide updated documents to account holders.

Signature Policies Banks keep a signature card on file with the signature of all parties to an account, whether it is held solely or jointly with other persons. Signature policies spell out who may do what, both in terms of the account as it exists at the time of opening and in the event of inconsistencies, disputes, or death of parties. Usually, in the event of disputes among parties, the bank refuses to pay items on the account until the dispute is resolved between the parties. The bank notes that it has no responsibility for a dispute, its resolution, or its choice to freeze the account.

Opening and Closing Accounts Policies governing opening requirements may include a specified minimum opening deposit, the presence of the person opening the account with proper identification, and the right not to open an account for a person if the bank so chooses. The bank also reserves the right to close an account at its discretion.

Bring in some copies of account rules or other governing documents. In small groups, try restating the ideas in the various provisions of the documents in the simplest language possible.

Deposit Collection This provision is similar to the check hold policy of the governing documents, except that it goes further in explaining the effect of uncollected deposits on the account. The bank also notes that it is not its job to collect deposits beyond using reasonable care in their processing. This statement often notes exactly when deposits are credited, such as the next business day after receipt at 3:00 or 4:00 P.M.

Overdraft Policies When an account has insufficient funds to meet its obligations, it is overdrawn. Depending on the type of account, the bank may pay the obligation, return the obligation to whoever presented it, or move funds from another account to cover it. Uncollected deposits may also cause an overdraft. Fees are charged in such cases, and a reference to the fee schedule usually appears.

Minimum Balance/Service Charges Here the bank specifies exactly the terms for when failure to maintain minimum balance charges apply. Reference to the fee schedule for service charges appears here.

Withdrawal Policies Requirements for withdrawing funds from the bank are explained here. These requirements vary with the type of account, but include maturity dates and penalties for early withdrawal of time deposits, occasions when withdrawals must be made in person, identification requirements, and various other requirements for withdrawing funds or obtaining cashier's checks.

Check Policies These policies include requirements for accurate dating of checks and timely deposit or presentation of them. A *stale check* is one dated six months or more before it is presented for payment or deposit. A *post-dated check* is one that is dated later than when it was written. A bank

may refuse to honor either. Additionally, some banks require that you use checks they sell or approve.

Account Statement Policies These policies deal with the bank statement sent by the bank. They may cover what is and is not included with each statement, the account holder's obligation to review the statement in a timely manner, and how discrepancies will be handled.

Other Policies Account rules usually include various other policies, including stop-payment policies, how the bank will handle inactive or dormant accounts, reimbursement of expenses incurred by the bank on the account holder's behalf, and so forth.

Waivers The account rules may also contain notices about various waivers, such as the customer agreeing to waive protest of dishonored items or the bank's willingness to waive certain fees. Doing so does not prevent the bank from enforcing the same provisions it waived at another time.

Governing documents and account rules serve as the legal basis for the relationship between you and your bank. If you do not like a provision or some of the account rules, you are free to choose another bank. In actuality, though, most account and deposit regulations are fairly similar from bank to bank. In their precision and specificity, they protect both bank and consumer.

How do governing documents and account rules differ?

_____

_____

THINK CRITICALLY ●●●●●●●●●●●●●●●●●●●●●●●●

1. Why do banks supply a separate set of account rules as part of the governing documents for each account?

_____

_____

_____

2. Do you think most people carefully read the documents associated with their bank accounts? Why or why not?

_____

_____

_____

3. Why does the government feel it is necessary to require that written copies of documents related to bank accounts be provided to customers?

_____

_____

_____

4. In what circumstances might a bank waive a fee it had charged?

_____

_____

_____

MAKE CONNECTIONS ●●●●●●●●●●●●●●●●●●●●●●

5. **SOCIAL SCIENCE** Learn more about consumer protection and the banking industry. Using research materials of your choice, make a timeline showing key events in the growth of fair and reasonable banking practices.

6. **PROBLEM SOLVING** If you had a dispute with a bank, how would you resolve it? What approaches would you take, and what further actions would you pursue if you could not come to an agreement? List steps that you would take to resolve a disagreement over an uncredited deposit, for example.

_____

_____

_____

_____

_____

_____

_____

_____

_____

CHAPTER 4

·················· REVIEW

CHAPTER SUMMARY

LESSON 4.1 Deposit Accounts

A. Transaction accounts are demand deposit accounts that allow unlimited transactions. The most common transaction account is a checking account.

B. Time deposits include savings accounts, money market deposit accounts, and certificates of deposit.

LESSON 4.2 Interest-Bearing Accounts

A. Interest is the price paid for the use of money. Simple interest is calculated with the formula $P \times R \times T = I$.

B. Compounding greatly expands the power of interest by adding the interest earned to the principal and paying interest on the new total for the next period. The formula for calculating compound interest is $F = P(1 + R)^n$. APR represents the annual percentage rate, and APY represents the annual percentage yield.

LESSON 4.3 Flow of Deposits

A. The flow of deposits includes all economic transactions, not just those between banks and the Federal Reserve.

B. The Federal Reserve influences the flow of deposits, but economic conditions (supply and demand) more greatly affect the way money moves.

LESSON 4.4 Deposit Regulations

A. For each account, banks provide a package of governing documents that include account rules, deposit rate schedules, fee schedules, check hold policies, and disclosure statements.

B. Account rules list policies in detail that apply to specific accounts, with references to other documents.

VOCABULARY BUILDER

Choose the term that best fits the definition. Write the letter of the answer in the space provided. Some terms may not be used.

a. annual percentage rate

b. annual percentage yield

c. Certificate of Deposit (CD)

d. compound interest

e. demand deposit

f. interest

g. money market deposit account (MMDA)

h. passbook savings account

i. statement savings account

j. time deposit

k. transaction account

_____ **1.** Price paid for the use of money

_____ **2.** Effective rate of interest when compounding is factored in

_____ **3.** Savings account earning a competitive interest rate from invested deposits

_____ **4.** Deposit held for or maturing at a specified time

_____ **5.** Savings account that provides you with a ledger of activity

_____ **6.** Deposit payable on demand whenever the depositor chooses

_____ **7.** Savings instrument with fixed interest rate and fixed maturity date

_____ **8.** Account that allows transactions to occur at any time and in any number

_____ **9.** Return calculated by adding interest to principal for next interval

_____ **10.** Nominal rate on which interest is calculated per year

REVIEW CONCEPTS

POINT YOUR BROWSER

banking.swep.com

11. What is a demand deposit?

_____

_____

_____

12. Name three forms of demand deposits.

_____

_____

_____

13. What is a minimum balance?

_____

_____

_____

_____

14. Name three types of time deposits.

_____

_____

_____

15. Why are savings accounts not subject to the Fed's reserve requirements?

_____

_____

_____

16. Describe a Certificate of Deposit and its maturity date.

_____

_____

_____

17. What do the letters in the formula $P \times R \times T = I$ represent?

_____

_____

_____

18. Explain the basic idea of compound interest.

_____

_____

_____

_____

19. What is the difference between APR and APY?

_____

_____

_____

20. What is the most significant factor influencing the flow of deposits in the United States?

_____

_____

_____

21. Name five main types of documents typically supplied with new accounts.

_____

_____

_____

APPLY WHAT YOU LEARNED

22. Why are transaction accounts the most liquid of all funds?

_____

_____

_____

23. What factors should a person consider when choosing an account?

_____

_____

_____

_____

24. Why is the annual percentage rate an ineffective measure for comparing accounts?

_____

_____

_____

25. Why won't the Federal Reserve's monetary policies completely control the flow of deposits in the U.S. banking system?

_____

_____

_____

_____

26. Why must banks provide customers with documents such as account rules and fee schedules?

_____

_____

_____

_____

_____

27. How do account rules protect both banks and consumers?

_____

_____

_____

_____

MAKE CONNECTIONS •

28. ADVERTISING Collect advertisements for checking and savings accounts that appear in print media. Evaluate the ads in terms of attractiveness, clarity, quality of product, and overall effectiveness. What makes a fair and good advertisement?

_____

_____

_____

_____

29. BANKING MATH Calculate the interest earned on a three-year Certificate of Deposit (CD) with an initial value of $12,500 earning 5.5 percent, compounded annually. What will be the final account balance? Then calculate the interest earned on a one-year CD with an initial value of $5,000 earning 7 percent compounded semi-annually. What will be the final account balance?

_____

_____

_____

_____

_____

_____

_____

_____

30. DESIGN Create a marketing brochure for a checking account. Select the features your account will offer, choose the type of customer you would like to attract, decide on a name, and design a brochure that will effectively and fairly present the features. You may wish to gather real brochures to use as models.

CHAPTER 5

NEGOTIABLE INSTRUMENTS

5.1 TYPES OF NEGOTIABLE INSTRUMENTS
5.2 PRESENTING CHECKS FOR PAYMENT
5.3 PROCESSING CHECKS
5.4 CHANGING FORMS OF PAYMENTS
5.5 SECURITY ISSUES

Careers in Banking

MARATHON COUNTY EMPLOYEES CREDIT UNION

Marathon County is a primarily agricultural county in north central Wisconsin. The Marathon County Employees Credit Union (MCECU) serves the needs of county government employees. The MCECU is a closed-charter credit union, which means that only eligible employees may join. MCECU offers a full range of financial services to its 2,400 member/owners, including checking and savings accounts, loan services, retirement plans, and credit cards. MCECU provides telephone and online banking as well as direct deposit, payroll deduction, and domestic and foreign wire transfers.

Tiny by comparison to many financial institutions, MCECU's eight employees provide friendly, efficient, and individual service. "We listen to our members," says President Anne Heggelund, "and we serve their needs."

THINK CRITICALLY

1. What advantages are offered by a closed-charter credit union as compared to a regular bank?
2. How might marketing services to credit union members be different from marketing services to bank customers?

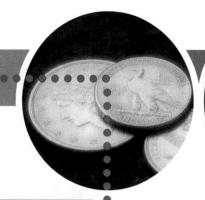

···········•· PROJECT ··········•

NEGOTIABLE INSTRUMENTS in YOUR WORLD

VIDEO
The Chapter 5 video introduces the concepts in this chapter.

PROJECT OBJECTIVES

- Expand awareness of payment systems
- Consider the use of negotiable instruments in daily life
- Consider the impact of technology on payment systems
- Increase awareness of security issues for both electronic and traditional payment methods

GETTING STARTED

Read through the Project Process below. Make a list of any materials you will need. Decide how you will get the needed materials or information.

- Make a list of negotiable instruments with which you frequently have contact or use often. Include instruments you receive and create.
- Make a list of electronic payment devices with which you frequently have contact or use often. Create as diverse a list as possible.
- Make a list of security measures for fraud prevention that you have encountered when writing or cashing checks.

PROJECT PROCESS

Part 1 LESSON 5.1 Discuss your use of negotiable instruments such as checks, drafts, or promissory notes. Discuss how those items eventually move money between accounts. Diagram this movement.

Part 2 LESSON 5.2 Discuss your own experience with cashing checks. List endorsement requirements and security measures you have encountered.

Part 3 LESSON 5.3 Create a model for the check-cashing process. Make either a poster-sized diagram or a 3-D model. Compare the poster or model to the diagram you made for Lesson 5.1.

Part 4 LESSON 5.4 Discuss emerging forms of electronic payment in your community and share your experiences.

Part 5 LESSON 5.5 Learn more about security issues and fraud prevention. Discuss ways that you can minimize the risk of fraud or other crimes involving negotiable instruments.

CHAPTER REVIEW

Project Wrap-up Hold a class discussion about payment systems in the banking industry. Make a list of possible payment systems that you envision to be in operation 20 years from now.

Lesson 5.1
TYPES OF NEGOTIABLE INSTRUMENTS ···

DEFINE the term negotiable instrument

IDENTIFY different types of negotiable instruments

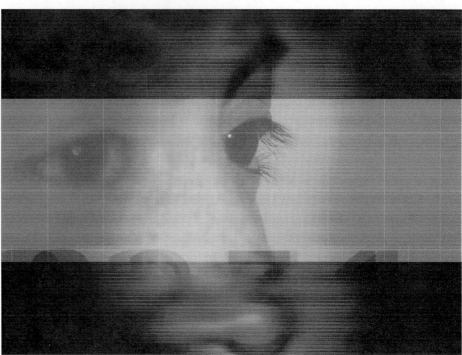

NEGOTIABLE INSTRUMENTS

Money is zipping around the banking system every day, 24 hours a day, seven days a week. The flow of deposits that carries both national and international economies moves constantly. In what forms does that money move?

When most people think of money, they think of cash, but only a small part of the money that moves in this country is cash. Increasingly, ledger entries add to one account and subtract from another without actual currency changing hands. Today, electronic transfers of one kind or another create these entries. Most large transfers within the banking industry have taken place this way for years. The electronic world is increasingly apparent to consumers, as electronic payment systems are becoming more and more a way of life in retail business as well. But, for many people, money moves

BANKING *Scene*

Midori Akita is finishing her career as a postal worker and moving from her home in New York to a small town in Florida. Each month, she will get funds from the government, her pension for her many years of service. As she prepares for her new life in Florida, Ms. Akita must consider many options about the best ways to receive, transfer, and handle her money. What financial choices does a person who moves to a new location face, and how should one best learn about them?

both to them and from them in the form of *negotiable instruments*, such as checks, drafts, and other written documents of value.

A **negotiable instrument** is a written order or promise to pay a sum of money, either to a specified party or to the person who holds it. Negotiable instruments include drafts, bills of exchange, and some promissory notes, but the most common form of negotiable instrument is a check.

The first documents that might be called checks appeared in Europe in the late 1650s.

What is Negotiable?

Don't let the word *negotiable* in *negotiable instrument* confuse you. The word means transferable. Consider that a check, like money, is a medium of exchange. The "negotiation" that goes on refers to the transfer of the instrument from one party to another. That transfer may mean passing the instrument between two people, or from one bank to another, or even from one country to another. The recipient or holder of the instrument negotiates the instrument in order to obtain its value. For example, your company gives you your paycheck. You negotiate the check by endorsing it and depositing it in your bank. Then you have use of its value.

Unless you and the bank agree that the instrument is negotiable, you won't be able to use it. The negotiation, however, may be restricted by one party or another in the transfer. As you might imagine, banks have a great interest in seeing that the negotiable instruments they receive for deposit are genuine and worth their assigned value. Most of the terms of negotiation relate to making certain an instrument does indeed possess real value, so that the bank in which you deposit it can negotiate the instrument to get the value from it just as you did.

What is an Instrument?

In the broadest sense, almost any agreed-upon medium of exchange could be considered a negotiable instrument. A Federal Reserve note is a written promise to pay on demand a certain value to the person who owns it. Certificates of deposit, bonds, Treasury bills and other securities, and even a winning lottery ticket may also meet that definition. In day-to-day banking, a negotiable instrument usually refers more narrowly to checks, drafts, bills of exchange, and some types of promissory notes.

CHECK**POINT**

What is a negotiable instrument? What is the most common form of negotiable instrument?

_____

_____

WORKSHOP

In small groups, make a list of checks that affect your daily life. Make a log to show the maker of the check, the type of check, and its purpose. Compare your list to those of other groups.

A negotiable instrument is a written order promising to pay a sum of money. It may be a **bearer instrument**, which is payable to the *bearer* (whoever holds it), or it may be an instrument with highly specified terms, including the date of maturity and the intended recipient. What makes it negotiable is that it can be used for value and is a medium of exchange.

Checks

Checks are the most common form of negotiable instrument and are the preferred method of payment for many debts. They offer convenience for both writer and recipient, a relatively high degree of safety, and a record of transactions. They are accepted for most transactions when supported by appropriate identification, and their common and recognizable form makes them a part of normal life for most people. There is a huge industry devoted to the printing, transporting, safeguarding, and processing of checks around the country. The Federal Reserve provides some of these services, but there are many private companies involved as well.

Most people immediately recognize standard features of personal checks.

- *Check number* is the number of the check being written.
- *Date* is the date the check is written. Post-dated or pre-dated checks violate most bank deposit agreements.
- *Payee* is the receiver of the funds. This line directs the bank to "pay to the order of" a specified party.
- *Amount* spaces allow for the amount of the check to be entered in both numbers and words, to minimize errors. In the event the words and numbers don't match, the amount written in words takes precedence.
- *Signature* is a valid signature of the maker of the check. Banks usually will not negotiate checks without a signature.
- *Memo* is an optional entry to note the check's purpose or other information.
- *Identification numbers* show the check number, the bank routing number, and the account number. These numbers are printed with magnetic ink in machine-readable characters, called magnetic ink character recognition (MICR) numbers.

THE GIRO IN EUROPE

A common form of payment in Europe that is almost unknown in the United States is the *giro*. From the Italian word for "circuit," a giro is a service provided by many European banks. Unlike a check, a giro is an order given by the payer, not to the payee but to his or her own bank, ordering it to transfer funds to the payee's bank. Giros cannot bounce like checks because if the payer lacks the funds, the payer's bank simply refuses the giro. Increasingly in Europe, giros have become electronic transactions. A written giro is rare in the United States, but most direct payment authorizations for recurring payments such as utility or insurance bills are in reality giros.

THINK CRITICALLY

Research more information on European banks. What differences in the American banking system as compared to more centralized European systems could explain why the check became far more common than the giro in the United States?

When you write a check, you may issue it to the person whose name is on the payee line, but you are really writing it to your bank. You are directing the bank to pay the sum "to the order of" the recipient.

As a percentage, check use per person is beginning to decline in the United States as a result of increasing numbers of electronic payments. According to the Federal Reserve, the total number of checks written rose steeply from 1980 to 2000, but only about 60 percent of noncash payments were made by check in 2000, down from 85 percent in 1979.

Drafts

A draft is a three-party instrument similar to a check. In fact, a check is one form of draft, but there are other forms. A **draft** is an order signed by one party (the *drawer*, or *drafter*) that is addressed to another party (the *drawee*) directing the drawee to pay to someone (the *payee*) the amount indicated on the draft. The payment may be at sight or at some defined time. If you (the drawer) were writing a draft, you would be directing your bank or other institution (the drawee) to pay the payee of the order the sum shown on the draft. You can see the similarity to what happens when you write a check. The terms for writers and receivers of drafts are the same as those used for checks. In fact, some credit unions provide "share drafts" instead of checks for their members. Most drafts are used for the purchase of goods and services when the transaction goes beyond the bounds of U.S. banking law.

Bills of Exchange

A **bill of exchange** is a negotiable and unconditional written order, such as a check, draft, or trade agreement, addressed by one party to another. The receiver of the bill must pay the specified sum or deliver specified goods on demand or at a specified time. Bills of exchange are a common form of internationally negotiable instruments.

Promissory Notes

A **promissory note** is a written promise to pay at a fixed or determinable future time a sum of money to a specified individual. You might not regard promissory notes as negotiable instruments, but if you think about it a moment, you can see why they are. Suppose you wrote an IOU to LaTasha for ten dollars. LaTasha, as it happens, owes Jamal ten dollars. Why couldn't LaTasha just give Jamal your IOU? You pay Jamal the ten dollars, and everyone comes out even. That is exactly what happens when certain promissory notes are used as negotiable instruments. These two-party instruments are legally binding documents with many specified terms that vary widely. For example, you might obtain a mortgage loan from ABC Mortgage Company, which might then sell the mortgage note to DEF Finance, which now owns your obligation.

Such trading practices on short-term notes make up a large part of a rapidly moving investment economy. *Commercial paper*, a short-term (270 days or fewer) note or draft issued by a corporation or government, is a common investment instrument. Remember that fast-moving overnight loans between banks make up a segment of the money supply.

CHECK**POINT**

List the standard features of a personal check.

_____

_____

THINK CRITICALLY ●●●●●●●●●●●●●●●●●●●●●●●●●

1. How is a negotiable instrument different from cash?

_____

_____

_____

2. What advantages might checks have over electronic payments?

_____

_____

_____

3. Why can a promissory note be considered a negotiable instrument?

_____

_____

_____

4. What risks might be associated with negotiable instruments?

_____

_____

_____

MAKE CONNECTIONS ●●●●●●●●●●●●●●●●●●●●●●●

5. BANKING MATH According to the Federal Reserve, 26 percent of checks are written to pay bills, 18 percent are written for point-of-sale transactions, 18 percent are written for income payments to individuals, and 11 percent are written for consumer-to-consumer payments. Using the American Banking Association's figure of 61 billion checks written annually, how many checks are written for each category?

_____

_____

_____

_____

6. TECHNOLOGY In groups, list every company or group you can think of that might be involved in the business of preparing or processing checks. Which of these groups might successfully adapt if electronic payment systems displaced checks? Which might go out of business? What effects might these changes have on the economy and the banking system?

_____

_____

_____

_____

_____

PRESENTING CHECKS FOR PAYMENT ••••••

GOALS

IDENTIFY bank requirements for honoring checks

LIST common forms of check endorsements

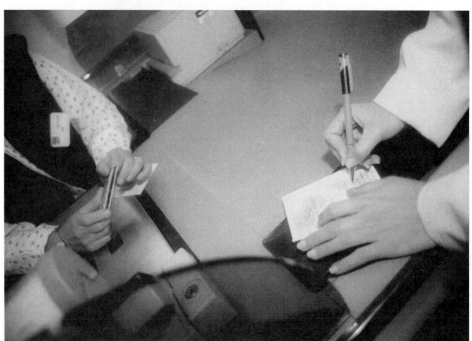

ELEMENTS OF NEGOTIABILITY

A check is a negotiable instrument. When you present a check to a bank for payment, the bank must assure that the check meets certain legal requirements. These conditions are commonly called **elements of negotiability**. The Uniform Commercial Code, Articles 3 and 4, covers notes, drafts, and checks. Every state has adopted these legal guidelines. They require a written, signed, unconditional promise or order to pay a fixed amount on demand or at a defined time to a specified person or to the holder of the instrument. There are practical considerations as well. When you bring a check to a bank to cash or deposit, the elements of negotiability directly affect how the bank looks at the check, the maker of the check, and you. After all, if the check you deposit turns out not to be a legal negotiable instrument, the bank is not going to get paid and neither are you.

BANKING *Scene*

After moving to her new neighborhood in South Florida, Midori Akita opened a checking account at a nearby bank. She used her final paycheck from the Postal Service to open the account. Her account representative politely requested two separate forms of identification, including one with a photograph. This request was no problem for Ms. Akita, who knew that the bank needed to be certain of both the check and its depositor. What was the bank trying to determine?

Written

The first requirement for a negotiable instrument is that it must be written. Remember that the law surrounding negotiable instruments was made long before electronic payment systems. In addition, written documents are easily transferable and universally recognized as legally binding. If a document conforms to the law, it is a negotiable instrument.

You might be surprised to note that there is no legally prescribed form for a check. A check is a written order to pay someone. There is not even a necessity that the "document" be written on paper. If all proper information were present, the check would be honored. There are old stories of checks written on various materials, tax payments made with "the shirt off one's back," or even written on a person's actual back. Whether these tales are true is hard to prove, but they illustrate that the information on the document is what matters, not the material of it.

Of course, checks written on shirts would wreak havoc in the automated check-processing system. Standards created by the American Bankers Association and the American National Standards Institute (ANSI) govern the size and placement of information on checks, as well as paper thickness, colors, and security features. Most checks are in one of three sizes—the standard, personal-check size and two larger sizes of checks common for payroll. These standards are for the industry's benefit, but they do not determine negotiability.

Discuss ways in which the elements of negotiability affect the writing and transfer of checks in daily life. Relate each element to a specific part of a check.

Signature

A document must be signed by a person capable of making the order or promise for it to be a negotiable instrument. Legally, a check is not payable if it does not bear the drawer's genuine signature. The bank that paid such a check would be liable, not the drawer. Like any legal document, the signature must be valid, but it does not necessarily need to be human. Machine signatures are perfectly acceptable if the bank obtains a resolution or agreement that liability for forgery resides with the customer using the machine.

Unconditional Promise or Order

To be negotiable, an instrument must make an unconditional promise or order to pay. First, the promise or order must be explicit. Authorizing a payment or acknowledging a debt is not enough. Second, the promise or order must be unconditional. Reasoning for this rule has to do with transfer. If the order to pay is conditional, a third party, who has no control or relation to any conditions set, may not be able to obtain the instrument's value. If its value cannot be transferred or obtained, an instrument is not negotiable.

Sum Certain

A negotiable instrument must state clearly on its face the principal amount to be paid, and it must be a monetary value. Although interest may be referenced, as may other documents regarding fees and charges, the principal sum in a note or order must be defined.

Payable on Demand or at a Defined Time

If a negotiable instrument bears no instruction as to when it is due, it is payable on demand, that is, immediately. It may show a time when it is payable, such as a promissory note does, but that must be a defined time. Checks are commonly payable on demand.

Words of Negotiation

Remember that *negotiation* applies to the ability of the holder to obtain its value, not to conditions or terms. Words of negotiation are instructions about how the instrument's value may be obtained. *Pay to the order of Keshia Smith* lets the instrument be negotiated by Keshia Smith with her endorsement, or to whomever she may later assign it. *Pay to the order of Cash* makes the instrument a bearer instrument, valuable to anyone who has it regardless of endorsement.

When you hand a check across the counter, the bank's representative will quickly check for all six elements of negotiability. Banks spend considerable time and effort training employees to understand and identify these elements. Recognizing them not only protects against fraud, but also allows the bank or other institution to know exactly how to handle a negotiable instrument.

What is meant by "elements of negotiability"?

_____

_____

ENDORSEMENT AND IDENTIFICATION

When you present a check to the bank for payment or deposit, the banker will ensure that the check has been endorsed. Although the maker of a check may have created a perfectly negotiable instrument, the actual negotiation of it involves the transfer of both the instrument and its value. *Endorsement* of the instrument allows it to be negotiated, not only by you but also by other parties later. After all, if the instrument cannot be used by others, it is not really negotiable. After you have endorsed the check, the teller may ask to see identification, especially if you seek cash or are depositing only a small part in your account (known as a *split deposit*).

Types of Endorsement

There are four primary types of endorsement, and each affects the degree of negotiability of the instrument. Some of these endorsement types have varying names, but they mean essentially the same thing.

Blank Endorsement A *blank endorsement*, sometimes called an *open endorsement*, is the least secure of the four main types of endorsement, but it is also the most negotiable. It is simply the signature of the holder.

For example, assume a check has been written to Maria Mills. Maria simply writes her name in the endorsement area

on the back of the check and does what she wants with the check thereafter. Maria must take care of this check, however. Once she signs it, it could be cashed by anyone. A check with a signed blank endorsement is a bearer instrument and is as good as cash to anyone who can find someone to accept it. It is a good idea not to endorse a check with a blank endorsement until the very moment you intend to cash or deposit it. Your signature implies that you have negotiated the check, and if you sign it and lose it, anyone who finds it may cash it.

Perhaps Maria intends to pass the check to someone else. Assume the check is for $100.00, and Maria happens to owe her cousin Martina exactly $100.00. Maria could use a blank endorsement and simply give the check to Martina. Martina could then endorse it again, called a *secondary endorsement*, and deposit or negotiate the check as she pleases. In fact, checks may receive multiple secondary endorsements as they work their way back to their originating banks.

The blank endorsement is the most common type of endorsement, and millions of people negotiate checks on a daily basis with it. Blank endorsements call for care, though, just as you would care for cash.

Restrictive Endorsement The holder of a check may wish to prescribe a little more carefully how the check is negotiated. A *restrictive endorsement* limits the use of the instrument to a means specified by the endorser. In theory, a restrictive endorsement ends further negotiation of the check. The most common restriction is "For Deposit Only," which limits the negotiation of the endorsed check to deposit in an account. By ending the instrument's transferability, a restrictive endorsement renders the instrument no longer negotiable.

Restrictive endorsements do not necessarily guarantee the end of negotiation, though. Perhaps an inattentive teller may not respond to the restriction properly, or perhaps the check might be deposited into another account than that of the intended payee. Such cases are more common when business accounts are involved, or when the payee has many accounts. More restrictive endorsements such as "For Deposit Only, Hobbit Corporation," or even the name of a particular account if a company has more than one, restrict negotiation more effectively.

Full Endorsement A *full endorsement* transfers the check to another specified party. From there, its negotiability depends on what that party does with it. Sometimes called a *special endorsement*, a full endorsement limits neither the transferability nor the further negotiability of the check. Suppose again that Maria Mills owes her cousin Martina $100.00. She could just endorse the check with a blank endorsement. She could just cash the check and hand Martina the cash. She could also use a full endorsement to transfer the check completely to Martina. In effect, it is just the same as if Martina had been the original recipient of the check. Martina must endorse the check whenever she wishes to negotiate it further, and she has the same range of options that Maria did. What the full endorsement provides is protection for the endorsed check. No one but Martina can use the check next.

Of course, negotiability is also determined by the next holder. Martina has to find a bank that will accept Maria's check, and she must identify herself and endorse the check to the satisfaction of the bank. If it is a different bank from Maria's, Martina's endorsement also acts as an *accommodation endorsement*, guaranteeing that the bank will eventually collect the money from Maria's account, wherever it may be.

Qualified Endorsement Another endorsement, the *qualified endorsement*, is an attempt to limit the liability of the endorser without limiting an instrument's further negotiability. The words "without recourse" appear in the endorsement, intending to move the instrument along without incurring liability if the check is no good. A qualified endorsement often guarantees payment if the person of primary liability does not pay.

Although qualified endorsements are not common, persons acting as representatives for others may use them. If, for example, a lawyer representing Martina Mills received a check for funds owed to her, the lawyer might simply transfer the check to her by endorsing it with a full endorsement but adding the words "without recourse." If the check were no good, assuming the lawyer had met other legal requirements for endorsement, neither Martina Mills nor any later holder of the check could require the lawyer to make good on the check.

The deposit agreements in the governing documents cover in detail when deposits are accepted, when funds are available from them, and what happens in cases in which the funds cannot be collected. Every account holder, especially those who receive checks from many sources, should be thoroughly familiar with his or her own bank's rules.

> **ENDORSE HERE**
> *Pay to the order of Martina Mills,*
> *without recourse*
> *A. Tourney Atlaw*
>
> DO NOT WRITE, STAMP OR SIGN BELOW THIS LINE
> RESERVED FOR FINANCIAL INSTITUTION USE*

You are walking down the street and notice a $20 bill. No one is around, and there is no way you can discern who might have dropped the bill. You congratulate yourself on your good fortune, think sympathetic thoughts about the person who lost it, pick up the bill, and go on your way. The next day, as you walk to your bank to deposit your paycheck, you notice a blue piece of paper on the curb. It's a check, in good shape, made out to John Dolan, whom you don't know. The check is drawn on your bank, and Dolan has placed a blank endorsement on it.

THINK CRITICALLY

How is the check different from the $20 bill? How is it the same? Knowing this check is a bearer instrument, what will you do with it? Discuss the issue with classmates.

Identification and Check Acceptance

Does the bank really care who you are if you present a check made out to Maria Mills and want to cash it? It sure does. Check fraud is a serious issue for banks, and there are ways that banks and companies work to prevent it. One of the ways banks protect themselves is to require adequate identification.

Banks may require as much or as little identification to cash or deposit a check as they wish. Some banks even require fingerprinting. The greatest risk to banks comes from personal checks cashed by new customers or noncustomers. A bank may charge fees for noncustomers, even for checks drawn on that same bank. It may make different rules for customers and noncustomers, and it may refuse to cash a check about which it is doubtful. Sometimes these policies make people feel they are being treated poorly, but a bank must balance customer service and risk management. When a bank cashes your check, it is essentially giving you money it has yet to recover, so it has a great interest in seeing that you are who you say you are and that the check is genuine.

CHECK**POINT**

Name the four main types of check endorsement.

_____

_____

THINK CRITICALLY •••••••••••••••••••••••••

1. How do elements of negotiability provide for the transfer and use of a negotiable instrument?

_____

_____

_____

2. Why do the words "pay to the order of" play such an important part in negotiability?

_____

_____

_____

3. What role does endorsement play in the negotiability of checks?

_____

_____

_____

4. If you were cashing a check at a bank and were asked to supply a fingerprint, would you be offended? Why or why not?

_____

_____

_____

MAKE CONNECTIONS ••••••••••••••••••••••

5. **COMMUNICATION** Create a flip chart or PowerPoint presentation on types of endorsements for checks. In your presentation, indicate the advantages and risks of each type as they apply to both safety and negotiability.

_____

_____

_____

_____

6. **SOCIAL STUDIES** Being able to open and maintain a checking account is a basic skill critical to participation in American economic life. Should such business skills be a required part of public education? What basic business skills should be taught? Write a one-page paper in which you clearly identify your opinion on these issues and provide logical reasons to support it.

_____

_____

_____

_____

_____

_____

PROCESSING CHECKS •••••••••••••••••••••••

IDENTIFY three key laws that make today's check-clearing process possible

EXPLAIN the sequence of events as a check is processed for payment

A NATIONAL SYSTEM OF PAYMENT

Checks are not only the most common form of negotiable instrument, but they also are a way of life in the United States. Next to cash, they are used most often for monetary transactions, and they are far safer and more convenient than cash for bill payment. The legal status of checks as negotiable instruments, and in many cases proof of payment, make them a dominant force in the economic life of the nation. Enhanced technology and communications have made the processing of checks more efficient and accurate. Although there is evidence that electronic payments are a growing trend, checks and check payments will remain a fact of economic life and the banking system for a long time.

As Midori Akita adjusted to her new life in Florida, she received a check in the mail from a brother-in-law in upstate New York as a retirement gift. She considered cashing it, but then remembered the account rules for her new account and thought it might be smoother to deposit the check. Still, her account rules noted that there might be a "hold" on the funds until the check cleared. Why might banks have such policies? What do you think is a reasonable time for a hold to occur?

Before reading the remainder of this lesson, work with a group and draw a diagram of what you think happens to a check as it is processed for payment. Later, compare your group's diagram to what you learn.

The Legal Structure of the Check Payment System

For a massive system of check processing to work, there must be clear and coordinated cooperation among banks. In the United States, with its unique blend of private and public institutions in the banking system, check payment depends upon the legal foundations that set up and maintain the banking system itself. Although many state and federal regulations govern the banking industry, three key legislative acts most critically affect the check processing system.

Federal Reserve Act of 1913 In establishing the structure of our banking system, the Federal Reserve Act of 1913 also established the fundamental relationship between the Federal Reserve and banks, as well as among banks. The Act created a national check collection system and other rules for payments. Today, the Fed is deeply involved in check collection and plays a leading role in the industry. It has fostered technological advance, beginning with automatic sorters more than 40 years ago and continuing through the latest state-of-the-art technology. The Fed has also used its regulatory authority to influence applicable legislative acts by Congress. In addition, the Federal Reserve has helped set and apply standards for checks and the technology that processes them. Not only the backbone of the banking system, the Federal Reserve is an up-to-the-minute participant in the check processing and collection system.

Uniform Commercial Code of 1958 The Uniform Commercial Code (UCC) of 1958 established a consistent code for commercial law transactions. Adopted eventually by all 50 states, the UCC largely eliminated the wide variation of legal regulation that could hamper the national payments system. Articles 3, 4, 5, and 9 of the UCC pertain to banking and negotiable instruments and contain terms, definitions, and regulations, many of which form the foundation of account agreements.

Expedited Funds Availability Act of 1987 The Expedited Funds Availability Act (EFAA) of 1987 was passed to combat an abuse of the check payment system practiced by a few banks. When checks were deposited, these banks did not credit the accounts until long after the checks had been paid by the banks on which they were drawn. Although the banks had credit for the checks in their funds, they would not make payments on them, creating in effect a "float" fund for their use at the expense of their customers. The EFAA directed the Federal Reserve to set rules that balanced the needs of consumers with the need for banks to protect themselves from uncollectible checks. Federal Reserve Regulation CC established these rules and procedures.

Why does the check processing and collection system depend on the Federal Reserve?

_____

_____

CHECK PAYMENT AND PROCESSING

What happens to your check after you write it and give it to the payee? How are the appropriate accounts adjusted and the check returned to you? Several steps occur as the check makes its way from you to the payee to your bank and back to you.

1. Suppose you write a check for $95.50 for this month's electric bill. You are the drawer or maker of the check. The electric company is the payee. Your bank, A National Bank, is the drawee. You mail the check to the electric company, the payee.

2. The electric company deposits your check in B National Bank, where it keeps its accounts. If it happens that the drawer and the payee of a check have the same bank, that bank handles the processing in-house. About 30 percent of all check-clearing ends here. If the banks are different, the processing continues.

3. B National Bank puts a magnetic code on your check showing the dollar total and sends it on to the Federal Reserve or other intermediary. Note that B National Bank has *not* credited the electric company's account for $95.50 yet, because the check has not cleared.

4. The Federal Reserve clears about one-third of the nation's checks. There are several large private banks, called *correspondent banks*, that also clear checks, and some have created check-clearing corporations. Whether processed by the Federal Reserve or other intermediary, the check is sorted, and the bank ID and the dollar amount are read from the magnetic codes.

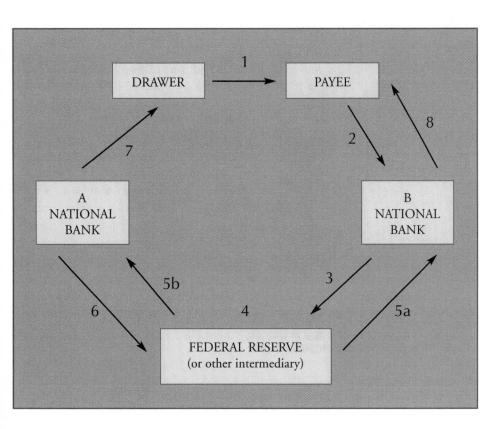

Float averaged $774 million a day in 2000, but legislation in the 1980s and electronic transactions both large and small are reducing the number from its high of $6.6 billion in 1979.

5. The Federal Reserve or intermediary credits B National Bank $95.50 in its account at the Federal Reserve. All financial institutions using the Fed to clear checks have an account at the Federal Reserve. Correspondent banks also have accounts at the Fed. Your check is then sent on to your bank, A National Bank. Note that at this point B National Bank has been credited with the $95.50, but A National Bank has not paid out anything. Thus, for this brief period, the same funds are counted in both banks. These funds are called *float*, and they distort both the money supply and reserve figures.

6. The A National Bank pays the Federal Reserve $95.50 and debits your account $95.50. If your account doesn't have $95.50 in it, the check is returned to B National Bank, and ultimately the electric company, unpaid. The penalties in your account agreement will apply. The electric company may have its own penalties as well.

7. The canceled check is returned to you, or perhaps you receive an image of the check or merely a transaction summary with your bank statement. Actual return of physical paper checks is declining because it is more costly than the digital-imaging systems banks increasingly use.

8. Finally, B National Bank credits the electric company's account for $95.50. In actuality, this might have happened earlier in the process, depending on B National Bank's policies for deposits. The entire process usually takes two to five days, and banks are required to make a depositor's funds available within five days.

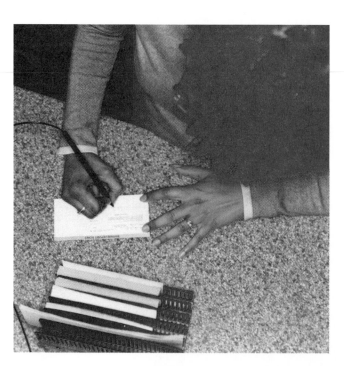

There may be some variation in these steps if a correspondent bank or other intermediary is used, or if somewhere along the line the check is converted into an electronic transaction rather than moving physically through the system.

The millions of checks written daily create a lot of float. Float has several causes, and there are separate names for each cause. *Malfunction float* is caused by machine breakdown. *Transportation float* refers to delays in moving checks from one place to another. The highest occurrence of transportation float happens in the winter. *Holdover float* occurs when banks are slow in processing transactions. Some banks have been accused of deliberately holding checks to create float in order to earn short-term interest.

CHECK**POINT**

What is float? What causes it?

_____

_____

THINK CRITICALLY ●●●●●●●●●●●●●●●●●●●●●●●●●

1. Could banks in the same city create an independent check-clearing network that didn't use any intermediaries? Why or why not?

_____

_____

_____

2. How does the foundation of the Federal Reserve make a national check-clearing system work more smoothly?

_____

_____

_____

3. Why does the Federal Reserve act to limit float?

_____

_____

_____

4. Why does advanced technology minimize float?

_____

_____

_____

MAKE CONNECTIONS ●●●●●●●●●●●●●●●●●●●●●

5. BANKING MATH According to the Federal Reserve, float averaged about $774 million in 2000, down from an $860 million average in the second half of the 1980s. What percentage decrease does this drop represent?

_____

_____

_____

_____

_____

6. PROBLEM SOLVING You have a roommate who routinely writes checks before receiving a paycheck. Your roommate claims the money will be deposited by the time the checks clear. Make a list of practical reasons why this idea is not a good one and the consequences it could bring.

_____

_____

_____

_____

_____

_____

LIST modern forms of payment systems

EXPLAIN how banks and other financial institutions use automated forms of payment

CONSUMER PAYMENTS

Although checks still make up the largest volume of payments in the United States, change is on the horizon. Other forms of payment now exceed the use of cash in dollar volume for transactions. With more rapid and more secure electronic capabilities, growth in electronic forms of payment is likely to alter forever the way payments are made and processed. The banking system already is adapting to these changes, but some of the newest possibilities also pose challenges for the existing system.

The growth of varied forms of payment is a product of two phenomena. One is the entrepreneurial spirit. Merchants and banks have always looked for ways to increase revenue. Providing alternative payment methods increases business by making purchasing easier. Revenue is further increased when fees are charged for the use of the new methods. Along with this opportunistic spirit, advancing technology is supporting creative, convenient,

Although Midori Akita had long had the option of having her pay-check deposited electronically, she had never used it, preferring to have the check in her hands. Now living in Florida, she is considering having her retirement checks go to her new bank through direct deposit. What questions might she ask about electronic funds transfer (EFT)?

rapid, and efficient forms of payment. Banks and the banking system are adapting to meet this evolution.

Charge Cards

Today's credit card industry grew from the use of charge cards. Because of the similarities, it may be easy to confuse the two. With a **charge card**, a consumer makes purchases but must pay the account in full at the end of the month. Most of the monthly bills are paid by check, with the card issuer doing the record keeping. Charge cards, in effect, lend the amount of purchases for a month. Originally charge cards were store cards, but eventually third-party companies formed networks of participating businesses to expand the market. Today, American Express is the most prominent national charge card.

Credit Cards

Credit cards allow consumers to pay all or part of their bills each month and finance the unpaid balance. Because of limits on interstate banking, credit cards did not become big business until banks devised a system using two banks (the card issuer's and the retailer's) that met regulations. Then the business exploded to become the competitive and powerful economic force it is today.

To make the system work, the credit slips (or records of them) function more or less like checks. The retailer sends the slips to its own bank, which pays the retailer, records the transactions, and sends the slips to a clearing system. The clearing system routes them to the issuing bank, which pays the retailer's bank and collects from the consumer.

Cash Cards

Cash cards are commonly used at an automated teller machine (ATM). Consumers can get cash, make transfers and deposits, or perform almost any other banking function at the machine by inserting the card and entering a *personal identification number* (PIN). Banks encourage the use of cash cards, as they are less expensive than human tellers and are usually available 24 hours a day. Some banks even charge for the use of a human teller in an effort to encourage ATM or online banking to hold down costs. Internet-working of different bank computers has made cash cards a way of life in the last 20 years, but the simple cash card is beginning to disappear. The same functions are often combined on a card that is also acceptable to retailers for payment. These cards are, in effect, debit cards.

Debit Cards

Taking advantage of current computer networking technology, **debit cards** transfer money from a person's designated account to the account of the retailer. A debit card allows an immediate *point-of-sale* (POS) transaction. The consumer swipes the card through a magnetic reader, enters a PIN, and authorizes the transfer. A record of the transaction appears on the consumer's bank statement, and the bank usually charges a monthly fee for use. Debit cards are rapidly growing in popularity as consumers become more comfortable with them. Checks still travel nicely by mail, but debit cards may replace them for point-of-sale transactions.

WORKSHOP

With a group, make a list of ways to pay for goods and services other than cash or check.

Smart Cards

Smart cards are credit, debit, or other types of cards with embedded microchips. The microchips store values and, unlike magnetic strips, use the embedded logic to change values and record transactions. Smart cards enable a wide variety of "electronic purse" programs. The use of smart cards has grown rapidly in Europe, but is just beginning to take off in the United States. Retail, security, and customer loyalty programs frequently use smart cards. Eventually, smart cards could combine all plastic-card functions on a single card.

Future Payment Systems

The future of payment technology seems almost unlimited. Online banking is growing, and experiments are underway with *e-checks*. An e-check is a digitally guaranteed type of electronic check to be transmitted on the Internet. Resolving security issues and establishing mutual acceptability networks are among the hurdles to overcome. Similar obstacles are faced by an even more radical concept, *electronic tokens*. Electronic tokens are a monetary system based on the exchange of digital money via computer. There is no inherent reason why such a system wouldn't work if enough people agreed to it, for it is in effect another type of fiat money. Problems of control and counterfeiting must be solved, and institutional and personal resistance to new intangible systems must be overcome.

Numerous digital ledger transactions already take place daily, and it may be only a matter of time before paper payments in any form become rare. Large-scale acceptance and gradual integration by the world's major financial institutions must occur before these innovations become common.

CHECK**POINT**

Name five payment systems other than cash or check.

_____

_____

BANK PAYMENTS

Innovations that are changing payment methods for consumers are also changing bank processes. Not only have banks implemented systems for recording and processing new forms of consumer payments, but they have also developed innovative systems for conducting their bank-to-bank transactions and internal operations as well.

EFT

EFT is an acronym for *electronic funds transfer*. Funds transfers occur between banks, between banks and the Federal Reserve, between banks and the government, and between banks and consumers.

Direct Deposit One common form of EFT is direct deposit. The Treasury Department encourages government employees and others receiving money from the government to have funds sent electronically directly to the bank. A statement arrives instead of a check, and the overhead cost of processing checks is eliminated. Safety, accuracy, and immediate use of the funds are reasons that many people prefer direct deposits. In 2000, the Treasury Department made 75 percent of its disbursements by direct deposit. More and more private employers encourage direct deposit as well.

Automatic Payments Automatic payments might be called direct deposit in reverse. Upon receiving a signed authorization, a bank makes defined payments to a specified recipient, including a record of the transaction with a statement. Recurring payments of an unchanging amount are good candidates for this service. The recipient is always sure of receiving funds on time, and the payer never has to write a check, nor does the bank or check-clearing house have to process it.

Automated Clearing Houses

Many transactions are handled by *automated clearing houses* (ACHs). The Federal Reserve led the development of ACHs in the 1970s and still operates most of them. Magnetic tapes exchanged among banks read streams of data into computers, ideal for large volumes of smaller payments such as

TECH TALK

EDI IMPLEMENTATION

Computers "talk" to each other by means of conventions, called protocols, for information exchange. EDI is an acronym for electronic data interchange, a set of standards for business-to-business exchange of information. As technology improves and extends further into the banking business, implementation of EDI becomes more critical to run such applications as online banking, smart card applications, and other forms of electronic commerce.

THINK CRITICALLY

Research more information on EDI systems. What sort of challenges do you think might be involved with implementing EDI?

payrolls or recurring payments. Although ACH technology is older and slower than online transfer, the cost per transaction is considerably less.

Online Transfers

For instant movement of high-dollar amounts, banks and the Fed use inter-bank online transfers. These online transfers take place via dedicated networks not for public use. The transfers are usually time sensitive, so the instant and final transfer of these funds is critical. *Fedwire*, the funds transfer system run by the Federal Reserve, handles transfers for federal funds, inter-bank dealings, and securities transactions. In 2000, for example, Fedwire handled about 300,000 transactions per day, averaging $3.5 million each. Another online system for private-sector transactions is the *Clearing House Interbank Payment System* (CHIPS), which specializes in large-dollar transactions for international business. A central computer keeps constant track of all interbank business. At the end of each day, banks settle their accounts by transferring money to accounts at the Federal Reserve.

The Leading Edge

Banks have a keen interest in pursuing leading-edge technology not only to attract and keep customers, but also to increase efficiency and lower costs for their own internal operations as well. Digital-imaging technology has the potential to save banks millions of dollars per year in storage, record keeping, postage, and labor costs. Instead of saving the actual processed check, a digital photo of the check becomes the document of record. A bank may send a customer reduced images of checks or merely a record of checks processed. If a customer needs a canceled check, the image can be retrieved from digital storage. Consider that a box of checks holds about 300. Imagine the space savings for the 61 billion checks written annually.

Electronic check presentment (ECP) is another means of making check-clearing more efficient. When a check is first processed for payment, a device reads the account information from the magnetic ink. Similar to credit card authorization, the check information is transmitted to the paying bank to immediately verify funds availability. This process virtually eliminates bad checks and float. In some versions of ECP, the depository bank sends a digital image of the paper check for processing, using digital-imaging techniques rather than the paper itself. This process, called *truncation*, eliminates the middle step of physical transport. Pilot programs of various types of ECP are in progress.

Those people whose business it is to produce, transport, and process paper checks have been hearing predictions of a paperless economy for decades. Yet check use, though declining as a percentage of total payments, is far greater in volume than it was 20 years ago.

Name three systems banks use for funds transfers.

_____

_____

_____

THINK CRITICALLY ●●●●●●●●●●●●●●●●●●●●●●●

1. Why do you think banks are interested in new systems of payment?

_____

_____

_____

2. Why might banks choose not to use up-to-the-minute technology for funds transfers or internal operations?

_____

_____

_____

3. Why might some consumers be uncomfortable with their banks' move to digital imaging for record keeping?

_____

_____

_____

_____

4. How does ECP eliminate float?

_____

_____

_____

MAKE CONNECTIONS ●●●●●●●●●●●●●●●●●●●●●

5. ECONOMICS Many businesses have a stake in keeping today's system of paper checks in place. The Check Payment Systems Association is an association of businesses and organizations committed to advancing, promoting, and protecting the check payment system. Look at the member list of the organization at www.cpsa-checks.org/memlisting.html. Visit some of the web sites of members. List some of the businesses these members are in, and list others you can think of that are part of today's check payment industry.

_____

_____

_____

_____

_____

_____

_____

_____

_____

6. COMMUNICATION Interview someone who works in the banking industry. Learn that person's thoughts about the future of payment systems. Summarize your findings in a brief report to the class.

Lesson 5.5
SECURITY ISSUES ••••••••••••••••••••••••••••••••

IDENTIFY security issues that banks face

LIST ways that banks and other financial institutions can combat fraud

SECURITY ISSUES IN BANKING

You might think of bank security in terms of the movies and television programs you have seen depicting bank robberies. Indeed, protecting your money physically at the site is an important mission of banks. Far larger dollar values are lost, however, through computer crime, vandalism, and various forms of fraud than through outright robbery. The average robbery nets less that $2,000, but the typical computer crime causes loss or damage exceeding a quarter of a million dollars. Various forms of fraud, some simple and some sophisticated, cost banks and consumers billions of dollars a year. Fighting and preventing these less visible crimes are a never-ending part of the banking industry. Like the rest of the industry, both the crimes and the prevention methods are changing with the times.

Settling into her new life in Florida, Midori Akita is pleased with her new bank. She reads daily in the papers, though, about frauds and schemes involving various forms of negotiable instruments. Many of them target senior citizens. How can she find out about the best ways to protect herself from such crimes?

Physical Security

It's easy to picture vaults and safe-deposit boxes when you think of physical security at banks. Locking devices are certainly part of the business, but physical security includes other considerations sometimes less obvious.

- **Building design plays a role in physical security.** Everything from resistance to attack to placement of sprinklers is a consideration in facility design. Planning the facility for technology, control of physical access to the building, location and security of records, and even the types and placement of furniture is part of an integrated security plan.

- **Surveillance and alarm technology continues to evolve.** Increasingly sophisticated devices with higher and higher resolution are appearing in banks. From closed-circuit television (CCTV) systems to monitoring software for all phases of processing operations, forms of surveillance are becoming increasingly complex.

- **Employee training is a critical factor in physical security.** Banks invest a lot of resources in teaching their employees how to recognize and what to do in an emergency. These procedures both lessen the risk of harm for staff and customers and minimize financial loss to the institution.

- **Transportation security is a part of physical security.** With the necessity of safeguarding cash and checks in transit, transportation security involves screening of employees involved in transportation. Companies providing this service are liable for the actions of employees.

Technology Security

The fastest-growing segment of banking security issues involves safeguarding the technology that makes doing business possible. With the rising use of online systems, both private and public, chances of loss through these systems rise as well. Anticipating the next clever scheme to vandalize or defraud a bank via technology is a difficult job.

- **Security technology itself helps with this challenge.** From anti-virus software to *autobots*, programs that constantly monitor all transactions looking for abnormalities, system administrators seek tools to prevent hackers from gaining access to records or systems. Providing such tools is a growing industry. *Firewalls*, programs that monitor and limit incoming and outgoing transmission, have become increasingly important as banks allow access to records for online banking via the Internet.

In small groups, list fraud prevention measures that you have personally experienced when writing, receiving, or negotiating checks.

- *Physical security of devices is an important part of technology security too.* From placement of equipment to access control, limiting potential damage to technology can prevent crime.
- *Administrative policies for both computer operators and bank employees play a role in safeguarding technology.* Some of these policies are as simple as insisting that employees log off each time they leave a terminal or requiring passwords to be changed frequently. Employee training helps explain the risk that the policies intend to avoid.

Fraud

Fraud in its many forms is the largest cause of loss to banks. From bad checks to complex and sophisticated schemes devised by organized crime, fraud is a never-ending challenge for the banking industry. With each new service or technology arises a new opportunity for fraud as well.

Check Fraud Check fraud has been around for a long time, but new technology has given criminals new tools to improve their work. Counterfeit and forged checks cost the banking industry $10 billion a year, with more than 500 million bad checks per year being presented.

The first and probably most important line of defense is teller training. Knowing how to verify a check and what to look for on a suspicious one is the focus of training efforts. Third-party verification businesses are growing, using biometric systems techniques such as fingerprinting and maintenance of exhaustive databases to help banks combat fraud.

Credit Card Fraud Credit card fraud has grown along with the giant credit card business. Various forms of identity fraud, forgeries, and scams cost billions per year. Often, it is merchants and banks who lose the most, as consumers may not be liable for all charges. The ease of gaining personal

information for fraudulent use makes credit card fraud hard to combat. The growth of the Internet has also contributed significantly to credit card fraud, sometimes by web site creators who design false sites merely to collect valid credit card numbers.

Loan Fraud Loan fraud is a growing area of concern for banks. Complex schemes to obtain loans that will never be collected are becoming more frequent. These sophisticated crimes are often high-dollar frauds, sometimes conducted by insiders and others in the loan-brokering and approval process. The FBI has recently increased its efforts to combat these crimes.

CHECK**POINT**

What are three primary security issues for the banking industry?

_____

_____

FRAUD PREVENTION

Fraud prevention occupies more resources of the banking industry than any other activity except routine processing. Fraud in its many forms is limited only by the imagination, knowledge, and nerve of criminals. Small-time theft is a cumulative problem, but recent trends spotlight a growth in more sophisticated schemes. In addition, the sheer volume of check and credit card transactions presents many opportunities for the unscrupulous.

Bank administration is an important part of fraud prevention. Adhering to established procedures, including technology security rules, insisting on careful record keeping, conducting audits, and investigating suspicious activities of employees or customers are part of an overall plan for security and fraud prevention.

Employee training may be the best return on investment for fraud prevention. Detailed checklists for ways to identify questionable or counterfeit checks, identification verification procedures (sometimes as simple as a telephone call), and frequent updates on new types of counterfeit and fraud schemes all help combat fraud on the front lines. Training should not be confined to tellers, however. Operations personnel, technicians, investment counselors, loan officers, and other personnel require frequent and current training. With the increasing complexity of many types of fraud, management also needs to stay alert for the latest trends.

Consumer education is an effort that banks see as increasingly worthwhile. Most frauds are crimes of opportunity, and if consumers protect their checks, credit cards, identities, and account information more carefully, committing fraud becomes a more difficult task.

Consumer Tips

Checks are the most common negotiable instrument and should be treated as carefully as cash. Here are some steps to prevent check fraud.

Poll five members of your community to see how many of these consumer tips they personally use to avoid check fraud. Write a brief summary of your findings.

- Use checks that have built-in security features. Many of these checks have a padlock icon on them to indicate the presence of enhanced security features such as watermarking and microprinting.

- Don't have your social security number imprinted on checks. Your SSN is usually enough for a criminal to get a credit card, bank account, or fake loan.

- Don't endorse a check until just before you cash or deposit it. It is better, in fact, if you sign the check in a teller's presence.

- Don't leave spaces on checks. Draw horizontal lines to fill any blank spaces, and write words close together, especially on amount lines.

- Reconcile your account regularly. Call your bank immediately if you notice any suspicious transactions on your statement.

- Shred statements, canceled checks, ATM slips, and credit card receipts, rather than just throwing them in the trash.

- Be careful on the phone, in person, and on the Web. Never give out account information or numbers to anyone you don't know or of whom you are not certain. Don't be afraid to contact authorities.

CHECKPOINT

What are the three best bank defenses against fraud?

_____

_____

BANKING MATH CONNECTION

Do you balance your checkbook? Many Americans don't, often just checking the balance at the ATM. An error could lead to problems, and deposit agreements require that you notify the bank of discrepancies within a defined time limit.

Your bank statement of October 15 says you have $1,114.72 in your account. Your checkbook register shows $1,146.57. You have made two deposits, written five checks, and visited the ATM three times since the statement was printed.

SOLUTION

Begin with ending balance from the Oct. 15 statement. $1,114.72

Add deposits made since the date of the bank statement.

Oct. 22	$900.00	
Oct. 25	54.00	
	$954.00	954.00
		$2,068.72

Subtract checks and debits in your check register
not shown on the bank statement.

Oct. 15	Check 1114	$ 62.00	
Oct. 15	ATM	50.00	
Oct. 18	Check 1115	97.15	
Oct. 21	Check 1116	610.00	
Oct. 22	ATM	20.00	
Oct. 24	Check 1117	18.75	
Oct. 24	ATM	20.00	
Oct. 26	Check 1118	44.25	
		$922.15	−922.15
			$1,146.57

Compare the result to your check register balance. Your calculation agrees with your checkbook register. If the account doesn't balance, recheck your math. Compare deposit slips and checks to make sure you entered them correctly and that the bank debited them correctly. Check for outstanding checks from previous statements that may still not have cleared. Check your statement also for automatic withdrawals or fees that you may not have recorded. Balancing a checkbook can be easy, provided you make clear entries for every transaction, calculate accurately, and perform the task promptly.

THINK CRITICALLY ●●●●●●●●●●●●●●●●●●●●●●●●

1. How does building facility design contribute to physical security of a bank?

_____

_____

_____

2. What background information would you require of a prospective employee? What steps would you take to verify the information?

_____

_____

_____

_____

3. What causes some bank employees to be careless about technology security?

_____

_____

_____

4. What steps do you personally take to minimize the chance of fraud with your accounts?

_____

_____

_____

MAKE CONNECTIONS ●●●●●●●●●●●●●●●●●●●●●

5. **TECHNOLOGY** Visit the web site of the Comptroller of the Currency at www.occ.treas.gov to learn more about fraud prevention and detection. Prepare a three-minute presentation on check fraud prevention measures, including teller training.

6. **CRIMINOLOGY** Crooks can be quite clever. Use the Internet or other research materials to learn about some specific forms of fraud that are currently problematic. Present a report to the class about how they work and how they can be prevented.

7. **COMMUNICATION** Do you believe that fraud can ever be effectively eliminated from the banking system? Write a short paragraph explaining your answer.

_____

_____

_____

_____

_____

_____

_____

_____

CHAPTER 5 REVIEW

CHAPTER SUMMARY

LESSON 5.1 Types of Negotiable Instruments
A. A negotiable instrument is a written order or promise to pay a sum of money to a specified party or to the person who holds it.
B. Checks are the most common form of negotiable instrument. Other forms include drafts, bills of exchange, and promissory notes.

LESSON 5.2 Presenting Checks for Payment
A. Elements of negotiability call for a written, signed, unconditional promise or order to pay a defined sum on demand or at a defined time.
B. Types of endorsement include blank, restrictive, full, and qualified.

LESSON 5.3 Processing Checks
A. The Federal Reserve Act of 1913, the Uniform Commercial Code of 1958, and the Expedited Funds Availability Act of 1987 provide the legal framework for today's check payment system.
B. Checks travel a circuit among drawer, payee, banks, and the Federal Reserve or other clearing house. Checks usually clear in two to five days.

LESSON 5.4 Changing Forms of Payment
A. Charge cards, credit cards, cash cards, debit cards, and smart cards are current forms of payment systems. New systems on the horizon are e-checks and electronic tokens.
B. Automated clearing houses, Fedwire, and CHIPS are computer systems that transfer high volumes of transactions between banking entities.

LESSON 5.5 Security Issues
A. Physical security, technology security, and fraud are three primary areas of concern. Growth of technology creates challenges in all three areas.
B. Fraud prevention is a major part of the banking business. Rigorous bank administration, employee training, and consumer education combat fraud.

VOCABULARY BUILDER

Choose the term that best fits the definition. Write the letter of the answer in the space provided. Some terms may not be used.

a. bearer instrument
b. bill of exchange
c. cash card
d. charge card
e. credit card
f. debit card
g. draft
h. elements of negotiability
i. negotiable instrument
j. promissory note
k. smart card

_____ **1.** A negotiable and written order addressed by one party to another
_____ **2.** Certain legal requirements that a check must meet
_____ **3.** Negotiable instrument payable to whoever holds it
_____ **4.** Commonly used at an ATM
_____ **5.** Transfers money directly from buyer's bank account to merchant's account
_____ **6.** A written order or promise to pay a sum of money to a specified party or the person who holds it
_____ **7.** Card with embedded microchips

banking.swep.com

8. What is a negotiable instrument?

_____

_____

_____

9. What does _negotiable_ mean as it applies to negotiable instruments?

_____

_____

_____

10. List the elements of negotiability for a legal negotiable instrument.

_____

_____

_____

_____

_____

_____

11. Identify four types of endorsement and the effects they have on a negotiable instrument.

_____

_____

_____

_____

_____

_____

12. Briefly explain the check-clearing process.

_____

_____

_____

_____

_____

_____

13. What is a correspondent bank?

_____

_____

_____

14. List four types of consumer payments other than cash.

_____

_____

_____

15. Give two examples of electronic funds transfer (EFT).

_____

_____

16. What are three prime areas of security concern for banks?

_____

_____

_____

17. Name three types of fraud with which banks must contend.

_____

_____

_____

18. Identify three major steps banks can take toward fraud prevention.

_____

_____

_____

APPLY WHAT YOU LEARNED

19. How are negotiable instruments similar to money?

_____

_____

_____

20. Why are there specific legal requirements for an instrument to be negotiable?

_____

_____

_____

_____

21. When you cash a check, why does the bank care whether or not you are the actual payee?

_____

_____

_____

22. How did the Federal Reserve Act of 1913 pave the way for the modern check-clearing process?

_____

_____

_____

23. Why is float harmful?

_____

_____

_____

24. How has the growth of the Internet increased opportunities for fraud?

_____

_____

_____

MAKE CONNECTIONS •

25. BANKING MATH Carlota's bank statement shows a balance of $674.32. Since the statement date, Carlota had deposits of $800.00 and $50.00. She has visited the ATM for withdrawals of $20.00, $50.00, and $20.00, and she has written checks for $42.11, $79.80, $600.00, $81.50, and $174.00. Her checkbook register shows a balance of $556.91. Is her account properly balanced?

_____

_____

_____

26. COMMUNICATION Predict the future of technological impact. Do you think checks and other negotiable instruments (not counting cash) will eventually disappear? Explain your thoughts in a two-page persuasive paper that gives clear reasons for your predictions.

27. ART/DESIGN Create a poster to educate consumers about the possible risks of careless check security. Provide at a glance an education in check fraud prevention.

28. TECHNOLOGY Learn more about encryption, one of the ways in which computer networks protect their data. What are the main methods, advantages, and issues surrounding secure data transmission today?

_____

_____

_____

_____

_____

29. SOCIAL STUDIES The growing availability of personal and financial information troubles many people. In groups, research privacy issues as they apply to banking and the Internet. Present a report on current problems, possible solutions, and potential legislation about protecting consumers' privacy.

CHAPTER
6

BANK LOANS

6.1 CONSUMER LOANS
6.2 GRANTING AND ANALYZING CREDIT
6.3 COST OF CREDIT
6.4 CREDIT AND THE LAW

Careers in Banking

CHELSEA STATE BANK

Chelsea State Bank has a unique market position, according to Executive Vice President and Chief Information Officer, Scott Tanner. Located in southeast Michigan, Chelsea and surrounding small towns provide most of the bank's customers, 97 percent of whom express complete satisfaction with their choice. With three branches and 57 employees, Chelsea State Bank is a little larger than most small town banks, but not so large that the personal touch is lost.

"Small town" doesn't mean "small time." Chelsea State Bank is high-tech. "We offer digital imaging of checks exclusively in this area," Tanner notes. The bank sends customers a single page of images rather than the actual checks. The bank has fully operational online banking, and will soon make images available online as well.

All employees participate in a profit-sharing program made possible by a tax-deferred contribution by the bank. "We look for good people first," Tanner says, "with good communication skills who are honest." He's not interested in people who "would be accurate, but rude." The bank conducts its own on-the-job training in banking skills. Tanner notes with pride that most of Chelsea State Bank's officers began as entry-level employees.

THINK CRITICALLY

1. Why might it be easier in some ways for a smaller bank to implement new technologies?
2. What qualities do you think a person needs for a successful banking career?

BANK LOANS and THE COMMUNITY

VIDEO
The Chapter 6 video introduces the concepts in this chapter.

PROJECT OBJECTIVES

● Learn more about consumer loans offered in your community
● Learn to carefully read information about consumer loans
● Compare local loan offerings in terms of interest and fees
● Recognize the impact of consumer loans on the economy

GETTING STARTED

Read through the Project Process below. Make a list of any materials you will need. Decide how you will get the needed materials or information.
● Make a list of financial institutions from whom you will acquire information.
● Vary the types of financial institutions from whom you gather information.
● As you collect information, think about how it compares to information in the content of this chapter. Translate marketing language for consumer loans into industry names by analyzing features of the loans. Categorize local loan offerings by comparing them to chapter content.

PROJECT PROCESS

Part 1 LESSON 6.1 Discuss in class your personal experience with various types of consumer loans. Who can apply for loans? How does one apply? What is expected of the customer?

Part 2 LESSON 6.2 Expand your awareness of loan offerings in your area. Begin with a list of local institutions, and find out about consumer loans from each. Divide the class into areas of responsibility for acquiring information about the loans.

Part 3 LESSON 6.3 Use the information from the chapter to compare the loans, identifying features, requirements, fees, and rates for each.

Part 4 LESSON 6.4 Make a chart projecting the total cost of each loan identified, using the information you gathered from the lender and the chapter. Who could benefit most from each type of loan?

CHAPTER REVIEW

Project Wrap-up Hold a class discussion about obtaining a loan. What things should consumers do as they prepare to apply for a loan? To borrow money responsibly, what information do you think consumers should have? Ask students to examine credit from the banking industry's point of view and analyze the impact of credit on a local financial institution and on the banking system as a whole.

Lesson 6.1
CONSUMER LOANS ••••••••••••••••••••••••••••

GOALS

DEFINE major terms associated with consumer lending

EXPLAIN the difference between installment loans and open-end loans

INSTALLMENT LOANS

Since the earliest days of human activity that could be considered banking, loans have been at the center of the business. Lending is the foundation of the banking industry, a mainstay of all business, and critical to the working of our economic system. When you consider that lending supports the banking industry and that banks, in turn, help stabilize the economy, then the lending process is key to our nation's soundness. Loans, responsibly used and administered, are a powerful financial tool. Like any powerful tool, they can also be dangerous when used without proper knowledge.

With increasing competition among banks and financial institutions, a wide array of loan products is available from which to choose. Most consumer lending falls under two categories: installment loans and open-end loans.

BANKING *Scene*

Jamar Brown needs a better car. He has saved $2,000 for a down payment and has researched the kind of car he wants. Now he needs to consider a car loan. He wants to find the best loan with terms that are right for his situation, but he is not sure where to start. What questions should Jamar ask himself as he prepares to seek a loan?

Installment loans are perhaps the most familiar of banks' consumer lending products. An **installment loan** is a loan for which the amount of the payments, the rate of interest, and the number of payments (or length of term) are fixed. An installment loan contract is a legal document obligating both parties to the written terms, so it is important for consumers to read and understand every word carefully.

Personal loans Personal loans do not require that a specific purpose be stated. You might take out a personal loan for a vacation, optional medical procedures such as cosmetic surgery or dental work, or almost anything you choose. There is an almost unending variety of terms and schedules for personal loans, based on the consumer's credit rating and the specific type of loan he or she seeks. There are many types of installment loans available, usually marketed according to purpose.

Automobile Loans Automobile loans may be the most common type of installment loan. After the automobile price is settled, the trade-in value and down payment negotiated, and the deal established, consumers usually finance the remaining balance with an installment loan. Although manufacturers have financing available through their own corporations, banks often offer competitive rates and establish relationships with dealers to provide the service. In the case of used cars, an installment loan may be the only kind of financing available. With installment loans, the term and payments are fixed and scheduled, based on the principal and the interest rate calculated on the balance. Typically, the better your credit rating, the lower the interest rate you get. Borrowers should always ask questions and read carefully the *Truth in Lending Statement* required to be given at the time of signing. Installment loans for cars, boats, and recreational vehicles are similar.

Home Equity Loans Home equity loans are an increasingly popular form of lending. These loans, based upon the difference between what a home is worth and how much the homeowner owes on a first mortgage, are in effect second mortgages. This type of loan generally carries a low interest rate, and interest charges may be tax deductible.

Education Loans Education loans help many students achieve an education they might not otherwise be able to afford. In many cases, loans are backed or subsidized by the government. Stafford loans for students and PLUS loans for parents are examples of government-backed programs. If the borrower for some reason defaults, the government may pay these loans. Because of government backing, there is less risk to the lending bank, so interest rates are often lower than those available for other loans. Students are not required to make payments while they are in school. Payments begin once a student is out of school. If the student meets certain need-based requirements, the government will pay the interest that accumulates on the loan until student payments begin. Employers may also help arrange loans through credit unions or the employer's bank for continuing education programs for employees.

In small groups, list as many items as you can think of that consumers purchase with installment loans. How well might these items sell if installment loans were not readily available?

Secured and Unsecured Loans

Although there are many types of consumer loans, they all fall into one of two categories. A **secured loan** is one in which some item of value backs the loan in case the borrower defaults on the loan. The item that secures the loan is called **collateral**. The bank could use the collateral, if necessary, to recover the financial loss of an uncollected loan. For example, if you take out an auto loan, the lender typically has a **lien** on the car, a legal claim to the property to secure the debt. The car will go to the lender if you fail to make the payments, and the lien is noted on the car's title.

Collateral offers the bank a degree of safety for its loan. In theory almost anything agreed to between borrower and bank could be collateral, but for most loans used to make a large purchase, the purchased item is the collateral. A banker might accept other things of value to secure a personal loan, such as a savings account, CDs, stocks or other securities, a personal possession of value, or any other financial asset. Be certain that banks don't want an inventory of used cars and diamond rings, though. They examine creditworthiness carefully before granting any loan, secured or otherwise.

An **unsecured loan** is a loan backed only by the reputation and creditworthiness of the borrower. Sometimes called a *signature loan*, these loans are typically for smaller amounts than secured loans. There may be exceptions for customers who do large volumes of business with the bank or have a great track record and credit rating. Commercial lending often blends secured and unsecured loans.

Lending Terminology

Loans are legal contracts between lender and borrower, and so they include precise language. With the many types of loans and many varieties of plans within those types, there may be a great deal of variation in details and numerous terms. Although banks are required to disclose the truth about their loans, it is still in the consumer's best interest to read carefully and understand everything in the loan agreement. Reputable bankers explain and answer questions about loan terms. It is in their interest to do so not only for good customer relations, but also to help ensure a smooth and steady income for their business.

Some fundamental terminology applies to nearly every loan.

- ***Principal is the amount borrowed.*** If you need $12,000 after your trade-in and down payment on a car, the $12,000 is the principal.

- ***Interest is the amount you pay to use the principal.*** The interest rate is the amount of interest, usually expressed per year as a percentage of the principal, such as 9.9 percent. The annual percentage rate (APR) is one of the most important figures to compare when considering loans. Rates for most installment loans are *fixed rates* for the life of the loan, but in some loans they may be *variable rates*, changing over time. *Indexed rates* are linked to some other rate, such as the Federal Reserve's prime rate (usually plus some other figure) to allow for changes in the economy.

It is important to know how interest is calculated. In some loans, interest is calculated on the declining principal balance as payments are made. In other loans, payments go toward the interest first, and then toward the balance, so there is no advantage in paying off the loan early. In such a case, you may owe more on the principal at the time of payoff than you would have if you had financed with a loan that charged interest on a declining balance.

- **Fees are other charges for the loan.** Examples are application fees, document preparation fees, late charges, and so forth. The loan agreement must specify all fees.

- **The finance charge is the total dollar amount to be paid for the loan.** The finance charge includes all interest calculations, fees, and other costs. It must be disclosed to the consumer. Sometimes the finance charge alone can be misleading. For example, if you borrowed $1,000 for a year with a loan fee of $10 and interest totaling $100, your finance charge would be $110. The APR would be 10 percent if you kept the whole $1,000 the full year, but you probably wouldn't. Assuming that you began to pay the loan back immediately in 12 equal payments of $92.50, you don't have the use of the full $1,000 for the year. The math gets a little tricky, but the actual APR would be 18 percent.

- **Total payments is the total amount a consumer must repay.** It includes the principal and the total finance charge. This figure must be disclosed at the time a loan is signed. The total payments figure reveals the effect of an interest rate over time. The APR, the finance charge, and the total payments are the three key figures to evaluate.

- **Payment is the amount the borrower repays each specified period.** The schedule of payments specifies exactly when payments are due and what penalties are assessed if payments are not made on time. Sometimes an *acceleration clause* brings the entire loan due if payments are missed. A missed payment may also be cause for a variable interest rate to increase. Payments are usually monthly and fixed for the life of the loan. Some loans may include a balloon payment (a single large payment) at the end of the loan. Although the balloon payment reduces the payments before it, paying the final large amount may be difficult.

What is the difference between a secured loan and an unsecured loan?

_____

_____

OPEN-END LOANS

Open-end loans are another type of loan with an almost endless variety of applications. The amount owed on an **open-end loan** is flexible, as is the term. The longer you use the money, the more you pay.

Credit Cards

You may not think of credit cards as forms of consumer loans, but that is exactly what they are. The issuer is lending you the money for a period of time and charging interest for its use. The principal changes as your balance goes up and down, but you are still borrowing and paying interest. Because the balance changes, finance charges vary as well. One variable is the method used to calculate the balance. Some cards offer a **grace period**, which is an amount of time you have to pay the bill in full and avoid any finance charges.

Most cards have an annual fee that is added to the balance. Transaction fees for cash advances or charges for exceeding your credit limit may apply. Some issuers charge a monthly maintenance fee even if you do not use the card. Late penalties for bills paid after the due date raise the cost of credit cards, and special delinquency rates may raise the APR significantly.

Lines of Credit

Other forms of open-end loans are the various line-of-credit plans that banks may offer. These may include a home equity reserve or an overdraft protection plan. Essentially, these plans allow consumers to establish a line of credit that they may draw on as needs arise. Borrowings may be for any amount up to an agreed-upon limit. As the balance is paid down, more money may be borrowed. Terms of agreement are similar to those of credit cards.

Credit card use is growing among college students. In 2000, 78 percent of undergraduate college students had at least one credit card, up from 67 percent in 1998. The average balance in 2000 was $2,748, up from $1,879 two years earlier.

What is an open-end loan?

_____

_____

ETHICS IN ACTION

Some credit card issuers offer teaser rates, extremely low rates for balance transfers or for a brief period of time. Later, the rates may change to normal or even high levels. Credit analysts note that moving your credit accounts too often can hurt your credit rating.

THINK CRITICALLY

Do you think that offering teaser rates is a misleading policy? Why or why not? Should credit lenders hold it against consumers who take advantage of such offers?

THINK CRITICALLY ●●●●●●●●●●●●●●●●●●●●●●●

1. Why do you think consumer loans have so many names and forms?

_____

_____

_____

2. What is the difference between the interest and the finance charge of a loan?

_____

_____

_____

3. Why might it be important for consumers to understand their credit card agreements?

_____

_____

_____

_____

4. In your opinion, how many credit cards are too many? Explain your reasoning.

_____

_____

_____

MAKE CONNECTIONS ●●●●●●●●●●●●●●●●●●●●●

5. COMMUNICATION With a partner, make a list of questions people should ask themselves to decide whether taking on debt makes sense for them. Include questions about needs, budgets, and possible changes in lifestyle. Convert the questions into a checklist for consumers that offers guidance for responsible borrowing.

_____

_____

_____

_____

_____

6. BANKING MATH According to one financial study, credit card debt in the United States at the end of 2000 was about $675 billion. This number represents about 40 percent of total consumer borrowing. Using these figures, what was the total amount of consumer debt at the end of 2000?

_____

_____

_____

_____

Lesson 6.2
GRANTING AND ANALYZING CREDIT ••••

GOALS

LIST steps in the credit-approval process

IDENTIFY major criteria in a person's credit rating

GRANTING CREDIT

Every borrower represents a potential risk to the lender. If you can't or don't pay off any loan you have, you not only ruin your credit rating, but you also hurt the bank as well. In fact, bad loans of various types are the number one reason banks get into financial trouble. Banks have to make sound decisions when it comes to loans, and they need defined methods of doing so. Consider, for example, that about 6 percent of all credit card charges ($675 billion total charges in 2000) *never* get paid. Add to that installment and mortgage loan defaults, and you can see why banks need to know what they are doing.

Before a bank is willing to advance its money (or more accurately, its customers' money) to you, it takes a number of steps to minimize the likelihood of a bad decision. Most of these steps are part of a well-defined policy of risk management.

BANKING *Scene*

Jamar Brown has found a car, saved a down payment, and chosen a lender. He is nervous about how the lender will make the decision on whether to grant the loan. Jamar recently changed jobs, and he doesn't have a long credit history. What might Jamar need to know about the credit-granting process?

Risk Management

Risk management for bankers is the practice of minimizing financial loss through effective policies. Banks face risks in operations, credit, liquidity, legal and regulatory compliance, and even marketing matters. Regarding credit granting, risk management policies include consideration of the bank's overall financial position, reserve requirements, cash flow, and ratio analyses of liabilities and assets. These factors all influence the credit-granting process, determining how flexible a bank can afford to be in granting credit. In addition, a bank's risk management policies are carefully scrutinized by bank examiners during an audit. Sometimes legal requirements complicate these issues. Banks must document that they comply with the law in such areas as extending credit fairly and equally throughout the community.

Credit-Approval Process

To ensure credit granting decisions are made in an accurate, efficient, and fair manner (and to be able to document them as such), well-run banks have written credit-approval procedures. Procedures and the specific standards for them may vary depending upon the type of loan and from bank to bank. Some of these steps may be combined, or for large loans may have several cycles of processing and underwriting for approval. Some of the procedures may be automated, such as with an online application, but the essential credit-approval process follows some basic steps.

WORKSHOP

In small groups, list specific ways that operations, credit granting, legal compliance, and marketing pose potential risks to banks.

- *Application* The first step in the credit-approval process is obtaining a complete and accurate application. This may seem self-evident, but it is critical, for much of the later processing of the loan depends upon the information provided here. It is not unusual for a credit application to fail because it lacked an important detail or gave inconsistent information. Even something as basic as a name can cause confusion. Is it George Walker Bush, George H. Bush, George Bush, Sr., or George Bush, Jr.? A social security number may clear up such problems, but an incorrect digit could ruin everything. A loan officer or other representative often works with the customer, guiding him or her through the application and clarifying exactly what information and what degree of detail is necessary. Often bank representatives help consumers with this step as part of a loan analysis or needs analysis, helping consumers decide what kind of loan may best meet their needs.

- *Documentation* The next step for the bank is gathering the necessary documentation for the loan. Some of this information may come from the application itself, depending upon how detailed it is. Other information includes such items as a credit report, employment verification, bank account information, appraisal of properties for secured loans, and so forth. Sometimes preliminary approval is granted based on these documents.

- *Processing* The bank builds a loan file, as the loan officer verifies statements on the application and checks information on all documentation the bank receives. The processing time depends upon the type and amount of the loan and the credit history of the applicant. The loan officer may ask for explanations or seek further information during this step.

- *Underwriting* When all required information has been gathered and verified, the loan officer forwards the loan file for **underwriting**, or reviewing the loan for soundness. The underwriter's job is to make sure the loan

is a prudent use of bank funds. The underwriter reviews the application package to make sure it is complete and makes an evaluation of the loan based on the assembled documentation. Underwriters evaluate the three c's: *collateral*, *capacity*, and *credit reputation*. Collateral refers to the security (if any) required for the loan. Capacity refers to the ability to repay, based on income, job history, and amount currently owed. Credit reputation, or credit history, is a record of how well the applicant has repaid debt in the past. Based on these factors, the underwriter approves or disapproves the loan.

Today, underwriting is increasingly automated. Sophisticated software programs provide statistical analyses and models based on vast quantities of data. Banks may sometimes grant a loan to applicants who don't meet standards, grant a loan with certain conditions, or offer a loan at subprime rates. **Subprime rates** are those higher than normal to offset the increased risk represented by a less-than-perfect borrower. The days when a banker might offer a loan based on acquaintance are disappearing. Many banks have less flexibility in underwriting than they once did, although they may offer more programs to meet varying needs.

- *Closing* At the closing, a bank representative discusses and explains the terms of the loan, and the borrower signs the documentation that has been prepared. Included with the documentation are disclosure statements required by law.

- *Funding* When the documents are signed, the bank either adds the funds to the borrower's account or issues a check.

Not all of these steps are followed for every type of loan nor in this exact order. However, some form of credit-approval process takes place for every loan, whether it is a credit card application through the mail or a loan officer working face to face with the consumer.

CHECKPOINT

What is underwriting?

_____

_____

ANALYZING CREDIT

When an underwriter (whether human or electronic) looks at your loan application, one of the key factors considered is your credit history. It is fairly easy to verify your income, how long you have had your job, and how much the car you want to buy is worth. It is not so easy, however, to predict how people will pay bills. The best way to predict the future is to see how a person has done in the past.

Consumer Reporting Agencies

A **consumer reporting agency (CRA)** is a company that compiles and keeps records on consumer payment habits and sells these reports to banks and other companies to use for evaluating creditworthiness. Sometimes called credit bureaus, CRAs also include information about whether a person has been sued, arrested, or has had financial judgments issued against him or her by a court. The three largest consumer reporting agencies are Equifax, Experian (formerly TRW), and TransUnion, but there are many such agencies. Among the three largest, records on almost every conceivable use of credit by every American exist. These comprehensive records form the foundation of credit analysis.

Most credit reports contain the following types of information.

- *Personal data* include names (including former ones), social security number, addresses, and employment history. Similar information for a spouse may also appear.

- *Accounts history* includes detailed history of active credit accounts, such as names and addresses of creditors, when an account was opened, co-signers, accounts status, whether the manner of payments (MOP) is timely, and whether the account is in default or a judgment has been issued. These records for active accounts typically show 24–36 months of history, and creditors keep reporting as long as the account remains open. Banks and credit unions, credit card companies, mortgage companies, finance companies, and department stores report this information regularly.

- *Delinquent accounts* are sometimes the only accounts reported to a consumer reporting agency. In these cases, the same sort of information as described above appears, as well as the current status of the delinquent account. Utilities, insurance companies, doctors, and landlords are typical reporters of this data.

- *Public records* include bankruptcies, judgments, liens, divorces, child-support arrearages, and criminal records. Private companies track and sell this data to credit bureaus.

- *Inquiries* are records of all who have requested a copy of the credit report within the last year. Although consumers have little control over these records, too many inquiries in a year can appear as if a consumer is having trouble obtaining credit.

With the enormous volume of credit records, errors inevitably enter into some records, and sometimes they are the first evidence of identity theft. Credit investigations have been criticized as not always being reliable. Reputable studies have reported that a large percentage of the credit reports reviewed had serious errors of some kind that could result in credit denial.

According to a non-profit consumer organization, the two main reasons for credit bureau errors are misidentification and deliberate fraud. Credit bureau statistics suggest that there are 500,000 to 700,000 cases of identity theft annually.

ONLINE IDENTITY VERIFICATION

With identity fraud on the increase, lenders and businesses are looking for ways to be certain customers are who they say they are, especially in online applications. Some new applications use networking technology to link credit applications directly to consumer reporting agencies to aid in verification.

Equifax's eIDverifier™, for example, is a software program that asks for verification information beyond social security number, driver's license number, and address. The program asks consumers to answer a multiple-choice questionnaire that is created from their own credit histories, answers to which only genuine consumers would know. These answers are compared to the Equifax data, and only if they match can the consumer move forward with the transaction.

THINK CRITICALLY

Search the Internet for more information about online identity verification systems, and write a short report on your findings. Does the use of such systems increase your confidence regarding online security? Why or why not?

Conduct research to learn what information to include in a letter of dispute to a consumer reporting agency. Write a sample letter to a credit reporting agency disputing an inaccurate entry on your report.

Although credit bureaus are private organizations, consumers are entitled to a credit report annually. In some states, one report per year is free. In most states, each report costs about $8. It is absolutely essential for consumers to ensure that credit reports are accurate. The Fair Credit Reporting Act guarantees consumers the right to review and dispute information in the reports.

Credit-Scoring Systems

A credit-scoring system can provide an efficient and unbiased method of evaluating credit. For many years, banks have used credit-scoring systems to evaluate the potential creditworthiness of loan applicants. These scores place a numerical value on the performance or status of an applicant in various categories. Income, debt, age (as long as it is not used to discriminate), years on the job, and even whether one has a telephone are the kinds of factors a credit-scoring system evaluates. The points in each category are added for a total score. There are many such systems in use, typically requiring a minimum score to qualify an applicant for a loan.

FICO

In recent years, the FICO credit-scoring system developed by Fair, Isaac and Company, Inc. has come to dominate the dozens of credit-scoring systems in use. The **FICO score** is a three-digit number that credit granters can use in making a loan approval decision. Using a sophisticated model, the FICO system weighs all categories of information, with the importance of factors depending on the amount and type of information available on the person being evaluated. The FICO system excludes income and the type of credit for which the applicant has applied. Also excluded are race, ethnic background, religion, gender, and marital status, all of which are prohibited by law from being factors used to make a credit decision. FICO uses the following criteria in its ratings. Percentages are approximate.

- **Payment history (35 percent)** includes a consumer's track record on many types of accounts, including credit cards, installment loans, mortgages, and other types of borrowing, as well as public records on collections, bankruptcies, judgments, and wage attachments. Details on late payments and how many accounts have no late payments appear.

- **Amounts owed (30 percent)** include the total amounts owed on all accounts, the types of accounts that are open, how many of those accounts have balances, whether certain types of accounts have balances, how much of a credit line is in use, and how much is still owed on installment loans compared to the original loan value.

- **Length of credit history (15 percent)** considers how long accounts have been established and how long it has been since each was in use. In general, a long, solid credit history increases the FICO score.

- **New credit (10 percent)** is often sought by people in financial trouble. Although shopping for the best rate is a good idea, too much new credit is a sign of overextension. FICO considers how many new accounts exist, how long since a new account was opened, how many recent requests for credit have been made, and what recent credit history shows.

- **Types of credit (10 percent)** are evaluated, including what types of accounts exist and how many there are of each. A "healthy mix" of credit yields a higher score than a dependence on a single type of credit account.

FICO scores range between 300 and 900, with about 620 being the point below which consumers may be regarded as high risk. The sophisticated (and secret) FICO scoring system is not without critics. Some analysts say that potential creditors depend too much on it, rather than carefully weighing all factors. Some consumer groups object to the fact that lenders do not have to release FICO scores, nor is FICO responsible for errors in content. If consumers don't know their scores, critics argue, how can they dispute? Recent actions by both credit bureaus and lenders toward more disclosure may help consumers understand both the credit-scoring system and their own ratings.

CHECK**POINT**

What is a consumer reporting agency?

_____

_____

THINK CRITICALLY ●●●●●●●●●●●●●●●●●●●●●●●

1. Why might underwriting standards vary at different banks?

_____

_____

_____

2. How do subprime rates offset the risk associated with borrowers who have less-than-perfect credit?

_____

_____

_____

3. How might a stranger having your social security number ruin your credit rating?

_____

_____

_____

4. Do any of the categories of personal information on a credit report strike you as being a violation of privacy? Discuss.

_____

_____

_____

MAKE CONNECTIONS ●●●●●●●●●●●●●●●●●●●●●

5. PROBLEM SOLVING Critique the methods and concepts of credit investigation described in this lesson. Then, working in groups, design your own credit-scoring system that produces a maximum score of 100. Assign point values to at least six types of information. State the weight of each type of information and how relevant you believe each is in predicting likelihood of payment.

_____

_____

_____

_____

_____

_____

6. CONSUMER AFFAIRS Visit at least three noncommercial web sites that provide information about how you can correct errors on your credit report. Summarize your findings.

_____

_____

_____

_____

_____

LESSON 6.3
COST OF CREDIT ••••••••••••••••••••••••••••••••

WHAT CREDIT COSTS

More than ever, the nation's economy runs on credit. Not only is it the foundation of banking income, but it is also the engine that makes possible growth and development throughout the economy, bringing into being the standard of living you know today. Credit is a convenient tool for consumers to use to enhance their lives. The credit industry grows by about 12 percent a year.

Like any tool, credit can be dangerous if misused. Today, credit debt is $1.2 trillion, and the number of people who are unable to meet their obligations is increasing. The easy availability of credit that results from fierce competition among lenders has allowed some consumers to accumulate more debt than they can manage. Instead of cutting back in a financial pinch, they simply add more debt to cover the shortfall. Eventually this can lead to disaster. Understanding the cost of credit and knowing how it is calculated helps consumers use it wisely. Banks want and need to make money

Jamar Brown has been approved for his car loan. His credit record, though brief, was good. While at the bank, his loan officer asks whether he would also like to apply for a credit card. She offers him several possibilities and options. Jamar has also seen many such offers in the mail. What should Jamar consider before he applies for a credit card?

on loans, but they have no interest in struggling to collect debt or losing what they lend in default. For this reason, banks have an interest in promoting consumer education. Many banks offer information on the best use of credit, and they are required by law to make full disclosure of the costs.

Reviewing APR and Finance Charge

The annual percentage rate (APR) is the amount of interest charged on the loan principal expressed as a yearly figure. APR does not include annual fees, transaction fees, penalties, loan origination fees, or other such costs.

The APR is a key aspect of comparing credit costs. Understanding the total finance charge depends on how interest charges are applied. How does the principal change? Lenders can calculate interest in many different ways, as long as they explain clearly what they are. Some of the methods are more advantageous to consumers than others. Finance charges may be very different, depending on which method is used. In many cases, the interest is charged on the declining principal balance.

Sum-of-Digits Method Sometimes the interest gets paid first, so paying ahead saves the consumer no money. This payment structure has essentially built in prepayment penalties, which may be fixed charges or may be based on the *sum-of-digits method*. This method takes the total finance charge, divides it by the number of months in the loan term, and assigns a higher ratio of interest to the early payments. For example, consider a 12-month loan. The sum of the digits 1 through 12 is 78. In the first month, 12/78ths of the total finance charge goes to interest. In the second month, 11/78ths, the third month, 10/78ths, and so on. Although the total cost to the consumer is the same, there is no advantage to paying early, because the interest is front-loaded.

Previous and Adjusted Balance Methods For open-ended credit, the finance charge is based on the rate multiplied by the balance. How the lender computes the balance matters in terms of the total finance charge. Some creditors take the amount owed at the beginning of the billing cycle and calculate interest on that figure, regardless of payments or charges. This method is called the *previous balance method*. Others subtract payments made during the billing cycle, but usually don't count purchases. This method is called the *adjusted balance method*.

Working in small groups, have group members independently interview 20 classmates, friends, family, and other people to find out how many separate consumer loan accounts they carry. What percentage of them are credit cards?

BANKING MATH CONNECTION

What portion of a credit card payment goes toward the principal? Suppose you have a balance of $1,500 on a credit card. Your minimum payment is 2 percent, or $30, on a card with an APR of 18 percent. How much of that payment will go toward paying the interest?

SOLUTION

The formula for finding the interest is

Rate ÷ 360 × 30 × Balance = Interest

Rate is the APR, in this case 0.18. Dividing it by 360 gives the rate per day, or 0.0005. Multiplying this figure by 30 provides the rate per month, and multiplying that product by the balance gives the interest.

Rate ÷ 360 × 30 × Balance = Interest
0.18 ÷ 360 × 30 × $1,500 = $22.50

In this example, $22.50 goes toward interest, and only $30.00 − $22.50 = $7.50 goes toward reducing your balance. It is going to take a long time to pay off the balance. Consumers should always pay as much beyond the minimum payment required as they can afford.

Average Daily Balance Method Probably the most common method is the *average daily balance method*. The balances for each day of the billing cycle are added and then divided by the number of days in the billing cycle to yield an average figure on which the finance charge is calculated.

Minimum Payments

Most credit cards require a minimum payment, usually 2 to 5 percent of the unpaid balance, every month. A recent trend toward lower minimum payments has increased bank profit, but has contributed to greater consumer debt. Although paying the minimum payment keeps the account in good standing, it doesn't reduce the principal much.

Term

For installment loans, length of term also affects the total finance charge. Lenders must disclose the total payments. This figure along with the APR and the finance charge helps consumers evaluate the cost of a loan accurately. The following chart from the Federal Reserve shows loan costs for three possible $6,000 loans.

	APR	Length of Loan	Monthly Payment	Total Finance Charge	Total Payments
Creditor A	14%	3 years	$205.07	$1,382.52	$7,382.52
Creditor B	14%	4 years	$163.96	$1,870.08	$7,870.08
Creditor C	15%	4 years	$166.98	$2,015.04	$8,015.04

Repaying the loan over a longer period reduces the monthly payment considerably. It also increases the total payments for this installment loan. So which loan is the best deal? The answer depends upon the individual consumer's needs and abilities. The least expensive loan is the shortest one with the highest payments. Perhaps a larger payment won't fit your budget, so paying a little more to use the money longer is a wiser decision than saddling yourself with a payment that is difficult to make. The consumer's credit rating may dictate which interest rate is available. Knowing and understanding the details of the cost of credit is critical for consumers.

Why is it a good idea for consumers to pay more than their minimum balances on open-end credit accounts?

_____

_____

THE IMPACT OF CREDIT

Could you imagine our society without the availability of credit? Our economic system would collapse almost overnight. Yet too much debt is not good for the economy at large, either. The more in debt consumers become, the less they can buy. The less they can buy, the slower the economy. If the economy slows, jobs may be lost, and the spiral of recession deepens. Healthy economic growth depends upon healthy use of credit.

Overextension

Consumers become overextended when they take on more debt than they can really afford. Some consumers mistakenly believe that just because someone approves them for credit, that must mean they can afford it. They take on two, three, four, five, or more new credit cards, thinking that they will have only a small balance on each without really totaling up the costs. They may be able to make minimum payments, but their overall debt load increases.

The effect of overextension on personal finances can be disastrous. If an emergency arises or a situation changes, such as a job loss, some consumers are suddenly in real trouble. A snowball effect may occur as late charges, penalty interest rates, and other fees apply.

One consequence of overextension is a ruined credit rating. Documentation of most credit problems stays in a consumer's file for at least seven years. During that time, new opportunities such as a great deal on the perfect house, an auto loan at an advantageous rate, or needed orthodontia may be inaccessible. In addition, with disposable income going to service debt, day-to-day life becomes more difficult. If you are barely making minimum payments and energy prices rise dramatically, your entire budget may collapse. Consumers have a responsibility to inform themselves about credit costs and use credit wisely.

The Role of Banks

Lenders are sometimes accused of creating problems for consumers by making credit too easily available without regard to the borrower's ability to pay. Fierce competition and the growth of subprime lending rates has led some banks to relax their underwriting standards. New regulations about such *predatory lending* practices are growing.

In the long run, excessive consumer debt is not in banks' interest. Banks need creditworthy customers, and practices that ruin the credit ratings of people serve no one. Collecting debt is expensive, if not impossible, on loans that are in default. Responsible lenders not only evaluate credit carefully and disclose costs as required by law, but they also help consumers make the best choices for their own particular situations. Customer service representatives will take the time to explain terms and answer questions fully. Still, the lending business is increasingly market driven, and consumers must understand and choose carefully the best use of financial resources.

Credit Counseling

Numerous agencies for credit counseling, both profit and nonprofit, exist to help overextended consumers. Most of their plans involve reorganizing debts and sometimes renegotiating terms. Banks and other creditors will often accept such arrangements rather than lose their money altogether. Consumers should look carefully, though, because some credit-counseling companies are simply looking for ways to offer more subprime loans or to make a profit from doing what the informed consumer could do alone. In extreme cases, a consumer may seek protection from creditors by declaring bankruptcy. Because doing so may have long-term consequences, professional legal advice is a worthwhile investment.

Why do consumers become overextended?

_____

_____

1. How can a consumer find the best deals on credit?

_____

_____

_____

2. What factors should consumers consider when choosing a loan?

_____

_____

_____

3. In your opinion, why has there been rapid growth in subprime lending?

_____

_____

_____

4. What danger signals might indicate to a consumer that he or she is becoming overextended?

_____

_____

_____

MAKE CONNECTIONS ●●●●●●●●●●●●●●●●●●●●

5. ART/GRAPHICS Design a chart that a person could use to compare loan products. Include spaces for all relevant information and factors.

6. BANKING MATH Assume a $3,000 balance, a 16 percent APR, and a 2 percent minimum payment requirement. How much is the minimum payment? How much of the minimum payment will go toward reducing the balance?

_____

_____

_____

_____

7. CONSUMER AFFAIRS Investigate credit-counseling agencies on the Internet. Summarize your findings of at least three types.

_____

_____

_____

_____

_____

_____

_____

CREDIT AND THE LAW ••••••••••••••••••••••••••

GOALS

EXPLAIN the purpose of consumer protection laws in lending

IDENTIFY important laws associated with consumer loans

CONSUMER PROTECTION

At best, credit policies are not always easy to understand, but in the past lenders sometimes made it purposely difficult. In a wave of consumer protection legislation during the 1960s, '70s, and '80s, Congress enacted several important laws to guarantee the rights of consumers. These *disclosure laws* require that details of lending agreements be specified in writing. Other important laws require far more than disclosure, guaranteeing equal access to credit for qualified consumers, accurate credit reporting, and freedom from unfair or deceitful collection practices. Banks are required not only to conform to federal and state laws, but also to document their compliance.

As Jamar Brown signs the papers on his car loan, he is asked to initial several places in the contract that point out terms and definitions. He also receives an itemized list of all charges, including the sale price of the car, APR, finance charge, total payments, and schedule of payments. He received similar forms relating to his credit application when he applied for the loan. Jamar was mostly interested in how much his payments were and when they were due. Why couldn't he just sign the whole package once? What was the purpose of so many forms and so many initialings and signatures?

In small groups, collect three sample copies of disclosure notices from local banks. Share your samples with each other. Study the wording of each carefully to see how it conforms to the requirements of TILA. Report your findings to the class.

Truth in lending

The **Truth in Lending Act** (TILA), Title I of the Consumer Credit Protection Act of 1968, was landmark legislation. Amended many times, it guarantees that all information about costs of a loan is provided in writing to consumers. Items that must be disclosed include the following.

- Total sales price
- Amount financed
- Annual percentage rate (APR)
- Variable rate information
- Total payments
- Schedule of payments
- Prepayment policies
- Late payment policies
- Security interest

In addition, the act provides for a *right of rescission*, which allows a consumer to change his or her mind about a loan until midnight of the third business day following the signing of papers. The law also prescribes complaint procedures and penalties.

Equal Credit Opportunity Act

The **Equal Credit Opportunity Act** (ECOA) prohibits the use of race, color, religion, national origin, marital status, age, receipt of public assistance, or exercise of any consumer right against a lender as a factor in determining creditworthiness. If a credit request is denied, the law also requires that the lender provide the reasons for the denial upon request.

CONSUMER LENDING IN JAPAN

The Japanese economic system, the most westernized of Asian economies, also depends on credit. From the first store card issued by Marui Department Store in 1960 to the present, the use of credit has grown dramatically in Japan. Japanese consumers face issues similar to Americans with their use of credit. Japanese bankruptcies are on the rise, especially as Japan has faced several waves of recession.

There are three primary consumer reporting agencies in Japan, one for banks, one for companies doing their own financing, and one for credit-granting companies. Although there are no laws limiting credit reporting in Japan, agencies abide by voluntary guidelines. According to *Credit and Collections World Magazine*, the guidelines do not allow reports to be used for employment screening or any purpose other than credit evaluation.

THINK CRITICALLY

What factors in a nation's economy would lead to a sophisticated system of credit reporting? What would likely be the result if the voluntary guidelines were not followed?

Fair Credit Reporting Act

The **Fair Credit Reporting Act** (FCRA) aims to protect the information that credit bureaus, medical information companies, and tenant screening services may collect. First enacted in 1971, the legislation provided the first legal oversight of the credit information industry. The FCRA establishes the following rights.

- Consumers must be told what is in their file and who has had access to the information.
- Consumers must be told if information in their file has been used against them. Anyone using a report to deny credit must supply the name, address, and telephone number of the agency that supplied the report.
- Consumers can dispute inaccurate information in their reports. The agency must investigate disputes within 30 days. The source must respond and advise all agencies of errors. If disputes cannot be resolved, consumers can add rebuttal statements to their files, a summary of which must appear in all future reports.
- Inaccurate information must be corrected or deleted. Although consumers cannot compel an agency to remove accurate data, agencies cannot reinsert disputed information without notifying the consumer.
- Credit bureaus cannot report information more than seven years old in most cases, or more than ten years old for bankruptcies.
- Access to consumer files is limited. The law specifies who may view the files and for what purpose. Penalties are imposed for violations.
- Consumers must authorize the release of reports to employers and the release of reports that contain medical information.
- Consumers may exclude themselves from credit-bureau lists sold for unsolicited credit or insurance offers. Telephone requests remove consumers from such lists for two years. Written requests remove names indefinitely.
- Consumers can seek damages for violations of the law.

Fair Debt Collection Practices Act

The **Fair Debt Collection Practices Act** (FDCPA) protects consumers from unfair collection techniques. Third-party collectors may not use deceptive or abusive tactics as they try to collect overdue bills. Such collectors may not contact debtors at odd hours, call repeatedly or in a harrassing manner, or threaten them in any way, even with legal action, unless it is actually contemplated. Nor may collectors reveal the debts or collection actions to other people, such as employers, in an attempt to embarrass the debtor. Penalties are prescribed for violations of the act.

Name four important pieces of consumer protection legislation.

_____

_____

OTHER LEGISLATION

The preceding four laws are the foundation of consumer protection, but there are many other laws that apply as well.

- **Fair Credit Billing Act** An amendment of TILA, specifies fair procedures for resolving billing disputes and prevents creditors from taking adverse action until the dispute is resolved.
- **Fair Credit and Charge Card Disclosure Act** Also an amendment of TILA, requires credit and charge card issuers to provide information about open-end credit in direct mail or telephone solicitations.
- **Home Equity Loan Consumer Protection Act** Also amending TILA, requires lenders to make appropriate disclosures about open-end loans that are secured by homes and places limitations on such plans.
- **Credit Repair Organization Act** Prohibits credit repair companies from misleading consumers about their services and costs and requires agreements to be in writing.
- **Gramm-Leach-Bliley Act** Compels banks and other financial institutions to protect the privacy of consumers. Institutions must develop written policies, notify consumers of them, and allow consumers the opportunity to "opt out" before a bank can sell some forms of personal information to others.

In addition to these federal regulations, many states have enacted similar laws intended to protect the rights and privacy of consumers.

Compliance

Authority for enforcing consumer protection acts varies with the individual law and the government agency associated with it. Some federal statutes are enforced by the Federal Reserve, some by the Federal Deposit Insurance Corporation (FDIC), some by the Federal Trade Commission (FTC), and some by courts in actions brought by consumers.

In addition, audits are conducted to test compliance at banks and other financial institutions. Examiners typically review randomly selected loan files for completeness of documentation. They also watch for patterns of credit granting and denial, look at the way disputes are resolved, and check to see that privacy regulations are being observed.

Banks spend an ever-increasing amount of time and money ensuring well-documented compliance with complex sets of regulations under various jurisdictions. Bank customers might be surprised to learn the amount of time that bank officers spend every day assuring that their banks follow consumer protection laws.

Name three other pieces of lending legislation.

_____

_____

THINK CRITICALLY ●●●●●●●●●●●●●●●●●●●●●●●●

1. What factors brought consumer protection laws into being?

_____

_____

_____

2. How might incomplete disclosure in an advertisement about a car loan have misled consumers before passage of the Truth in Lending Act? Give an example.

_____

_____

_____

3. Why is it in a bank's best interest to provide complete disclosure in a lending agreement and documentation of compliance to all lending laws?

_____

_____

_____

4. Some bankers feel that the banking industry is overregulated. What probably leads them to feel this way?

_____

_____

_____

MAKE CONNECTIONS ●●●●●●●●●●●●●●●●●●●●●

5. COMMUNICATION Work in teams to conduct a poll of at least 30 people. Find out how many of them have examined their credit reports in the last 12 months. How many of them have been the victim of an erroneous entry in a credit report? How many are aware of key provisions of FCRA?

_____

_____

_____

_____

6. PROBLEM SOLVING Conduct research to learn about the responsibilities of a consumer reporting agency when it receives a letter disputing information on a credit report?

7. CONSUMER AFFAIRS Review the privacy policy of a local bank's web site. Report your findings.

_____

_____

_____

_____

CHAPTER 6 ...... REVIEW

CHAPTER SUMMARY

LESSON 6.1 Consumer Loans

A. Installment loans are the most common form of consumer lending. They may be secured or unsecured. The principal, interest, fees, finance charge, total payments, and schedule of payments must be fully explained by law.

B. The amount owed on an open-end loan is flexible, as is the term. Open-end loans include credit cards and lines of credit.

LESSON 6.2 Granting and Analyzing Credit

A. A lender must determine whether extending credit is a sound decision.

B. Many lenders base credit decisions on reports from consumer reporting agencies (CRAs). CRAs and lenders often use credit-scoring systems.

LESSON 6.3 Cost of Credit

A. The cost of credit varies with annual percentage rate and term and depends on the method of calculation. Minimum payments reduce balances slowly.

B. Consumers should pay close attention to their credit standing because poor credit can result in numerous long-running financial problems.

LESSON 6.4 Credit and the Law

A. Four main laws (TILA, ECOA, FCRA, and FDCPA) provide the foundation for consumer protection in lending. Other federal and state laws apply as well.

B. Banks must document their compliance with all applicable state and federal regulations and spend considerable resources doing so.

VOCABULARY BUILDER

Choose the term that best fits the definition. Write the letter of the answer in the space provided. Some terms may not be used.

a. collateral

b. consumer reporting agency (CRA)

c. Equal Credit Opportunity Act

d. Fair Credit Reporting Act

e. Fair Debt Collection Practices Act

f. FICO score

g. grace period

h. installment loan

i. lien

j. open-end loan

k. secured loan

l. subprime rate

m. Truth in Lending Act

n. underwriting

o. unsecured loan

_____ 1. Period for which no interest charges accrue if balance is paid in full by due date

_____ 2. Guarantees that all information about costs of a loan is provided in writing

_____ 3. Loan with fixed amount of payments, rate of interest, and length of term

_____ 4. Loan backed by some item of value in case the borrower defaults

_____ 5. Dominant credit-scoring system

_____ 6. Loan backed by only the reputation and creditworthiness of the borrower

_____ 7. Company that compiles and sells credit records

_____ 8. Item used to secure a loan

_____ 9. Reviewing a loan for soundness

_____ 10. Loan with flexible principal and term

_____ 11. Protects consumers from unfair collection techniques

REVIEW CONCEPTS

POINT YOUR BROWSER

banking.swep.com

12. Give three examples of installment loans.

_____

_____

_____

13. What is a secured loan?

_____

_____

_____

14. What is a lien?

_____

_____

_____

_____

15. What is the difference between the interest rate and the finance charge?

_____

_____

_____

_____

16. Why are credit cards a form of consumer lending?

_____

_____

_____

_____

17. What is a line of credit?

_____

_____

_____

18. List six steps in the credit-granting process.

_____

_____

_____

_____

_____

_____

19. What are the three c's?

_____

_____

_____

20. What is a credit-scoring system?

_____

_____

_____

_____

_____

_____

_____

21. Why are credit investigations sometimes criticized?

_____

_____

_____

22. What five items appear in most credit reports?

_____

_____

_____

_____

_____

_____

APPLY WHAT YOU LEARNED

23. Should FICO scores be released to consumers? Why or why not?

_____

_____

_____

24. Name four consumer protection laws related to lending.

_____

_____

_____

25. What factors should a person consider before obtaining a loan?

_____

_____

_____

26. Why is it important to pay every bill on time?

_____

_____

_____

_____

27. Why is having many credit card accounts a risky practice?

_____

_____

_____

_____

28. What kinds of abuses are consumer protection laws intended to eliminate?

_____

_____

_____

_____

29. Why do responsible and ethical bankers sometimes oppose further consumer protection legislation?

_____

_____

_____

_____

MAKE CONNECTIONS •

30. SOCIAL STUDIES Using the Internet, research one of the laws discussed in Lesson 6.4. Prepare a detailed report on its history, its provisions, and its effect on the lending industry. Write a three-page report on what you learn.

31. ECONOMICS Analyze the impact of credit on the banking system as a whole.

_____

_____

_____

_____

_____

32. ART/DESIGN Prepare a brochure for consumer education that highlights effective and safe ways to choose and use credit. Outline the costs of credit to make others aware of its potential dangers. Include information on government agencies that consumers can contact for more information.

33. COMMUNICATION Interview an executive or loan officer of a local bank on the subject of consumer lending. Gain insight into the officer's daily life, changes in the business in the last few years, and the effects of regulation. Present your findings to the class in an oral report.

CHAPTER
7

MORTGAGES

7.1 MORTGAGE LENDING
7.2 MORTGAGE LOAN PROCESSING
7.3 MORTGAGES AND THE LAW
7.4 GOVERNMENT-BACKED LOANS

Careers in Banking

BANK ONE

Bank One is a large multi-state bank that characterizes big banking in the United States. With its 86,000 employees in the United States and 10 other countries and 1,800 banking outlets in 14 states serving 8 million households, Bank One is by no means a small operation. However, the corporation takes pride in its local impact, highlighting its state-by-state impact on its web site. Bank One also notes its overall contributions to the economy and the community, citing the $57 billion in Community Reinvestment Act, small business, home, consumer, and community development loans it has made, as well as the $130 million it pays in sales taxes and $36 million in personal property taxes. It maintains a Community Development Corporation to invest in developments that fulfill a public purpose and promote community welfare.

Bank One's benefit package is competitive and comparable with other organizations. The Corporation points with pride to numerous programs it supports in local communities, such as the Paint Your Heart Out program, the Building Up Conscientious Students program, and the Women's Business Center.

THINK CRITICALLY

1. What factors most determine an employee's choice of employers?
2. How can large multi-state corporations develop strong ties to local communities?

PROJECT

MORTGAGES and YOU

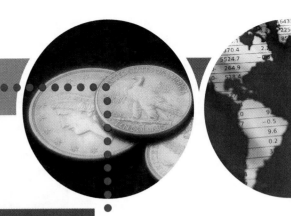

PROJECT OBJECTIVES
- Become aware of the many ways that mortgage lending intersects your life
- Recognize mortgage lending and other services when you encounter them
- Note bank offerings of mortgage lending and financial services in your community
- Identify various government-backed loan programs

VIDEO The Chapter 7 video introduces the concepts in this chapter.

GETTING STARTED
Read through the Project Process below. Make a list of any materials you will need. Decide how you will get the needed materials or information.
- Keep an ongoing list of things you encounter in your daily life that relate to mortgage lending and banking functions that you study in this chapter.
- As you make your list, and as you go through the chapter, jot down questions that occur to you about concepts that confuse you.
- Identify outside resources such as magazine articles and web sites that provide more information on topics in the chapter.

PROJECT PROCESS
Part 1 LESSON 7.1 Before studying the chapter, share what your experiences are in the four areas of study for this chapter. Make a list of what you know as a group.

Part 2 LESSON 7.2 Look for examples in your community of mortgage lending and services at work. Bring in a variety of articles and advertisements that relate to mortgage lending. Relate them to concepts in the lesson.

Part 3 LESSON 7.3 Learn more about legislation that affects mortgage lending. Identify a bank's responsibilities to the consumer when issuing mortgage loans.

Part 4 LESSON 7.4 Gather more information about various types of government-backed loan programs that interest you. Compile a list of useful web sites.

CHAPTER REVIEW
Project Wrap-up As a group, assess what you now know about mortgage lending and services. Use the list you made for Part 1 as a starting point, and expand and refine those understandings. Create a summary, outline, or chart of the knowledge you have gained about these four areas of the banking industry.

MORTGAGE LENDING ●●●●●●●●●●●●●●●●●●●●●●

GOALS

DEFINE the term *mortgage*

IDENTIFY several types of mortgages

WHAT IS A MORTGAGE?

Private banks have grown in the nineteenth and twentieth centuries from banks that did business only with other businesses to banks that sought to serve the needs of individuals. Nowhere in the twentieth century has this growth been more evident than in the growth of mortgage lending. Tax breaks, growing equity, rising value, and a sense of security provide incentive to undertake long-term debt. The idea of getting a mortgage to buy one's own home is the essence of the American dream, and in good times or bad, owning real estate is one goal that remains constant.

Mortgage lending is a good business for banks, too, although by percentage, it's not as great as it once was. The crush of competition, not only between banks but also from companies that specialize in mortgage lending, has reduced the banks' dominance in this field. Mortgage lending is now the third source of revenue in banking, behind wholesale banking and services.

When Laquinta Harris finished college, she found a good job in her career field of web design. After a few years, she paid off her student loans and began to feel more financially secure. She tired of living in an apartment and began to consider buying her own home. She didn't know anything about mortgages. What kinds of information might she want to research?

Total mortgage lending continues to rise. In 2000, new mortgages, called *mortgage origination*, exceeded $1 trillion. Of that $1 trillion, more than half consisted of refinancing existing debt, while the rest was entirely comprised of new business. As interest rates dropped in 2001, only a slowing economy kept the business from expanding even further. The mortgage business is linked to numerous other segments of the economy, such as construction and durable goods, and often provides a good idea of how the economy as a whole is doing.

The term *mortgage* comes from Old French language and Anglo-Saxon law. It literally means "dead pledge," and it was the most serious obligation one could undertake. At that time, property was conveyed to the creditor, who held it until a debt was repaid and then conveyed it back. If the debt wasn't paid on time, the creditor kept the property. Over time, the idea of the property as security remained, but restrictions eased, and now in almost all cases the borrower has full use and title to the property. Today, a **mortgage** is a note, usually long-term, secured by real property. Essentially, the mortgage places a lien on the property that is not released until the debt is paid. If the mortgage is not paid, the creditor seeks a court-ordered sale of the property called a **foreclosure**, and the debt is paid from those funds.

The obligation of a mortgage today is no less serious than it was hundreds of years ago, though. For most people, the largest and longest debt they will ever incur is a mortgage. It's a serious investment, usually five or more times the cost of a new car. Because it usually involves land, a mortgage is tied to government by deeds and title records in ways that are unique. It's also a serious obligation for the lender, and nowhere will a borrower's capability and record be more carefully examined than in an application for a mortgage.

Home ownership is often referred to as the American dream. Take an informal poll of as many homeowners as you can to learn about their experiences with home ownership and mortgages.

CHECK**POINT**

What is a mortgage?

_____

_____

TYPES OF MORTGAGES

There are many names and variations in loan products, and such is the case in the mortgage business as well. Whatever a mortgage is called, though, it essentially falls into one of three general categories: fixed rate mortgages, adjustable rate mortgages, and other forms of financing.

Fixed Rate Mortgages

Fixed rate mortgages, also called *conventional mortgages*, are loans with a fixed interest rate for the life of the loan. Payments on the loan itself (not including insurance and taxes, which may be included in payments) are set for the life of the loan. Terms are set, too. The most common terms are 30- and 15-year terms, but other terms are available.

Consumers are comfortable with fixed rate mortgages because there are few surprises. Once the interest rate is set, it remains the same, and the consumer has a pretty good idea of what housing costs are going to be. If interest rates rise, the consumer is still paying that original rate, which will look better and better as years pass. If interest rates fall, the consumer might lose money, but he or she has the option to refinance, that is, get a new mortgage, at a lower rate. Interest rates are usually somewhat higher for fixed rate mortgages than for other types.

For banks, a fixed rate mortgage offers a reliable source of income, or more often, a negotiable instrument to resell. There is some risk for the bank, however. If interest rates do rise, the holder of the note is making money on less than a market rate. This risk is the reason why interest rates are usually higher for fixed rate mortgages and why those mortgages are sold and resold, as holders try to maximize revenue.

One type of fixed rate mortgage that is sometimes confusing is called a **balloon mortgage**. In a balloon mortgage, the interest rate and payment stay fixed, but at some specified point, perhaps five years, the entire remaining balance of the loan is due in one single "balloon" payment. Although balloon mortgages allow some people to get mortgages who would not otherwise qualify, they are risky. Few people can pay off a house in five years, so as that balloon payment approaches, they must refinance. If they can't, they are likely to lose their houses and ruin their credit ratings.

Adjustable Rate Mortgages

Adjustable rate mortgages (ARMS), as the name implies, are those with rates that change over the course of the loan. Usually the interest rate and payments are fixed for some period of time at the outset but then change according to some index value. Initial rates and payments may be extremely low but are adjusted later to a rate closer to the normal rate, including some addition to make up for an artificially low start. Such *teaser rates* bring in business, but the borrower must make up for it and takes a risk that rates won't rise beyond what is affordable. There are lots of variables with ARMs, so it's extremely important for borrowers to understand their loans thoroughly. The chart on the following page summarizes some of the things that vary.

The many possibilities of ARMs offer both opportunity and potential confusion for borrowers. When overall interest rates are low, ARM rates usually don't vary much from conventional rates. In times of rising interest, ARMs may offer a good starting point for those hoping rates will later fall. If a homeowner plans to be in a house only a few years, an ARM might be an excellent way to get the most house for the least money. Still, most consumers are more comfortable with conventional mortgages, making them a large majority of the lending business.

Other Forms of Financing

Other forms of financing involve various ways that lenders calculate or adjust interest or other values. Most often these vary to suit particular circumstances not well adaptable to conventional financing.

Buy-Down In a **buy-down mortgage**, the borrower buys down, or prepays, part of the interest in order to get a lower rate. The borrower pays *points* to the lender at the outset, and the lender agrees to lower the rate so much per point. How much the interest drops is agreed to by lender and borrower as part of the deal. It's important to understand that a point is *not* an APR percentage point. A **point** is a value equal to 1 percent of the loan.

In groups, list other costs associated with owning a home. Discuss whether these costs are offset by the advantages of home ownership.

For example, 2 points on a $200,000 home would be 2 percent of $200,000, or $4,000. The principal on the loan remains $200,000, but the interest for the life of the loan would be lowered by some rate agreed to by lender and borrower. For its part, the lender usually forgoes some long-term income for the sake of more cash up front. If the lender is planning to sell the note, this may earn the lender more money. The borrower, by paying more up front, may save far more in the long run.

ARM Variables		
Variable	**Definition**	**Explanation**
Interest Rate	The rate the lender charges for the loan, expressed as an annual percentage rate.	Initial rates for ARMs may be close to other rates, or they may be much lower, depending on the lender's product. Eventually, after adjustments over time, they are usually slightly lower than conventional mortgages, dependent on the index. Some ARMs offer a fixed rate for several years at the outset of the loan.
Payment	The amount, usually per month, that a borrower repays the lender. Mortgage payments often include principal, interest, taxes, and insurance.	Payment calculation typically varies with the interest rate, although some lenders may also use a formula that begins with a low payment not related directly to the interest rate. Taxes and insurance, if included, may vary over time in any mortgage.
Index	The measure to which the lender's interest rate is tied. Usually this is a U.S. Treasury security rate plus some figure or percentage.	Each lender may choose any index it wants, and some are better than others for the buyer. Fully understanding the index and its past performance and comparison shopping for ARMs are keys to consumer success.
Formula	The means by which the payment's relationship to index and to principal is calculated.	Each lender may use its own formula, so long as it is clearly specified in documentation. Comparing products side by side and seeing actual payment numbers helps the evaluation process.
Adjustment Interval	The length of time that a given rate and payment are in effect.	Adjustment intervals also vary with each lender's loan product. Some may be as short as three to six months. One year is typical. Whether a long adjustment interval is advantageous to lender or borrower depends upon the formula used and how stable the index has been over time.
Periodic Cap	The maximum amount, usually a percentage, by which an ARM can increase or decrease on an adjustment date.	This feature can protect both lender and borrower from rapid changes in interest rates. For example, a flex limit of one-half percent on any adjustment date keeps change from being too dramatic.
Lifetime Cap	The specified overall maximum or minimum rate of an ARM, regardless of index.	The cap sets a top and bottom interest rate, also called a floor, between which the rate and payment vary. If the floor is 5 percent, and the cap is 12 percent, for example, the rate may not vary outside that range regardless of index.

Shared Appreciation Mortgage (SAM) Although this form of mortgage is not new, it is having something of a comeback in the competitive lending business. A **shared appreciation mortgage** can lower interest rates for borrowers who agree to share later with the lender some part of the amount the house appreciates. Appreciation is the amount that a house increases in value. With a SAM, the lender receives a part of that increase, often 50 percent. Say a borrower buys a house worth $150,000, and when the borrower sells it five years later, it's worth $200,000. The lender would receive a lump sum payment of $25,000 at payoff in addition to the remaining principal. In housing markets with little appreciation, a SAM can let a borrower get a low-rate loan without costing a lot at payoff. But SAMs also limit profit on the house for the borrower, who must share the appreciation and, thus, may lack a new down payment on another house after paying the lender. In markets that appreciate rapidly, SAMs can be very profitable for banks and allow borrowers to have a house they might not otherwise be able to afford, as long as they are less concerned with future value.

Refinancing Refinancing is one of the hottest segments of the lending industry. Essentially, refinancing is starting over with an entirely new loan, using part or all of the loan funds to pay off the old mortgage. If interest rates are low, consumers save money by getting new mortgages at lower rates. Banks and other lenders earn money on fees, points, and closing costs of the new loan and add business (usually at the expense of other lenders) at the new rates. Prepayment penalties for the old mortgage may also raise the cost of refinancing, although some states do not allow prepayment penalties on mortgages. Generally, the lower the refinancing rates, the higher the fees and points. Borrowers need to understand and consider all costs carefully.

The process for refinancing is the same as obtaining the original mortgage in most cases, and all steps and underwriting conditions apply. It used to be said that the new interest rate had to be at least two percentage points lower than the old one to make the cost of refinancing pay off, but competition in the business has led to low-cost, zero-point, low-fee offerings from some lenders. Refinancing is also a good time for consumers to consider another type of mortgage if they are unsatisfied or struggling with the ones they have.

Home Equity Loans Home equity loans are another active area in the lending industry. **Equity** is the difference between what an item is worth and what is owed on it. Depending on the area and the economy, homes may appreciate in value 3 to 6 percent or more per year. A home worth $160,000 at purchase might easily be worth $185,000 in five years' time.

Homeowners can use the difference between what they owe and what their homes are worth to secure a loan. Let's say a borrower purchases a $160,000 house with $20,000 down and after five years has a remaining principal of $135,000. The house appreciates during that time and is now worth $185,000. The homeowner has equity of $50,000. That home equity may be used to secure a loan up to or even beyond the value of the equity.

Home equity loans take one of two forms. One type is a simple loan, a single disbursement of money for the borrowed amount. Another type is a line of credit, sometimes with paper checks or accompanying credit cards. Borrowers have a credit line up to the equity limit. As they pay down the balance, they can add new expenses to the line if they choose.

In many respects, a home equity loan is just another consumer loan, but there is a big exception. It's a second mortgage. It is secured by the home. If borrowers are unable to repay the loan, they may lose their homes. In recent years, the easy availability of home equity loans has led some borrowers into trouble. Some irresponsible lenders have also extended credit to people who are not really in a position to repay, a predatory lending practice that can lead to disaster. Responsible lenders underwrite home equity loans carefully, but consumers should be very cautious about borrowing against their largest and most important asset.

Reverse Mortgages A **reverse mortgage** is not a mortgage used to purchase a home. It is really another form of consumer loan tied to the appreciated value of a property. In most cases, reverse mortgages are limited to homeowners 62 years or older. With a reverse mortgage, a homeowner receives a sum from the lender secured by the value of a home and does not pay the loan back as long as he or she lives there. Typically, a senior homeowner owes less on a mortgage because he or she has been paying on it for many years. Also, the house may well have appreciated considerably since purchase. The lender is repaid, including fees and interest, when the borrower sells or dies. Borrowers may receive their funds in lump sums, a credit line, or a monthly payment direct from the lender, or some combination of the three.

The advantage of a reverse mortgage is that it allows homeowners the opportunity to get cash from the value of their homes without selling and moving. Although loan advances are not typically considered income by the Internal Revenue Service, obtaining a reverse mortgage may affect eligibility in some other government benefit programs and can affect taxes and estate planning considerably. Equity in the home declines throughout the life of a reverse mortgage, and the homeowner is still responsible for taxes, insurance, and maintenance. As with any loan, there are many variations in features, terms, and lenders, and it's wise to shop for the best terms. Those considering a reverse mortgage should thoroughly understand all terms of the mortgage, as well as all other aspects of their retirement, financial, and estate planning.

That advice holds true for any type of mortgage from any type of lender. For most people, mortgages represent the largest debt for the largest financial transaction they will ever undertake.

CHECKPOINT

What is the basic difference between conventional and adjustable rate mortgages?

_____

_____

_____

1. What incentives make home ownership and the undertaking of long-term debt attractive to consumers?

_____

_____

_____

_____

2. Explain the advantages and disadvantages to the consumer of balloon mortgages.

_____

_____

_____

_____

3. Why might a consumer choose an adjustable rate mortgage over a fixed rate mortgage?

_____

_____

_____

_____

_____

4. What is a _point_ and why do some consumers choose to pay points on their mortgages?

_____

_____

_____

_____

_____

MAKE CONNECTIONS ●●●●●●●●●●●●●●●●●●●

5. HISTORY Though it changes, land lasts forever. Pick an area, a neighborhood, a small town, a subdivision, or even an individual property and trace the history of its owners. You may need to do some initial research to learn how to conduct a search of county records.

_____

_____

_____

_____

_____

6. RESEARCH Refinancing is a big portion of the lending business. Learn more about refinancing using resources such as the Internet, newspapers, and magazines. Write a brief report on your findings.

MORTGAGE LOAN PROCESSING •••••••••••••

GOALS

DESCRIBE the components involved in obtaining a mortgage

EXPLAIN the mortgage approval process

OBTAINING A MORTGAGE

Because of the typical size of the loan, lenders scrutinize mortgage applications closely. The potential risk involved is greater for the bank both in terms of the amount of the loan and the liquidity of the collateral. Banks don't want to own houses.

Lenders typically require a down payment of 5, 10, or 20 percent for a mortgage. (FHA and other government-sponsored loans, which you'll learn about in a later section, may require less, as do some other programs.) A larger down payment not only lowers the cost of the monthly payment, but also affects how the lender views the borrower. Lenders may make the loan if a down payment is high, even if the borrower's credit rating is not ideal.

In addition, a higher down payment allows a borrower to have more house for the same monthly payment. Most lenders don't want a person's housing costs to exceed 25 to 28 percent of gross monthly income. Total

Laquinta Harris has done some research on mortgages and now has a better understanding of the loan process. She has been looking at some real estate properties and is now ready to obtain a loan. Where should she start?

debt should not exceed 36 percent, including housing costs. For the same monthly payment, a borrower could get a house worth about $170,000 with a 20 percent down payment, as opposed to one worth $135,000 with 5 percent down. A higher down payment may also avoid a requirement of private mortgage insurance.

PITI

Monthly payments to the lender usually consist of **PITI** or Principal, Interest, Taxes, and Insurance. These are the housing costs that the lender considers in the loan analysis and are itemized on the monthly mortgage statement.

Principal is the remaining unpaid balance of the mortgage. The figure shown on the statement may not be the payoff amount but merely the remaining principal calculated currently. The payoff figure may differ based on the type and terms of the loan.

Interest is the amount of the monthly payment that goes toward interest. In the early years of a mortgage, this is by far the largest figure. Because interest is usually deductible, the tax advantages of a mortgage make home ownership doubly attractive.

Taxes include local real estate taxes. Most lenders require an amount to be paid to them in advance, called **escrow**, from which they pay the real estate taxes. Many loans also allow for an additional amount for an escrow buffer so that the escrow fund never falls below a set level.

Insurance refers to property insurance and sometimes private mortgage insurance. To protect the lender against potential loss, almost all mortgages require the homeowner to maintain adequate property insurance against fire, storms, and other calamities. The lender collects the insurance premium as part of the payment to make sure its security is covered. *Private mortgage insurance* (PMI) protects the lender against loan default. PMI is not typically required for those whose down payment is 20 percent or greater, and it can be eliminated once the principal balance reaches 20 percent of the original loan value.

As with all types of loans, specific terms, methods of calculation, and costs may vary, and it is a good idea for borrowers to have legal counsel about the details of mortgages.

WORKSHOP

Working in groups, develop a list of potential losses that homeowners' insurance may cover. Consider losses that may occur inside and outside the home.

BANKING MATH CONNECTION

Private Mortgage Insurance (PMI) rates may vary, but a typical PMI rate is $\frac{1}{2}$ of 1 percent of the borrowed principal. The formula for calculating the monthly PMI cost is

Rate $\times$ Principal $\div$ 12 = PMI

Calculate the monthly cost of Private Mortgage Insurance (PMI) for a principal balance of $140,000.

SOLUTION

If PMI were required for a principal of $140,000, the calculation would be

Rate $\times$ Principal $\div$ 12 = PMI
0.005 $\times$ $140,000 $\div$ 12 = $58.33

What is Private Mortgage Insurance?

_____

_____

_____

THE APPROVAL PROCESS

Few things in financial life are as nerve-wracking for many consumers as the mortgage approval process. The many details, close examination of finances, and legal language intimidate many borrowers, producing considerable anxiety. Although the process is detailed, it is getting simpler and certainly faster.

Application, documentation, underwriting based on credit reputation and capacity, and closing are all part of the credit analysis and credit-granting process. The process is more detailed for mortgages, largely because the transfer of real property brings into play more legal issues than a simple contract. Here are the basic steps.

- *Application* for a mortgage may be more involved than for other forms of loans, and accuracy and completeness are essential. Unlike many small consumer loans for which a quick credit check is sufficient, every detail of a mortgage application will be evaluated carefully. Missing, incomplete, or wrong information will delay the process at the very least and may result in denial of the loan.

- *Documentation* for a mortgage loan must also be complete and accurate. Often, it takes some time to assemble full documentation, which usually includes a professional appraisal of the property. Lenders pay attention to the **loan-to-value** (LTV) relationship, which is the value of the loan compared to the value of the asset. Most lenders prefer to lend no more than 95 percent of the appraised value of a house so that their risk is supported. It's not merely a question of what you're willing to pay the seller, but also what the house is really worth that may determine whether you get a mortgage. Other documents include complete credit reports, employment and/or income verification, and verification of existence and source of the down payment. If you borrow the down payment, that debt must be considered as well. Most lenders like to see that the down payment has been deposited for some period of time before the application (60 days is best).

- *Underwriting* is the critical step, as documents arrive and are verified and reviewed. Some lenders have loan processors who verify completeness and accuracy separate from the underwriters, and some combine both functions. As with any loan, *collateral, capacity,* and *credit reputation* determine whether a mortgage is a good investment for the bank. Mortgage underwriters look hard at a borrower's ability to repay as measured by a debt-to-income ratio and the track record of a borrower over a long period of time. Often, underwriters may want more information or a letter of explanation about some circumstance or item in the credit record.

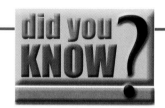

In 2000, online mortgage sales accounted for approximately 1.3 percent of total U.S. mortgage loans, or about $13 billion. That number is expected to rise as software gets better and consumers get more comfortable using the Internet.

Applicants can't hide much from a thorough underwriter, and completeness and fullness on applications is the best approach. Sometimes underwriters may modify the terms of a mortgage one way or another to fit the circumstances. Although mortgage underwriting is becoming automated by software, the underwriting process for mortgages is still the most careful and painstaking part of obtaining a mortgage.

- **Drawing Documents** is another carefully considered step in the process. The sale of a home involves many documents between lender and borrower. As you'll recall, many promissory notes are negotiable, and mortgages are often sold for servicing many times. It is essential that all

documents be accurate and all terms and requirements met so that the note remains negotiable no matter where it eventually goes. Once the note is signed, the bank prepares the funding.

- **Closing** requires the signing of all documents involving the transfer of the property from one party to another. These documents go beyond the scope of just the mortgage. Closing costs, including fees for application, origination, title search, surveys, appraisal costs, inspections, taxes, attorneys, escrow, and recording are paid, as well as any points and applicable realtor fees. Frequently, a title company, which specializes in researching and transferring property between owners, will handle the closing.

- **Recording** the mortgage/deed of trust at the county recorder's office makes the mortgage public record. Records may be available online, either from a recorder or from another company that compiles such records.

Although the process of obtaining a mortgage is often longer and more involved than obtaining other types of loans, the lending business, like other aspects of the financial industry, is changing. Lenders need to lend money, and competition among lenders makes it easier than ever before for borrowers to apply and be approved. Still, the risk to both lender and borrower is greater for a mortgage if things go bad, so it's best for consumers to understand as much as they can about the process and their own capabilities before undertaking a transaction that will have lifelong implications.

What are the basic steps of the mortgage approval process?

_____

_____

THINK CRITICALLY ●●●●●●●●●●●●●●●●●●●●●●

1. Why is the mortgage loan application process longer and more involved than that for other consumer loans?

_____

_____

_____

2. Why do you think a lender might overlook less than perfect credit for a borrower with a large down payment?

_____

_____

_____

_____

_____

_____

3. Why do lenders (or the holders of a mortgage) usually want taxes and insurance included as part of the payment?

_____

_____

_____

4. What types of information do you think are requested on a mortgage loan application?

_____

_____

_____

MAKE CONNECTIONS ●●●●●●●●●●●●●●●●●●●●

5. RESEARCH Online mortgage sales are now a big business. Find a mortgage financing web site and write a short description of the mortgage loan process used by the financier.

_____

_____

_____

_____

_____

_____

6. BANKING MATH Most lenders prefer that a mortgage payment not exceed 28 percent of your gross monthly income. Assuming that you make $40,000 per year, what is the maximum PITI that the bank would deem acceptable?

_____

_____

_____

MORTGAGES AND THE LAW ••••••••••••

GOALS

DESCRIBE consumer protection laws that apply to mortgage lending

DESCRIBE laws directly related to mortgage lending

CONSUMER PROTECTION LEGISLATION

Because of the importance of home ownership and the relative monetary value of mortgage notes compared to other loans, numerous laws affect mortgage lending. Parts of consumer protection legislation apply to mortgage lending as well. Most of these laws are designed to protect consumers from unfair practices relating to lending, collecting, or maintaining privacy as described below.

- The Truth in Lending Act (TILA) promotes informed use of consumer credit by requiring disclosures about its terms and costs.
- The Equal Credit Opportunity Act (ECOA) prohibits creditors from discriminating against applicants on the basis of race, color, religion, national origin, sex, marital status, and age.

When Laquinta Harris conducted her research on mortgages, she learned about many laws related to mortgage lending. Laquinta wondered how any of these laws really applied to her. In what ways do these laws affect Laquinta?

- The Fair Credit Reporting Act (FCRA) is designed to promote accuracy, fairness, and privacy of information in the files of consumer reporting agencies (credit bureaus).
- The Fair Debt Collection Practices Act (FDCPA) prohibits abusive practices by debt collectors.
- The Gramm-Leach-Bliley Act requires that financial institutions protect the privacy of consumers.

Many of the provisions of these laws apply specifically to the mortgage lending industry with targeted sections and enforcement specifications for various agencies such as the Federal Trade Commission (FTC), the Federal Deposit Insurance Corporation (FDIC), and the Federal Reserve.

How do consumer protection laws apply to mortgage lending?

_____

_____

MORTGAGE LEGISLATION

Other laws exist that relate directly to mortgage lending. Complying with this legislation and documenting compliance requires considerable effort and expense on the part of financial institutions. A few of these laws are described below. Most of these laws have been amended numerous times since their passage, and amendments on many of them are pending. Most states also have similar measures, although they may not always be consistent with federal legislation.

Community Reinvestment Act (CRA)

Congress passed the Community Reinvestment Act (CRA) of 1977 in response to widespread complaints that some banks refused to lend to residents of certain neighborhoods, a practice called **redlining**. The law requires that banks document their lending decisions and demonstrate an effort to serve their local communities. CRA investments increase home ownership and help stabilize neighborhoods, which is good for the local economy. Periodic government examinations monitor compliance with the law.

Some critics of the law note that the statute is enforced only when banks merge or expand. They point out that the Gramm-Leach-Bliley Act, though imposing new requirements on privacy, weakened the CRA by slowing the cycle of examination for many banks.

Many lenders, however, struggle with the CRA, both in terms of the burden of compliance and their

need to follow sound banking practices. It's not always easy to balance the desire to lend liberally in local communities with the need to meet strict (and increasingly inflexible) conditions for making good loans, which are subject to government examination.

Home Mortgage Disclosure Act (HMDA)

The Home Mortgage Disclosure Act (HMDA) of 1974 was a forerunner of the CRA. It requires banks and other financial institutions to record and report data on home lending in order to identify possible discriminatory patterns. As a practical matter, it set into motion the huge record keeping responsibilities of compliance regarding home mortgages. In 2000, for example, there were about 19 million loan records reported by 7,713 financial institutions. These data become the basis for statistical analysis and compliance monitoring by various agencies.

Home Ownership and Equity Protection Act (HOEPA)

Congress passed the Home Ownership and Equity Protection Act (HOEPA) in 1994 to protect consumers against predatory lending. Provisions of this act also apply to second mortgages and refinancing. If a loan's annual percentage rate (APR) is 10 points higher than a rate on a Treasury Bill for the same length of time (for example, fifteen years on a fifteen-year note), the loan is a high interest rate loan, also called a HOEPA loan. Loans with noninterest fees of more than $465 or 8 percent of the loan value are also HOEPA loans. For HOEPA loans, lenders must make disclosures three days before closing, may not pay a contractor directly, may not require balloon payments due in less than five years on most loans, and are limited in the type of prepayment penalties allowed. Lenders also may not make loans that do not adequately consider the borrower's ability to repay. The fierce competition in the hot subprime lending business has sometimes led lenders into extending credit to people who do not fully understand that they are securing the money with their homes, who do not have the ability to repay, and who do not fully understand the high cost of subprime loans. In some cases, a few lenders deliberately engage in such practices to obtain properties they then resell. HOEPA is intended to discourage such equity stripping and educate those consumers who may not be fully informed.

WORKSHOP

Working in groups, list discriminatory mortgage lending practices that may have occurred in the past or present.

ETHICS IN ACTION

Former Senator Phil Gramm of Texas commented on the difficulty of writing banking legislation that protects consumers without harming banks by saying that it is impossible to regulate something that cannot be defined. He was referring to predatory lending practices, which numerous acts and amendments have attempted to prohibit.

THINK CRITICALLY

Where is the line between strict business practices and taking advantage of someone? What, in your opinion, is predatory lending? How would you recognize it in contract terms, in advertising, and in discussions with a customer?

Some consumer groups regard HOEPA's triggers as still too high and would like the law tightened. Some lenders believe that existing consumer protection and disclosure laws are sufficient. In an effort to discourage unscrupulous lenders, they believe such regulations burden honest ones, hurt competition and, thus, hinder access to credit by people who may need it most.

Real Estate Settlement Procedures Act (RESPA)

Congress enacted the Real Estate Settlement Procedures Act (RESPA) of 1974 to protect consumers from hidden costs or expensive surprises at closing time. The law requires disclosures to be provided to the borrower at various times during the transaction. At the time of application, the borrower must receive a booklet explaining various real estate settlement services, a good faith estimate of what closing costs are likely to be, and a Mortgaging Service Disclosure Statement, which indicates whether the lender will service the loan or sell it to another lender. Before closing, the lender must also disclose any business relationships with other service providers in the transaction. The lender may not require the borrower to use such parties, such as titling companies or attorneys, affiliated with the lender. At the time of closing, the borrower is entitled to an itemized list of actual closing costs and an Initial Escrow Statement showing anticipated principal, interest, taxes, and insurance (PITI), including the amount collected beforehand (escrow) for taxes and insurance. An escrow analysis must be done once a year, and any surplus more than $50 must be returned to the borrower.

RESPA also prohibits giving or accepting fees in exchange for referrals of settlement service business. The law bans kickbacks and fee splitting for settlement businesses and outlaws fees for services not actually performed.

The Homeowners' Protection Act of 1998 requires that lenders drop private mortgage insurance (PMI) when equity reaches 22 percent in loans closed after July 29, 1999.

HOUSING IN JAPAN

The cost of a home in Japan is one of the highest in the world. The average Japanese homebuyer may pay over 6 times his or her annual salary for a new home and land. Even so, Japan is the number two housing market, after the United States. There are a number of factors contributing to Japan's high housing costs. One of the biggest factors has been a lack of foreign competition in the building materials market. In the past, there have been very few building materials manufacturers in Japan. This led to decreased competition and little price differentiation among products. In 1995, Japan's Ministry of Construction set out to reduce the purchase price of a house. A campaign was launched to introduce imported packaged housing into Japan. The Ministry of Construction is also revising Japan's Building Standards Law for construction to allow the introduction of new building methods and techniques (such as those used in housing designs of U.S. homes). Due to new policies of the Japanese government that allow increased imports of foreign building materials, housing costs in Japan are falling.

THINK CRITICALLY

Why is the Japanese housing market so attractive to foreign building suppliers? Why do you think there's an increasing demand from Japanese homebuyers for foreign designs?

CHECK**POINT**

What is redlining and what legislation was enacted to address it?

_____

_____

THINK CRITICALLY ●●●●●●●●●●●●●●●●●●●●●

1. Why is there a need for consumer protection legislation related specifically to mortgages?

_____

_____

_____

_____

2. What is the purpose of escrow in a mortgage?

_____

_____

_____

_____

3. Why might financial institutions look at mortgage legislation as being burdensome?

_____

_____

_____

_____

4. Which of the laws related to mortgage lending discussed in this section do you believe is most important? What are your reasons?

_____

_____

_____

_____

MAKE CONNECTIONS ●●●●●●●●●●●●●●●●●●●●●

5. HISTORY Select one of the laws that apply to mortgages and use the Internet to research the history of the law. Present your report to the class.

6. COMMUNICATE Talk with a loan officer at your local bank about how mortgage laws affect the officer's job responsibilities. Summarize your discussion below.

_____

_____

_____

_____

_____

7. RESEARCH Using the library or Internet, find out what path someone should take if he or she encounters discrimination while trying to obtain a home mortgage loan.

Lesson 7.4
GOVERNMENT-BACKED LOANS •••••••••••

EXPLAIN the concept of government-backed loans

IDENTIFY government-backed programs to encourage home lending

EQUAL·JUSTICE·UNDER·LAW·

WHAT IS A GOVERNMENT-BACKED LOAN?

The government sometimes acts as a partner to the banking industry, as well as to people and businesses. Numerous government programs help banks help people get loans they need.

With these programs, the Federal government offers a number of ways to help people obtain financing for worthwhile purposes. In most of these programs, the banks provide funding and the government absorbs some of the risk. The government backs the loans by promising to repay them should the borrower default. In order to minimize its own risk, the government also examines the borrower's finances and has eligibility requirements for participation. Some states even operate such programs, and consumers can get more information on these and federal programs from prospective lenders. Lenders want to make loans, and they are happy to work with the consumer and government agencies to find financing solutions.

Laquinta Harris learned quickly that she didn't have the resources or the track record to obtain conventional funding for a home loan. She turned to the government. She had gone to college on government-backed loans, and it occurred to her that there might be similar programs to help new homeowners. What might be a good way for Laquinta to start searching the vast amount of information available from the U.S. government?

How do banks and the government work together to provide loans?

_____

_____

FEDERAL MORTGAGE PROGRAMS

The Federal government has been interested in housing programs since the Great Depression of the 1930s. At that time, many new programs came into being to help people who had lost everything in the crisis. Probably the most familiar of the many programs that President Roosevelt and the Congress introduced is the social security program. Many other programs to help the unemployed, farmers, and others, including those who were struggling with housing, arose as well. The Federal Housing Administration, established in 1934, supported both homebuyers and banks by replenishing funds available for home lending. Today, there are many such programs with varying missions, services, and operations, but the twin benefits of both supporting homeowners and backing the banking industry continues.

Federal Housing Administration (FHA)

The Federal Housing Administration is the oldest of the many government agencies working to help homeowners. The banking industry was in trouble during the Great Depression, but it was not the only industry in trouble. Two million construction workers were out of work, as well as millions of others, and all the businesses they supported with their incomes were faltering. The FHA was an attempt to get the housing industry back on its feet. By guaranteeing loans and providing mortgage insurance, the FHA helped to reverse the tough climate for borrowers. Before the FHA was established, mortgages were typically limited to half of a property's value and had to be repaid in three to five years, typically with a balloon payment. Few people could afford such terms, even fewer in an economic disaster. The FHA made it possible for banks to offer better terms without shouldering all the risk. Helping to pioneer the long-term loans that make home ownership possible, the FHA changed the face of lending.

Today, what was once the FHA is now the Office of Housing, and it is part of the Department of Housing and Urban Development (HUD). It still performs the same services, guaranteeing loans with low down payments—often as little as 3 percent—to help people obtain housing who perhaps could not otherwise afford it. These loans, still called FHA loans, are not direct loans from the program, but they guarantee the lender that the mortgage will be paid. If it isn't, the agency repays the lender. The loans are arranged through lenders and may be fixed or adjustable rate mortgages. The FHA 203(b) loan program for conventional loans is most common, but there are many variations and even resources for getting help with the down payment. The mortgage insurance premium is charged up front (usually 2 to 2.25 percent of the loan, with another 0.5 percent per year) and goes to defray the costs of administering the program. Almost anyone can qualify for an FHA loan, subject to some credit and residency restrictions, and there

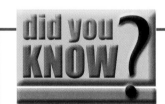

Today, the home ownership rate is about 68 percent, compared to about 40 percent before the FHA revolutionized the lending industry by insuring long-term loans.

are limits to the size of the loan. The FHA program pioneered the government's entry into the mortgage business and has backed over 30 million mortgages.

Fannie Mae

The Federal National Mortgage Association (FNMA) was so often referred to by its acronym that the corporation came to be referred to as Fannie Mae, which is now its registered trademark. Fannie Mae was also born of the Depression. It was created in 1938 to help lenders find funds to make available for mortgages. If the FHA was a source of help for consumers, Fannie Mae was a source of help for lenders. Fannie Mae is a government-chartered corporation that buys mortgages from the originating institutions and either keeps them or exchanges them for securities which it guarantees. The effect is that there is a pool of money available to lenders for mortgage loans. In the Depression, this made money available quickly to lenders to expand the available funds, as it still works today.

To participate, lenders must be licensed to originate mortgages, have a net worth of at least $250,000, be bonded and insured, and have written policies for underwriting and loan servicing, among other requirements. Although once a part of the FHA, Fannie Mae is now an independent corporation. Today, Fannie Mae is the largest source of home mortgage funds. More than 2,600 lenders are approved by Fannie Mae.

Freddie Mac

The Federal Home Loan Mortgage Corporation, nicknamed Freddie Mac, operates a similar program. Freddie Mac also buys home mortgages from banks and other lending institutions and combines them into large groups, selling interest in the groups to investors. Expanding the market for mortgages as negotiable instruments in this way expands the amount of funds invested in the lending and housing businesses. Created in 1970 as a fully independent corporation, Freddie Mac has financed about 15 percent of all mortgages in the United States since its beginning. Like Fannie Mae, Freddie Mac also lends for multi-family dwellings and rehabilitation projects. Freddie Mac also invites lenders to participate, with eligibility requirements similar to those of Fannie Mae.

FANNIE MAE DU AND FREDDIE MAC LP

As underwriting of mortgage loans becomes increasingly automated, government-chartered agencies that work with private lenders have developed tools for their lending clients. Fannie Mae's Desktop Underwriter (DU) and Freddie Mac's Loan Prospector (LP) are two automated systems that are helping streamline the underwriting communications between agencies and the client lenders.

The desktop programs are based on statistical models of FHA underwriting data to create an automated scoring system specifically designed with FHA criteria in mind. As a result, these customized automated underwriting systems streamline the often cumbersome process of working through the agencies and the FHA. The systems are FHA approved and can return a routine underwriting decision and conditions within an hour. Lenders enter data from their own sites, using a standard Residential Loan Application. Although they are not the only ways to get FHA approval for Fannie Mae and Freddie Mac funds, these two software programs are the wave of an interconnected future in underwriting.

THINK CRITICALLY

What type of information had to be factored into the DU and LP programs in order for them to be reliable? What are some elements of the underwriting process that make it difficult to automate?

Ginnie Mae

A third government initiative, unlike the other two, remains part of the Federal government. The Government National Mortgage Association, called Ginnie Mae, is part of the Department of Housing and Urban Development (HUD). Originally an arm of the FHA, it split. It neither buys nor sells mortgages, but it backs securities issued by holders of pools of mortgages. By guaranteeing the worth of the securities, Ginnie Mae attracts investors, and the pool of funds for mortgages remains high. Ginnie Mae encourages funding for FHA, VA, and other low-income housing, assuring that there will be funds available for these programs.

Veterans Administration (VA)

Loans from the Department of Veterans Affairs (DVA) have helped millions of service men and women get government-backed loans with low down payments. Veterans may get loans with no down payment, no prepayment penalties, and negotiable interest rates. Similar to the FHA loan program, VA loans allow qualified veterans to buy, build, remodel, or refinance a home. In general, to qualify for a VA loan, a person must meet one of the following criteria.

- Have served 181 days of active duty between 1940 and 1981 or 24 months for those who served after 1981, or discharged with a service-related disability in less time (certain exceptions apply for Gulf War veterans)

- Have served six years in the National Guard or Selected Reserves, completing all weekend and active duty time

Work as a class to compile a list of government programs that have an impact on the economic life in your local community. Be as specific about the program and its benefits as you can.

- Be an unremarried spouse of a service person killed in action or who died of a service-connected disability
- Be a spouse of a prisoner of war or a service person missing in action

In some cases, the VA may declare other persons eligible, such as Public Health Service officers, merchant seamen with WWII service, members of service academies, and others.

NCHSA

At the state level, many programs also exist that help families buy homes. The National Council of State Housing Agencies (NCHSA) is a national organization of Housing Finance Agencies (HFAs) throughout the states that provide and administer programs for lower-income and other people who seek help at the state level to buy or renovate a home. There is an HFA in every state. There are also 350 affiliated profit and nonprofit agencies that work in this field. These agencies and firms have a variety of programs for affordable housing.

Other Government-Backed Loans

There are many other government-backed loan programs as well. For example, the U.S. Department of Agriculture's (USDA) Rural Housing Service offers both direct loans and grants from the government as well as guaranteed loans. Designed for low- and moderate-income rural residents, the program also offers opportunities for lenders and developers by making doing business in rural areas a safer investment. The Farm Service Agency, formerly the Farmers Home Administration (FmHA), is an agency of the U.S. Department of Agriculture

that provides credit assistance to farmers, both by guaranteeing and sometimes making loans. Borrowers are offered 30- to 40-year loans at fixed interest rates as low as 1 percent.

It's not easy to find every government loan program that's out there. *The Catalog of Federal Domestic Assistance* available in government depository libraries or online from the General Services Administration at www.cfda.gov is a good place to start looking. It provides information on agencies and programs with which individuals may be able to work.

CHECKPOINT

How do the FHA and VA make more loans available?

_____

_____

THINK CRITICALLY ●●●●●●●●●●●●●●●●●●●●●●●●

1. How do government-backed loan programs help the economy?

_____

_____

_____

2. What benefits do government-backed loans provide to lenders?

_____

_____

_____

_____

3. Why do you think there are limits to the size of FHA loans?

_____

_____

_____

_____

4. How do Fannie Mae, Freddie Mac, and Ginnie Mae make more mortgage funds available?

_____

_____

_____

_____

MAKE CONNECTIONS ●●●●●●●●●●●●●●●●●●●●●

5. COMMUNICATION Using the Internet or the library, gather information about FHA, Fannie Mae, and VA loans. List some of the requirements and restrictions that must be adhered to when applying for these loans.

_____

_____

_____

_____

_____

_____

_____

_____

6. HISTORY Visit the Fannie Mae Foundation web site at www.fanniemae foundation.org. List some of the information available.

_____

_____

_____

_____

CHAPTER 7 ••••••••••••••••••••••• REVIEW

CHAPTER SUMMARY

LESSON 7.1 Mortgage Lending
A. A mortgage is a note secured by real property. For most people, a mortgage is the largest and longest debt they will ever incur.
B. Mortgage lenders provide many types of loan products for buying a home, including fixed and adjustable rate mortgages, buy-downs, shared appreciation mortgages, refinancing, home equity loans, and reverse mortgages.

LESSON 7.2 Mortgage Loan Processing
A. Mortgages involve large amounts, so lenders scrutinize mortgage applications. Payments consist of principal, interest, taxes, and insurance (PITI).
B. There are six basic steps in the mortgage approval process: application, documentation, underwriting, drawing documents, closing, and recording.

LESSON 7.3 Mortgages and the Law
A. Consumer protection legislation applies to mortgage lending and other loans.
B. Lenders must comply with numerous housing-specific laws and document compliance.

LESSON 7.4 Government-Backed Loans
A. The government backs some loans by guaranteeing to repay the lender if the borrower defaults.
B. Mortgage programs like FHA loans, VA loans, and others make loans possible to people who might not otherwise qualify.

VOCABULARY BUILDER

Choose the term that best fits the definition. Write the letter of the answer in the space provided. Some terms may not be used.

a. adjustable rate mortgage
b. balloon mortgage
c. buy-down mortgage
d. escrow
e. equity
f. fixed rate mortgage
g. foreclosure
h. loan-to-value
i. mortgage
j. PITI
k. point
l. redlining
m. reverse mortgage
n. shared appreciation mortgage

_____ **1.** Value of loan compared to value of asset
_____ **2.** A mortgage in which the borrower prepays part of the interest to get a lower rate
_____ **3.** Discriminatory act whereby banks refuse to lend to residents in certain neighborhoods
_____ **4.** Mortgage with changing interest rate
_____ **5.** A note secured by real property
_____ **6.** A value equal to 1 percent of loan principal
_____ **7.** A mortgage in which the entire remaining balance of the loan is due in one single payment
_____ **8.** Principal, interest, taxes, and insurance
_____ **9.** Conventional mortgage
_____ **10.** When the mortgage is not paid, the creditor seeks a court-ordered sale of the property
_____ **11.** The difference between what an item is worth and what is owed on it

REVIEW CONCEPTS

12. What is a mortgage?

_____

_____

_____

13. What is a foreclosure?

_____

_____

_____

_____

14. List four types of mortgages.

_____

_____

_____

_____

15. How does a buy-down mortgage work?

_____

_____

_____

_____

16. What is equity?

_____

_____

_____

_____

17. What does the acronym PITI represent?

_____

_____

_____

_____

18. What is the LTV ratio and why is it important to lenders?

_____

_____

_____

_____

19. What is underwriting?

_____

_____

_____

20. List three consumer protection laws that apply to mortgage lending.

_____

_____

_____

21. What are the consumer and business implications of the Community Reinvestment Act (CRA)?

_____

_____

_____

_____

_____

22. To comply with RESPA, what must lenders disclose to borrowers?

_____

_____

_____

_____

_____

_____

23. How do government-backed loans differ from conventional loans?

_____

_____

_____

_____

24. Why was the FHA established?

_____

_____

25. Identify a government-backed mortgage program and explain what it does and the eligibility requirements.

_____

_____

_____

_____

26. Why does obtaining a mortgage initiate the most thorough credit review most consumers will ever undergo?

_____

_____

_____

27. What factors does a lender judge in order to assess consumer capability?

_____

_____

_____

28. How do disclosure laws protect consumers?

_____

_____

_____

_____

29. Why does the government have an interest in guaranteeing loans for private purposes?

_____

_____

_____

MAKE CONNECTIONS ●

30. BANKING MATH Calculate the monthly PMI (private mortgage insurance) for a principal balance of $125,500. Assume the PMI rate is $\frac{1}{2}$ of 1 percent of the borrowed principal.

_____

_____

31. TECHNOLOGY Use the Internet to learn more about the impact of technology on the real estate and mortgage industries. Prepare an oral report on what you learn.

32. HISTORY Learn more about past discriminatory practices, such as redlining, that led to various consumer protection laws in the mortgage lending industry. Write a one-page report on the topic. Contrast the business and consumer implications of the Community Reinvestment Act.

33. COMMUNICATION Interview a mortgage lender in your community. Find out what lenders like to see from an applicant, and make a top-ten list of things homebuyers can do to increase their chances of getting mortgages for their dream homes.

_____

_____

_____

CHAPTER 8

COMMERCIAL LENDING

8.1 COMMERCIAL LOANS
8.2 COMMERCIAL CREDIT ANALYSIS
8.3 SMALL BUSINESS LOAN PROGRAMS

Careers in Banking
UNITED BANK

United Bank, based in St. Petersburg, Florida, is a locally owned community bank with assets totaling $227 million. It offers both personal and business services. In particular, United Bank prides itself on its commitment to help small-to-medium size businesses manage their borrowing needs. It offers a complete range of loan services, including credit lines, real estate mortgages, term loans, and Small Business Administration (SBA) loans. United Bank was named the top SBA lender in the state of Florida for fiscal year 1999.

United Bank is dedicated to the communities in which it resides. A few of the organizations it supports include the American Red Cross, Cystic Fibrosis Foundation, Florida Gulf Coast Art Center, Police Athletic League, St. Petersburg Area Chamber of Commerce, and Tampa Bay Black Business Investment Corporation.

United Bank considers its employees its greatest asset. It expects employees to show commitment by delivering the best service possible to customers. United Bank offers some commission-based positions, such as the Mortgage Loan Originator, a 401(k) savings plan, and an Employee Stock Ownership Plan (ESOP).

THINK CRITICALLY

1. What makes some banks more successful than others in the commercial lending market?
2. Would you like to work in a position that compensates on a commission basis? Why or why not?

PROJECT

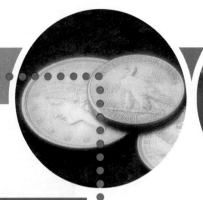

COMMERCIAL LENDING at WORK

VIDEO
The Chapter 8 video introduces the concepts in this chapter.

PROJECT OBJECTIVES

- Learn more about commercial lending and services
- Understand the various credit analysis tools used in commercial lending
- Compare the different types of SBA loans

GETTING STARTED

Read through the Project Process below. Make a list of any materials you will need. Decide how you will get the needed materials or information.

- Make a list of financial institutions from which you will acquire information.
- As you go through the chapter, jot down questions that occur to you about the commercial lending process.
- Identify outside resources such as magazine articles and web sites that provide more information on topics in the chapter.

PROJECT PROCESS

Part 1 LESSON 8.1 Look for examples in your community of commercial lending and services at work. Bring in a variety of articles and advertisements that relate to commercial lending or business services. Relate them to concepts in the lesson.

Part 2 LESSON 8.2 Expand your awareness of the credit analysis process for commercial loans. Work in groups and research various topics related to credit analysis.

Part 3 LESSON 8.3 Gather more information about various types of small business loans and programs that interest you. Compile a list of useful web sites.

CHAPTER REVIEW

Project Wrap-up As a group, assess what you now know about commercial lending and services. Draw up a formal plan to obtain a business loan. The plan should include the purpose of the loan, the types of financing available, and a list of financial records the lender will need.

COMMERCIAL LOANS ·······················

LIST purposes for commercial loans

IDENTIFY types of commercial loans

THE NATURE OF COMMERCIAL LENDING

Just as consumer loans allow you to have things you could not otherwise readily afford, commercial lending makes it possible for businesses to accomplish what they might otherwise never achieve. **Commercial lending**, as its name makes clear, is lending to business enterprises. Commercial lending is for businesses, but commercial lending practices may apply to individuals as well, such as a person who is buying rental property. Although perhaps less visible to the everyday citizen, commercial lending is actually a larger dollar market than consumer and mortgage lending. If you're trying to finance a $200,000 house, imagine financing a $2 million building. If you're concerned about paying utilities and taxes on a house, multiply that by the needs of a typical business and its employees.

Gloria Velez successfully obtained a house mortgage and was happy with the way that transaction went. Her job sometimes frustrated her, and she began to toy with the idea of starting her own business. To do this, she realized she would need to obtain a loan. Before going very far with the idea, she knew she would have to write some sort of a business plan. What are the components of a good business plan?

Banks and other financial institutions are keenly interested in this market and usually maintain specialists dedicated to commercial lending. Large banks dominate this field, although some small banks establish niches in their own communities. Although the underlying principles of sound lending apply to commercial as well as consumer lending, some of the products and analyses differ in their complexity and tools. The best commercial loan officers understand thoroughly the business their customers are in and look for effective and efficient ways to structure financing. Business needs may be variable as well as complex, and creative financial solutions can make the difference between success and failure. A private citizen can probably live without financing debt (although not easily in today's world). Almost no business can. One key to success in commercial enterprises is growth, and the careful acquisition and use of debt makes growth possible. Commercial loans are good business for lenders, businesses, and the people they serve.

Commercial Purposes

Commercial lending markets and customers may vary widely in size and scope. Whether it's a small one-person printing franchise in your neighborhood or a multinational hotel empire, businesses face many of the same challenges in terms of remaining adequately capitalized. Some of the purposes for commercial lending include the following.

- **Real Estate** Commercial real estate requirements differ from private residential mortgages, although many of the analyses are similar. Because facilities often need to be developed or redeveloped, and there may be local government issues involved, acquiring commercial real estate is a large and complex process. Even for investment real estate for residential purposes, the lending analysis is not quite so simple as for buying a home and requires a close look at the property as a business asset.

- **Construction** Closely linked, and often part of the same financing package as real estate loans, construction loans are a significant part of the commercial lending business. The size of construction loans often makes them subject to careful analysis of the value, purpose, and even design of the construction, as well as the overall financial position of the borrowing business. In order to assess whether the construction supports the loan value, underwriters must judge the worth of the building within it business function and its potential market value beyond the business.

- **Equipment** Most businesses need equipment to operate, and equipment is often the greatest start-up cost of new businesses. Because the value of equipment over time changes, equipment loans are often tied to the

WORKSHOP

In small groups, list specific examples of several different forms of commercial real estate, construction, equipment, and operations costs that demonstrate the wide variety of purposes of commercial lending.

overall cash flow, business plan, and financial position of the borrower as well as to the equipment itself. This change in value, called *depreciation*, requires that the loan officer understand fully the function, use, and effective lifetime of the equipment for the business.

- *Operations* Cash flow is an unending concern of business. Whether funding is needed to purchase inventory or supplies, meet unexpected expenses, or even hold the company through a difficult time, operations expenses are often part of a commercial lending package. Here, perhaps, is where a loan officer may need the most in-depth understanding of a business to assess the risk adequately. Operations expenses are sometimes seasonal or cyclical, as in agriculture and textile industries, and ongoing patterns of lending and repayment are part of the day-to-day life of these businesses. Many financial institutions involve themselves deeply with client businesses on a daily basis, managing cash flow, lines of credit, debt servicing, and operations costs as part of a total business relationship with the customer.

CHECK**POINT**

Name four purposes for commercial loans.

_____

_____

TECH TALK

ONLINE HELP FOR ENTREPRENEURS

Owning your own business and being your own boss appeals to many people. You can turn to the Internet to help fulfill this dream. The Internet offers vast amounts of information on business opportunities. There are web sites that provide guidance for starting a business. Some help you write a business plan and marketing plan and help you track your goals. Many sites can provide information on getting a business loan and help you evaluate your self-worth before applying for a loan. Other web sites offer businesses for sale across the country. Several web sites offer tips, strategies, and techniques to help an entrepreneur find and buy the right business at the right price.

Business loans can even be obtained directly online. You can review current interest rates and use the calculator provided on the web site to estimate your payments. Quotes can be obtained from hundreds of commercial lenders that are more than willing to compete for your business. You can get pre-qualified, apply for a loan, and get an answer within days. With the help of the Internet, you may be closer than you thought to being your own boss!

THINK CRITICALLY

Would you consider applying for a business loan online? Explain your answer. What are the advantages and disadvantages of using the Internet to obtain a loan?

TYPES OF COMMERCIAL LOANS

There is a wide range of commercial loan products available, and they offer considerable flexibility. Like consumer loans, commercial loans are secured or unsecured, depending on the type of loan, and vary widely in terms and rates. Just like individuals, businesses have credit ratings too, and the type and availability of funds depends on their track record and income prospects.

Term Loans

Most **term loans** finance permanent working capital, equipment, real estate, business expansion or acquisition of another business. Terms and rates vary with the asset securing the loan or the expected life of the asset. Many varieties of commercial loans are available such as fixed, adjustable rate, and balloon loans. Adjustable rate loans operate just as they do in the consumer sector, with rates tied to indexes as outlined in the loan contract, usually including caps (maximum rates) and floors (minimum rates). Balloon loans, although somewhat risky for the individual, are more common in commercial lending because they often offer more advantageous rates. As the loan matures, the borrower may sell the property to meet the balloon or may refinance the note. Still, careful analysis is necessary because business conditions at maturity may be hard to estimate and refinancing can become difficult or expensive.

Short-Term Loans

Most **short-term loans** are for a year or less, and a business may have many of them in sequence or even concurrently to finance expenses. Most short-term loans are used for seasonal or cyclical business costs, such as increasing inventory or maintaining the business until predictable receivables arrive. Short-term does not necessarily mean small. Short-term financing is a regular part of big business, and large short-term loans are common. Depending on the credit rating of the business, short-term loans are frequently unsecured, leading to trouble for lenders and borrowers if business goes poorly. Monitoring business conditions and performance is an important part of the loan analyst's job. Most short-term loans require a lump-sum payment at maturity. However, businesses often refinance short-term debt as well, rolling debt servicing into part of their ongoing operations costs.

Lines of Credit

Lines of credit for businesses work just as they do for individuals. The lender provides cash in the form of regular amounts, single disbursements, or a credit account to a business to cover routinely occurring expenses. Credit lines often finance contract work (which may not be paid until complete), inventory, or receivable intervals. They may also be used for day-to-day expenses, depending upon the lender's relationship with the borrower. Essentially, a line of credit is an open-ended loan, and though it has no specific term, its rates and conditions vary with the particular lending agreement.

Real Estate and Equipment Loans

Particular commercial mortgage loans for real estate and equipment are tied to and secured by the asset being purchased. These loans may also vary in terms and rates, but, depending on the equipment or real estate, they are typically long-term notes with 10- to 20-year repayment periods. Usually, the loan-to-value relationship (LTV) is limited to around 75 percent for real estate and anywhere from 60 to 80 percent for equipment. Second and third mortgages are also available for commercial real estate in amounts dependent on the first mortgage principal and the property value. However, second and third mortgages affect the overall debt structure of the business.

Contract Financing

Contract financing is secured by the value of a specific contract and allows for an orderly flow of funds to a company or organization performing services under contract. Funds are advanced as the work is performed, and contract payments often go directly to the lender until the obligation is satisfied.

Bridge Loans

Bridge loans are a particular form of short-term loan used to cover expenses until long-term financing is in place. Bridge loans are especially important in start-up enterprises or in complex transactions where many separate purchases, developments, or sales depend upon each other. Timing may be difficult to coordinate in such deals, and bridge loans offer a way to keep the business rolling.

Leasing

Many lenders finance leases for businesses, usually with lease terms of three to five years. The advantage of leasing is that it can allow businesses to possess needed equipment for less total cost than they would be obligated for if they bought the equipment. Lenders review the business and the equipment just as they would any other type of loan. At the end of the lease period, the business might return the equipment, buy the equipment, or renew the lease.

Asset-Based Loans

Another type of financing is called **asset-based lending**. Banks analyze profit and loss (P&L) statements, tax returns, and business plans to make lending decisions based on business income. Lenders of asset-based loans secure the loans with the overall assets of the business, including equipment, inventory, and accounts receivable, rather than just business income or a specific piece of equipment. A form of asset-based lending called **factoring** advances cash to a business in exchange for its receivables. This allows the borrower to increase its cash flow. The amount advanced is usually some percentage of the accounts. The factor then collects the invoices, forwarding the money to the borrower, less fees and interest kept by the factor. Most businesses seeking asset-based lending are those that do not easily qualify for other types of loans, such as new businesses without a track record or businesses with high potential that has not yet been realized.

Leasing is very popular in the business world. It offers the following advantages.

Low initial cost
Fixed rates
Longer terms
Smaller payments
Tax advantages
Equipment obsolescence insurance
Working capital preservation

What is a bridge loan?

_____

_____

THINK CRITICALLY ●●●●●●●●●●●●●●●●●●●●●●

1. Identify three major differences between consumer lending and commercial lending.

_____

_____

_____

2. Why is it essential that loan analysts understand the nature of a business, not just the balance sheets, to determine the soundness of a loan?

_____

_____

_____

3. How is it possible that a bank might make poor loans to a long-time commercial customer?

_____

_____

_____

MAKE CONNECTIONS ●●●●●●●●●●●●●●●●●●●●●

4. COMMUNICATION Interview a realtor to determine what the differences are in selling commercial real estate and residential real estate. Uncover differences in the lending analysis process for both types of real estate.

_____

_____

_____

_____

_____

5. SOCIAL STUDIES Small and new businesses are a vital part of our economy. These businesses could not survive, however, without financial backing. How do you think commercial loans help the economy?

_____

_____

_____

_____

_____

_____

6. COMMUNICATION Learn more about commercial lending. Interview a commercial loan officer of a local bank. Have the loan officer explain the job to you. Find out the parts of the job that are the most difficult, the most pleasurable, the most dependent on training, and the most dependent on experience. Present a brief oral report to the class on what you learn.

Lesson 8.2
COMMERCIAL CREDIT ANALYSIS ··········

GOALS

IDENTIFY basic ratios used in commercial underwriting

LIST other items used to evaluate commercial loans

EXPLAIN the importance of disclosure in commercial loans

COMMERCIAL CREDIT ANALYSIS TOOLS

Commercial credit analysis is not in principle a great deal different from the process used for consumer loans. The same general steps and ideas apply but with one significant addition. Assessing an individual's capability to repay is usually simply a question of verifying employment and income. Analyzing a business can be far more complicated, because not only are past income records studied, but underwriters must also estimate the likelihood of the profitability of the business in the future.

In the case of large corporations, evaluating those prospects can be an extremely complex process. Lenders hire or employ professional financial analysts to carefully study as much as can be determined about a company's financial position. Whether a company is large or small, the financial analysis for a particular loan often comes down to the results of three measurements. Though making the measurements may be complicated, the results determine whether the loan makes sense.

To prepare for starting her own business, Gloria Velez has developed a business plan. She intends to share this plan with the lender when applying for a loan to finance her new business. Besides the business plan, what other things do you think Gloria will need to provide the lender to help her obtain a loan?

Debt Ratio

Debt ratio for businesses is not much different from the debt ratio of consumers. **Debt ratio** is the total obligations compared to the total income. The formula for calculating debt ratio is simple. Debt ratio equals the debt obligation divided by income for some period of time.

Debt ratio = Debt ÷ Income

For example, in a given month, if your income is $3,000 and your monthly debt is $1,500, you have a debt ratio of $1,500 ÷ $3,000 = 0.5, or 50 percent. If you have a debt ratio of 200 percent, in which your debt is twice your income, you have a problem. Lenders usually will not consider a candidate with a debt ratio above 40 percent.

Assessing the debt ratio may be a major task in the case of a corporation, for merely compiling all the numbers can be a large job. Most of the processing of a commercial loan application is an attempt to verify the numbers that the prospective borrower provides.

Loan-to-Value (LTV) Ratio

Another critical ratio is loan-to-value. The **loan-to-value ratio** is the principal amount of the loan divided by the value of the securing property, just as it is in residential mortgages.

Loan-to-value ratio = Principal ÷ Market value

Lenders for commercial mortgages tend to be more conservative than for residential ones. Lenders look for a loan-to-value ratio of 80 percent maximum and often will not lend more than 60 percent of the appraised value.

The principle of loan-to-value gets complicated when you consider other types of business property such as equipment. Unlike real estate, which usually appreciates, or becomes more valuable, most business property depreciates, or loses value. Although depreciation offers tax breaks, it complicates securing a loan. Information technology equipment, for example, which becomes obsolete quickly, depreciates so rapidly that it's virtually worthless in a few years. How much can you get for a used computer? Lenders analyze those types of loans by carefully considering the overall health of company finances.

Debt Service Coverage Ratio

A more sophisticated tool for assessing a company's overall debt structure is the debt service coverage ratio. Used extensively for commercial real estate, it provides a look at a company's overall position. The **debt service coverage ratio** (DSCR) compares net operating income to the total cost of debt. Net operating income is gross income minus expenses, taxes, insurance, utilities, and so on. Note that net operating income does not include the cost of debt for mortgages or other debts for equipment, services, and other such things. Compiling these numbers may not be a simple task because there may be many items from many sources to be considered and verified. When net operating income is divided by the total cost of debt service, it yields the debt service coverage ratio.

Debt service coverage ratio = Net operating income ÷ Total debt service

Consider a small business with a $650,000 net operating income on a gross income of $1 million. Assume that the total cost of servicing the debt of the business, including all principal and interest but not counting taxes or insurance, which were taken out already to derive net operating income, is $520,000. Dividing $650,000 by $520,000 yields a DSCR of 1.25.

A lender wants to see the highest DSCR possible, for the higher the DSCR, the more net operating income is available for debt service. The higher the total debt service cost rises, the lower the DSCR falls. A ratio of less than 1.0 indicates a negative cash flow. Different lenders may require different levels of DSCR. Conservative lenders might seek 1.25 or higher, while other lenders would accept 1.20 or 1.10. Only rarely will a lender accept a DSCR near or below 1.0, and then only when there are strong mitigating reasons, such as other sources of potential income or a clear indication of a future upsurge of net operating income.

CHECK**POINT**

List three analytical tools used to evaluate commercial lending.

_____

_____

OTHER EVALUATION

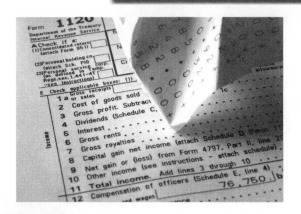

In order to perform ratio and other analyses of a company's finances, lenders want full access to company financial records. Remember that verification of capability is far more complex and difficult in the case of a business than in the case of an individual. In addition, changing business conditions may alter a company's profitability rapidly. Only by understanding the true nature of a company's financial position can a lender hope to make a sound decision.

BANKING MATH CONNECTION

Banks typically use the debt ratio, the loan-to-value ratio, and the debt service coverage ratio to determine if a commercial loan is viable. Using the following data, calculate each ratio.

Monthly income	$4,500
Monthly debt	$1,250
Loan principal	$30,000
Market value	$45,000
Gross income	$160,000
Net operating income	$100,000
Total cost of debt	$85,000

SOLUTION

Debt ÷	Income	= Debt ratio
$1,250 ÷	$4,500	= 0.28 or 28 percent

Principal ÷	Market value	= Loan-to-value ratio
$30,000 ÷	$45,000	= 0.67 or 67 percent

Net operating income ÷	Total debt service	= Debt service coverage ratio
$100,000 ÷	$85,000	= 1.18

Typically, lenders want to examine the following.

- Federal and state income tax returns for three years
- Company financial statements for three years (all assets and liabilities and proforma profit and loss statements)
- Year-to-date profit and loss and balance statements
- Projected cash flow estimates for at least the coming year
- Valuations and appraisals for collateral used to secure the loan
- Written business plan (for small businesses)
- Personal financial statements of owners (for new or small businesses)

Only by knowing the complete picture can a lender make an informed decision about a loan. As in all of the lending industry, competition has sometimes led lenders to less strict underwriting, which can lead to defaulted loans. Bank examiners review commercial lending policies just as they do consumer loans, and in times when larger numbers of bad loans are being made, examiners conduct more stringent examinations.

WORKSHOP

Working in small groups, compile a list of things that should be included in a business plan to be presented to a potential lender.

CHECKPOINT

Why does a lender need access to a company's financial records?

_____

_____

_____

You work as the accountant for a large manufacturing company. The company has fallen on hard times recently due to increased competition throughout the industry. The company is seeking a loan to buy new, state-of-the-art equipment to improve its operations, in turn making it more competitive in the market. After reviewing the company's finances, the president of the company is concerned that it cannot obtain a loan in its current financial state. She asks you to "rework" the financial statements and inflate earnings by reducing some of the recent debt taken on by the company. She thinks this will help secure the loan. The president feels that no harm is done because the company will increase profits in the long run with the new business it will acquire after the acquisition of the new equipment.

THINK CRITICALLY

Do you agree or disagree with the president? Explain why. If the loan is obtained and financial disaster ensues, whom will this ultimately affect?

DISCLOSURES

Unlike consumer lending, most commercial lending is regulated only by the terms of the loan agreement and some state laws. The assumption is that both parties to the loan are business professionals and can comprehend and negotiate the loan agreement with terms to which all parties agree. Still, it is in the interest of the business relationship to make sure that all terms are

explained and understood, as both parties seek to prosper from the loan.

Although it is fraud to falsify records for the purposes of acquiring a loan, desperate businesses hoping to refinance large amounts or forestall collapse sometimes provide inaccurate or incomplete information. Sometimes close relationships between lenders and businesses themselves lead to poorly underwritten loans. A financial collapse can doom not only the company that undertook the loan, and sometimes the lender, but also the personal finances and even the pensions of employees who had no part in the fraud. It is the ethical and professional responsibility of all parties to commercial lending to see that loans are honestly and soundly underwritten.

CHECK**POINT**

Why isn't commercial lending as heavily regulated as consumer lending?

_____

_____

THINK CRITICALLY ●●●●●●●●●●●●●●●●●●●●●●●

1. Why is the credit analysis process so much more detailed for commercial loans versus consumer loans?

_____

_____

_____

2. What does a company's debt ratio reveal to the lender?

_____

_____

_____

3. What things can a lender learn from reviewing a company's financial statements?

_____

_____

_____

MAKE CONNECTIONS ●●●●●●●●●●●●●●●●●●●●●●

4. BANKING MATH Assume that a small business owner has come to you with a loan request. Your careful analysis of the records shows a net operating income of $875,000 and total debt of $798,000, including the new loan. According to the debt service coverage ratio, is this a good candidate for a loan? Why or why not?

_____

_____

_____

5. RESEARCH Locate the web site of a commercial lender. Gather some background information on the lender and list some of its services and the various types of loans it offers.

_____

_____

_____

_____

6. PROBLEM SOLVING Assume you just obtained a loan to finance new equipment for your business. You later discover that the lender did not disclose all terms of the loan and that your interest rate will not remain fixed throughout the life of the loan as you had discussed. What recourse can you take?

_____

_____

_____

_____

_____

SMALL BUSINESS LOAN PROGRAMS ······

GOALS

DESCRIBE the purpose of the SBA

EXPLAIN SBA loan eligibility requirements

IDENTIFY SBA loan options

THE SMALL BUSINESS ADMINISTRATION

Just as our government thinks it is a worthwhile investment to back mortgage loans and expand available money for such loans, so too does our society support small business. When you think of business, you often think of giant corporations, but most Americans work for small businesses. A small business might be defined in a variety of ways, but the Small Business Administration defines a small business as one that has 100 or fewer employees in wholesale or trade businesses and 500 or fewer in manufacturing or mining businesses. According to the White House, 99.7 percent of U.S. businesses meet this definition, and 53 percent of the private work force and 47 percent of all sales belong to this group.

BANKING *Scene*

Gloria Velez learned quickly that she didn't have the resources or the track record to obtain conventional funding for a business loan. She kept her job, but began to work hard on her own time at learning more about running her own business. She turned to the government. She had gone to college on government-backed loans, and it occurred to her that there might be similar programs to help new businesses. What might be a good way for Gloria to start searching the vast amount of information available from the U.S. government?

Of course, small businesses can and do seek financing through many commercial channels. Commercial lending is available from many sources. Many small or new firms, however, don't easily qualify for standard commercial loans. As in consumer lending, credit scoring is critical in commercial lending. Things may not be easy for those small firms that don't have cash flow or collateral to qualify.

The **Small Business Administration** (SBA) offers a number of financial, technical, and management programs to help businesses. The SBA also grew out of a Depression-era agency, the Reconstruction Finance Corporation (RFC), a lending program for businesses of any size hurt by the Depression. The Department of Commerce's Office of Small Business, primarily an advisory agency, and RFC functions were combined in 1952 into the Small Business Administration.

Today, the SBA continues its mission of education and assistance for small businesses. There's nothing small about the project, though. Nearly 20 million small businesses have received SBA assistance in one form or another. Today, the SBA's help with 219,000 loans worth more than $45 billion makes it the nation's largest financial backer of businesses.

The financial assistance the SBA provides to small businesses comes in the form of loan guaranties. The loan guaranty program guarantees a lender that if the borrower defaults the SBA will repay most of the loan. The SBA guarantees a maximum of 85 percent of the loan funds, depending on the size of the loan and terms.

Borrowers apply to and receive funds from lenders, who must approve the loans. The SBA reviews the loans as well and provides the lender a written authorization of the guaranty. The lender sets rates, usually 1 to 2 3/4 percent over prime rate. Payments go to the lender. Although there is more paperwork involved for both borrower and lender, the added trouble allows the lender to make loans it probably couldn't make without the assurance of SBA backing, and borrowers get funding they probably couldn't get on their own.

Lenders are familiar with SBA loans, and many have SBA application forms on site. SBA certified lenders are those that work frequently and well with the SBA, and they have some authority to make their own decisions within the program. They also get faster SBA service. The SBA also maintains a preferred lender program for its best and most reliable lenders. In exchange for a lower rate of guaranty, preferred lenders have full authority to approve SBA loans on their own.

Still, an SBA loan is no free lunch. Borrowers must meet standards set by both the SBA and the lender. Although these standards may be more relaxed than those for other commercial loans, applications are still examined for soundness. Neither SBA nor the lender wants to get stuck with a bad loan.

WORKSHOP

Working in small groups, come to an agreement on a definition of a small business. Then compile a list of small businesses in your community.

CHECK**POINT**

How do SBA loans differ from standard commercial loans?

_____

_____

_____

SBA ELIGIBILITY

Most businesses are eligible for SBA loan guaranties, but the SBA makes a decision on a case-by-case basis, based on the type of program. In general, eligibility is determined by the following.

- *Type of Business* Businesses must be operating for profit in the United States or its possessions, have reasonable owner equity, and use other financial alternatives including personal assets of owners. Some types of businesses are ineligible. Charitable or religious groups, real estate investment, lending, pyramid sales plans, gambling businesses, and businesses engaged in illegal activities may not participate.

- *Size of Business* The SBA has precise definitions of a small business. It must be independently owned and not dominant in its field. When businesses are affiliated, all affiliated parties must meet the size standard for its field of operation, which varies from industry to industry. For example, the retail and service-size standard is $3.5 to $13.5 million in revenue, while for agricultural businesses, $3.5 million is the upper limit.

- *Use of Loan Funds* Although SBA-backed loans may be used for most business purposes, funds cannot be used to finance floor plan needs, to purchase real estate when a commitment has already been made to a developer or for investment, to pay delinquent taxes or to make payments to owners, or to pay existing debt unless it can be shown that refinancing will benefit the business and is not the result of poor management.

Certain other conditions apply in special circumstances, based on the particular field in which the business is engaged.

What three factors determine SBA loan eligibility?

_____

_____

SBA LOAN TERMS AND CONDITIONS

A borrower seeking an SBA loan must expect to meet all the criteria for a commercial loan. In general, the borrower needs a down payment, at least 20 percent and as much as 35 percent in some cases. Most importantly, the borrower needs to demonstrate that he or she has the experience and knowledge required to run the business successfully. The SBA expects that the loan will be repaid from the normal business cash flow and, therefore, joins the lender in seeking full documentation of the operation of the business. As you saw earlier in this chapter, lenders require Federal and state income tax returns, company financial statements, up-to-date profit and loss statements, projected cash flow estimates, personal financial statements of the owners, and a well-written business plan. Like the lender, the SBA wants to see as much collateral for a loan as possible, but it treats collateral as one part of the overall credit picture.

Maximum loan amounts and the size of the guaranty vary with the particular loan program, as do terms and other conditions. Loan terms may vary from 5 to 25 years, depending on purpose. Interest rates are set by the lender but are subject to SBA maximums. Whether the interest rate is fixed or variable is also between the lender and borrower.

7(a) Loan Guaranty

The 7(a) Loan Guaranty program is the SBA's most popular loan program and the foundation of the agency. In 1999, the agency guaranteed more than 43,000 loans totaling more than $10 billion. Businesses can use the funds to expand or repair facilities, purchase equipment or make improvements, finance receivables, or in some cases, refinance existing debt or purchase land or buildings. The legal maximum for a 7(a) loan is $2 million, but in practice, the SBA says it can generally issue a guaranty up to $1 million.

SBA*LowDoc* and SBA*Express*

The SBA*LowDoc* and the SBA*Express* loan programs both offer quick turnaround time on loans up to $150,000. Both programs generally follow the 7(a) guidelines. The SBA*Express* program uses preferred lenders for an even quicker response.

CAPLines

The CAPLines loan program supports short-term lending for seasonal, contract, or other cyclical capital needs with either short-term loans or revolving lines of credit. Generally, 7(a) guidelines apply.

SMALL BUSINESS NORTHWARD

The United States is not the only country that believes its government should support small business. Though the banking system of Canada differs from that of the United States, both Canadian and American governments guarantee small business loans in similar ways. The Canada Small Business Finance Act (CSBFA) continued a program begun in 1961 to advise businesses and guarantee up to 85 percent of small business loans. Since 1997, the program has been financially self-sustaining. One study found that the program is one of the best, with administrative costs and default rates lower than those of similar programs in Germany, the United Kingdom, Japan, and the United States.

THINK CRITICALLY

What factors might account for higher administrative costs and default rates on small business loans in the United States?

Talk to several small business owners about their experiences as entrepreneurs. Compile a list of pros and cons of owning your own business.

Microloans

The SBA Microloan program makes funds available to nonprofit intermediary lenders to help small, newly established businesses. The maximum loan amount is $35,000, with an average of $10,500. The lending intermediary agrees to provide technical assistance and advice, and the borrower may be required to undergo training or meet planning requirements.

Special-Purpose Programs

There are several special-purpose programs targeted to particular needs or businesses. The U.S. Community Adjustment and Investment Program (CAIP) helps businesses hurt by the North American Free Trade Agreement (NAFTA). The DELTA program helps small businesses affected by defense contract reductions, and there are Economic Injury Disaster loans available in special circumstances.

In addition, the SBA also operates a Small Business Investment Company (SBIC) program, consisting of about 40 for-profit corporations that raise and distribute venture capital to promising businesses. The program has been around since the 1950s but expanded greatly in the 1990s. The SBICs have SBA guidelines about how and with whom they invest but operate independently of the SBA on a day-to-day basis. Federal Express and America Online are examples of companies that received funding from SBICs.

CHECK**POINT**

What general ctiteria must a borrower meet to obtain an SBA loan?

_____

_____

THINK CRITICALLY ●●●●●●●●●●●●●●●●●●●●●

1. Why does our society support small business?

_____

_____

_____

2. Compare an SBA loan to a standard commercial loan. Why would someone choose one loan over the other?

_____

_____

_____

_____

3. Why do you think most charitable and religious groups are not eligible for SBA help?

_____

_____

_____

_____

4. Why is a well-written business plan an important factor in getting an SBA loan?

_____

_____

_____

_____

MAKE CONNECTIONS ●●●●●●●●●●●●●●●●●●●●●

5. **COMMUNICATION** Interview a person in your community who runs a small business. Find out how he or she obtained start-up capital, what the greatest challenges are in running a small business, and what advice or assistance this person has obtained and from what sources. Summarize your interview in a one-page report.

6. **HISTORY** Learn more about the history of the Small Business Administration. Find out how it changed from an organization intended to support business in general to one dedicated to small businesses. Write a one-page report on the history of the agency.

7. **SOCIAL STUDIES** Visit the Small Business Administration's web site at www.sba.gov. Learn more about emergency relief funds for businesses affected by the September 11, 2001 attacks. Outline the details here.

_____

_____

_____

_____

_____

_____

CHAPTER 8 ······················· REVIEW

CHAPTER SUMMARY

LESSON 8.1 Commercial Loans

A. Commercial lending is defined as lending to business enterprises. Commercial loans are available for real estate, construction, equipment, and operations.

B. There are numerous types of commercial loans including long- and short-term loans, lines of credit, real estate and equipment loans, contract financing, bridge loans, leases, and asset-based loans.

LESSON 8.2 Commercial Credit Analysis

A. Credit analysis of businesses involves an in-depth evaluation. Debt ratio, loan-to-value, and debt service coverage ratio are some of the credit analysis tools used.

B. To complete a credit analysis, the lender will require full access to a company's financial records.

C. Commercial lending is regulated only by the terms of the loan and some state laws. Commercial loans must be carefully underwritten to avoid financial disaster later on the part of the lender and borrower.

LESSON 8.3 Small Business Loan Programs

A. The Small Business Administration (SBA) offers financial and educational assistance for small businesses. The SBA guarantees a lender that the loan will be paid if the borrower defaults.

B. Eligibility for an SBA loan is determined by the type of business, the size of the business, and the use of loan funds.

C. There are several SBA loan options for small businesses. Loan terms and conditions vary with each program.

VOCABULARY BUILDER

Choose the term that best fits the definition. Write the letter of the answer in the space provided. Some terms may not be used.

a. asset-based lending

b. bridge loan

c. commercial lending

d. debt ratio

e. debt service coverage ratio

f. factoring

g. loan-to-value ratio

h. short-term loan

i. Small Business Administration

j. term loan

_____ **1.** Amount of loan divided by the property value

_____ **2.** Loans to business enterprises

_____ **3.** Loan used to cover expenses until long-term financing is secured

_____ **4.** Comparison of net operating income to the total cost of debt

_____ **5.** Financing for permanent working capital, equipment, and real estate

_____ **6.** Loan secured with the assets of a business

_____ **7.** Financing for a year or less

_____ **8.** Agency that offers financial, technical, and management programs to help businesses

_____ **9.** A form of lending that advances cash in exchange for a business's receivables

_____ **10.** Total obligations compared to total income

REVIEW CONCEPTS

banking.swep.com

11. What is commercial lending?

_____

_____

_____

12. List one purpose for commercial lending and describe how the loan might be used.

_____

_____

_____

13. What is depreciation and how might it affect a loan?

_____

_____

_____

_____

14. List five types of commercial loans.

_____

_____

_____

_____

15. What is a line of credit and how would a business use it?

_____

_____

_____

_____

16. What are the costs and benefits of factoring to a business?

_____

_____

_____

17. Explain the loan-to-value ratio. What do lenders consider an acceptable loan-to-value ratio?

_____

_____

_____

_____

18. What is the debt service coverage ratio (DSCR) and why does a lender prefer to see the highest possible DSCR?

_____

_____

_____

_____

19. List five things a lender will need to get from the borrower when considering a commercial loan.

_____

_____

_____

_____

_____

_____

20. How does the Small Business Administration define a small business?

_____

_____

_____

_____

21. Explain how the Small Business Administration helps businesses obtain loans.

_____

_____

_____

_____

22. List four purposes for which an SBA loan cannot be used.

_____

_____

_____

_____

_____

23. Describe the SBA 7(a) loan program.

_____

_____

_____

_____

_____

24. Why are banks and other lenders so interested in the commercial loan market?

_____

_____

_____

25. Why do many businesses choose to lease equipment rather than buy it?

_____

_____

_____

_____

26. How do disclosure laws differ for consumer and commercial lending?

_____

_____

_____

_____

27. Why does the government have an interest in guaranteeing loans for small businesses?

_____

_____

_____

MAKE CONNECTIONS ● ● ● ● ● ● ● ● ● ● ● ● ● ● ● ● ● ● ●

28. BANKING MATH Calculate the debt service coverage ratio for a small business that has a gross income of $1,400,000, a net operating income of $800,000, and total debt service of $650,000.

_____

_____

29. TECHNOLOGY Learn more about venture capital that is used to fund many high-tech enterprises. Visit the Small Business Investment Company (SBIC) web site at www.sba.gov/INV and prepare an oral report on how the program works.

30. COMMUNICATION Small or new businesses may need to submit a business plan to obtain financing. What is a business plan? What makes a good one? Visit the Small Business Administration's web site at www.sba.gov. and find information about starting a business. Study the information about the contents of a business plan. List the three major elements here.

_____

_____

CHAPTER 9

SPECIALIZED BANK SERVICES

9.1 INTERNATIONAL BANKING
9.2 INSURANCE AND BROKERAGE
9.3 CASH MANAGEMENT
9.4 TRUSTS

Careers in Banking

FIRST TENNESSEE NATIONAL CORPORATION

Headquartered in Memphis, Tennessee, First Tennessee National Corporation is a national, diversified financial services institution and one of the fifty largest bank holding companies in the United States. It provides banking and other financial services to its customers through various regional and national lines of business.

First Tennessee National Corporation is committed to an environment in which employees come first, enjoy the benefits of ownership, and are recognized as the reason the bank has a high customer retention and satisfaction rate. With over 600 locations nationwide, the corporation offers many career opportunities throughout its organization and various subsidiaries.

A trust officer is responsible for administering estate, custody, and individual trust accounts for the Trust division. Qualifications include a bachelor's degree in a business discipline, good verbal and written communication skills, the ability to work independently, and the ability to evaluate situations and make appropriate business decisions.

THINK CRITICALLY

1. How do you think the employees contribute to the bank's high customer retention rate and satisfaction?
2. Would you like to work in a position with little direct supervision?

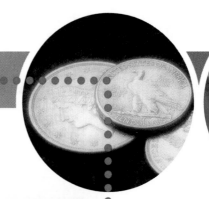

SPECIALIZED BANK SERVICES for CONSUMERS

VIDEO
The Chapter 9 video introduces the concepts in this chapter.

PROJECT OBJECTIVES

- Learn about the specialized services banks offer
- Learn about recent banking legislation and changes in the business environment
- Recognize different types of insurance products
- Compare the various types of financial planning products

GETTING STARTED

Read through the Project Process below. Make a list of any materials you will need. Decide how you will get the needed materials or information.

- Make a list of financial institutions from which you will acquire information.
- Make a list of terms for which you need definitions or about which you need more information.
- As you collect information, think about specific people, businesses, or circumstances in which the services would be useful.

PROJECT PROCESS

Part 1 LESSON 9.1 Discuss in class what you know about globalization. Identify economic interests in your community that are affected by international trade.

Part 2 LESSON 9.2 Expand your awareness of the insurance and brokerage services offered by banks in your area. Begin with a list of local institutions and find out what types of services are offered by each. Divide the class into areas of responsibility for acquiring information.

Part 3 LESSON 9.3 Learn about cash management services from the point of view of the customer. Find businesses that use such services locally, and find out how and why they use them.

Part 4 LESSON 9.4 Learn about trust services offered by local banks and how they are structured. Make a chart that compares the various offerings and their costs.

CHAPTER REVIEW

Project Wrap-up Hold a class discussion about specialized bank services. How do they fit into your overall understanding of the way banks do business? What qualities of these services are unique? How do they compare to other parts of the banking business? What do you predict for the future of these types of services?

Lesson 9.1
INTERNATIONAL BANKING ·············

GOALS

IDENTIFY three types of financial institutions engaged in international banking

DESCRIBE international services offered by banks

STRUCTURE OF INTERNATIONAL SERVICES

You don't need a textbook to tell you that the world of finance is increasingly an international one. The changing economy in the 1970s introduced waves of new imports to American life, and the computer and telecommunications revolution of the 1980s and 1990s eliminated national boundaries in many ways. Companies looking for new markets sought to sell to developing nations, and expanding economies in the Pacific Rim altered the balance of economic power. Changes in geopolitics, such as the end of the Soviet Union and the emergence of the People's Republic of China, realigned trading partnerships. New trade agreements and economic alliances such as the North American Free Trade Agreement and the European Union shifted the way the world does business, as did the growth of multinational corporations with branches in many countries.

Behind all this trade is money, and international banking is a huge and growing segment of the banking industry. Foreign banking organizations,

Amelia Lopez owns a small business. The market for the firm's major product is growing rapidly in South America, and she wants to investigate the advantages and disadvantages of selling her product there. What issues should Amelia consider? Where can she get sound advice about this possible venture?

their branches, agencies, and subsidiaries hold about a quarter of all U.S. commercial bank assets. American banks, too, have added international presence. With more and more U.S. companies operating abroad and involved in international trade, banks are expanding their services to provide the expertise that is needed. International banking can be a complicated business, with traders needing to understand the differences among currencies, governments, languages, laws, customs, and even computer systems that affect funds transfers. It is a vital business for the future of banking, because in the global economy, more business will have an international component. Banks that can help provide smooth, efficient, and trouble-free flow of funds and credit around the world may find a profitable and growing business.

International Lending Relatively few banks specialize in international lending. Only about 750 of more than 14,000 U.S. commercial banks have international lending departments with a smaller number having foreign branches or subsidiary corporations abroad. Although the number of these banks is small, both the scope and the size of their international business is expanding rapidly, and more banks are likely to expand into this area.

World Bank The *World Bank* is a partner in strengthening economies and expanding markets to improve the quality of life for people everywhere, especially the poorest. Unlike aid programs, the World Bank doesn't make grants but lends money to developing countries and expects the loans to be repaid. A member of the World Bank Group, the International Finance Corporation (IFC) promotes sustainable private sector investment in developing countries to reduce poverty and improve people's lives. The functions of the IFC include the following.

- Financing private sector projects located in the developing world.
- Helping private companies in the developing world mobilize financing in international financial markets.
- Providing advice and technical assistance to businesses and governments.

Other Services Lending is not the only international service. The number of banks that are helping companies conduct business overseas is growing. Other international services offered range from foreign exchange to collection of payments from overseas customers. Banks with knowledge of international business offer companies help in a complex world with which a firm may have little experience. It makes good business sense for companies to buy expertise they may not possess.

Foreign Banks

Many types of foreign-based banks, branches, agencies, subsidiaries, and holding corporations share features with U.S.-based banks doing international business, and they are supervised accordingly. Foreign bank branches and agencies may be chartered either by Federal or state governments. They may offer a full range of banking services, but most of their business involves short- and long-term commercial loans. Although foreign branches can accept deposits of any size from foreigners, they can accept deposits only greater than $100,000 from U.S. citizens and residents (in order not to harm domestic banks), and deposits made after 1991 are not insured by the FDIC.

Since 1991, the responsibility for supervising the branches and agencies of foreign banks operating within the United States has belonged primarily

WORKSHOP

As a class, make a list of factors that complicate regulating banks that do overseas business, as compared to those that do only domestic financing.

to the Federal Reserve. It annually examines the banks' policies of **r**isk management, **o**perations, **c**ompliance, and **a**sset quality (ROCA). If an examination reveals problems with a foreign bank, the Fed has a range of actions it can take. Usually, a letter of commitment explaining how a problem will be corrected from the bank to the Fed is required. Occasionally, further legal action occurs, and in extreme cases, the activities of a foreign bank in the United States will be terminated.

U.S.-Based International Banking

The *Office of the Comptroller of the Currency* (OCC) charters and supervises U.S. national banks that do international business. The OCC has the power to remove bank officers and directors, negotiate agreements to change banking practices, issue orders to stop certain practices, and levy financial penalties for unsound practices. The Federal Deposit Insurance Corporation, whose director is the Comptroller, reviews the safety of international banking operations.

Other Types of International Operations

Edge corporations or *agreement corporations* are financial corporations that are federally chartered and allowed to engage only in international banking or other financial transactions related to international business. Edge corporations must verify that every transaction is related to international business.

Correspondent banks act as points of contact for other banks that do not have a branch, agency, subsidiary, or corporation in the host country. These banks are subject to the banking regulations of the host country. The Federal Reserve, as well as other international banking organizations, works to communicate and standardize international banking policies to ensure a more stable flow of funds.

Special Considerations

Think of the potential hazards of doing business overseas. Different economic conditions, different currencies, different political systems, and even different cultural practices add a degree of uncertainty to doing business overseas that is not a part of domestic business. For bankers involved in underwriting such business, these other elements of risk must be considered.

- *Financial Risk* Financial risk may not seem all that different compared to domestic banking, and indeed, the evaluation of credit risk is similar. However, acquiring reliable information about a creditor's financial position may be considerably more difficult. The format, quality, and relative detail of financial statements around the world vary considerably. Many of these statements are unaudited, and in some cases, they are unreliable. Although international banks do share information, there are sometimes political barriers to the free flow of accurate information, especially when the potential borrower is a government itself. The task of assessing risk is considerably harder.

- *Currency Risk* The risk posed by variations in exchange rates between countries is called **currency risk**. In every transaction, the lender or borrower is at some degree of risk because of currency risk, as relative values fluctuate with economic and political conditions. The value of currencies compared to each other at the outset of the term may not be at all the same later in the term. Although many lenders minimize their risk by dealing only in U.S. dollars, some countries must convert those dollars

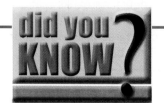

As of December 2000, foreign banking organizations operated or controlled 348 branches, 111 agencies, 79 commercial banks, and 18 edge or agreement corporations within the United States.

into local currency to use them. If the exchange rate changes, more local currency may be required to repay the loan than was expected at the outset. Banks need to be able to assess this risk as accurately as possible, which is not always an easy task.

- *Country Risk* The term for the entire range of political, legal, social, and economic conditions that may put international business at risk is **country risk**. International bankers spend a lot of time trying to assess country risk. Analysts consider the likelihood of political or social changes or unrest, the economic condition and prospects of the country, whether a government might seize private assets or renounce foreign debts, and whether the government is able to ensure the stability of its currency. These analyses produce varied classifications of risk for international business. A bank's activities in a foreign country in light of the country's risk classification are part of the Fed's regulatory examination of a bank.

The political and cultural environment is not the same in other parts of the world as it is in the United States. Bankers must be vigilant to protect not only their own interests but also avoid being unwitting allies of people who have illegal or harmful intent. The Bank Secrecy Act of 1970, updated again in 2000, intended to create a "paper trail" for currency so that people could not deposit, invest, or exchange money in such a way as to conceal its illegal source, called *money laundering*. The Foreign Corrupt Practices Act of 1977 requires banks to follow strict accounting procedures in their international dealings and prohibits offering or accepting bribes. Commerce Department regulations prohibit exporters and banks from complying with boycotts that discriminate against U.S. citizens or companies on the basis of race, color, religion, sex, or national origin, and require reporting of them.

The financing of illegal activities came into sharp focus after the terrorist attacks of September, 2001. Among its many provisions, the USA Patriot Act of 2001 attempted to make money laundering more difficult. The law prohibits establishing correspondent relations with foreign "shell" banks, banks that had no physical presence in their host country. It also requires "due diligence" on the part of banks to know the identity and source of transactions as well as to report suspicious transactions. Some privacy advocates whose fierce objections had led to the withdrawal of expanded "Know Your Customer" provisions in 1999, worried that the Patriot Act gave banks and government too much power. Even so, the law passed quickly and went into effect October 26, 2001, with most of its provisions in place by summer 2002.

CHECK**POINT**

What is an edge corporation? Name three types of risk for international banking.

_____

_____

INTERNATIONAL SERVICES

Banks offering international services help their customers negotiate, finance, ship, transfer, and collect their international accounts. Specialists in international finance and the export-import business help clients make their way through the sea of documents that are part of doing business across national boundaries.

Trade Financing

There are numerous forms of trade financing for international business. Some may take the form of simple domestic loans to be used for capital in an import or other international venture. Some may be direct loans to foreign governments through government-run banks or industries. Funds may go to foreign banks in the form of deposits or other loans as a means of making an indirect loan to a foreign business. Sometimes a direct loan may be made to a foreign business or individual. Loans for complex syndications of businesses may be very complicated but are not uncommon. In all cases, banks must review international financial statements, the borrowers themselves, and any other parties involved, such as parent companies, banks, and government institutions. Bank management must estimate if it can safely extend credit based on its own financial position; the financial condition of the borrowers and other parties; the bank's own marketing objectives; and the financial risk, currency risk, and country risk involved.

Letters of Credit The most common type of trade financing involves a letter of credit. A **letter of credit** is an instrument given by a bank on behalf of a buyer (applicant) to pay the bank of the seller (beneficiary) a given sum in a given time provided that documents required by the letter are presented to the issuing bank. The required documents usually consist of an invoice, transportation documents (listing the cargo), insurance, and other verification

EXPORT-IMPORT BANK OF INDIA

In some foreign countries, governments run banks rather than merely supervise them. Such is the case of the Export-Import (EXIM) Bank of India. Founded in 1982, EXIM Bank was created by an act of the Indian Parliament, and the government of India wholly owns it. Its purpose is to finance, facilitate, and promote India's foreign trade. EXIM Bank has eight offices in India and overseas offices in Budapest, Johannesburg, Milan, Singapore, and Washington, DC. It has expanded services to include financing at competitive rates to buyers of Indian goods in foreign countries.

THINK CRITICALLY

Of what potential benefit is the Indian government's involvement in export-import banking? Why might a foreign buyer benefit by financing through a bank of the seller's home country?

that the goods have been delivered. Until those documents have been accepted by the issuing bank, the letter of credit is of no value. When the documents are accepted, the bank debits the buyer's (applicant's) account, wires the specified amount to the correspondent bank of the seller (beneficiary), and the buyer can collect the shipment. In this way, both buyer and seller have some guarantee of the performance of the other, and the bank's funds are secured by the documentation for the goods. A *standby letter of credit* assures the seller of the buyer's creditworthiness by guaranteeing the bank to pay the seller in the event of nonperformance by the buyer.

Drafts and Wires Similar to a check, a draft is an order signed by one party (the *drawer*, or drafter) that is addressed to another party (the *drawee*) directing the drawee to pay someone (the *payee*) the amount indicated on the draft at sight or some specified time. Banks dealing in international banking can provide drafts in the specified currencies of many nations if necessary, so that the draft can be negotiated within that country. Banks can also provide international wire transfer. Messaging is not necessarily limited to ledger entries of funds but may also include letters of credit or any other communication or documentation necessary for international business.

International Collections Banks perform international collections services based on their relationships with correspondent banks and their knowledge of international commerce.

Foreign Currency Exchange Foreign currency exchanges are essential for international transactions. For example, before a U.S. importer can purchase commodities from Japan, it must first obtain Japanese yen to pay for them. Banks can provide this service. Banks may exchange currency through foreign exchange markets or may have correspondent relationships with banks in other countries for the trading of currency. A **foreign exchange rate** is the value of one currency in terms of another. Current foreign exchange quotations must be used to calculate the exchange. For example, the table below shows the exchange rates for select countries as of March 1, 2002.

Standby letters of credit are charged an origination fee, which varies based on the size of the letter and the security pledged. Typically the fees range from one to three percent of the size of the letter of credit.

Currency	U.S. $	Yen	Euro	Can $	U.K. £	Aust $	SFranc	FFranc	DMark
Last Trade	*N/A*	*Mar 1*	*Mar 1*	*Mar 1*	*Mar 1*	*Mar 1*	*Mar 1*	*Mar 1*	*Mar 1*
U.S. $	1	0.007504	0.8642	0.6282	1.418	0.5192	0.5858	0.1317	0.4416
Yen	133.3	1	115.2	83.72	189	69.19	78.07	17.55	58.85
Euro	1.157	0.008683	1	0.7269	1.641	0.6008	0.6779	0.1523	0.511
Can $	1.592	0.01195	1.376	1	2.258	0.8265	0.9325	0.2096	0.703
U.K. £	0.705	0.00529	0.6093	0.4429	1	0.366	0.413	0.09282	0.3113
Aust $	1.926	0.01445	1.664	1.21	2.732	1	1.128	0.2536	0.8505
SFranc	1.707	0.01281	1.475	1.072	2.421	0.8863	1	0.2248	0.7538
FFranc	7.595	0.057	6.564	4.771	10.77	3.943	4.449	1	3.354
DMark	2.264	0.01699	1.957	1.423	3.212	1.176	1.327	0.2981	1

To calculate what $1,000 U.S. dollars would be worth in euros, use the exchange rate from the table for U.S.$ to Euros: $1,000 × 1.157 = $1,157.

To calculate what 1,157 euros would be worth in U.S. dollars, use the exchange rate for Euros to U.S.$: $1,157 × 0.8642 = $1,000 (rounded).

Factors affecting exchange rates for the currency of a given country are interest rates, rate of inflation, trade balance (if a country's exports exceed its imports), and economic forecasts for that country. The demand for a given currency will be strong if the country is experiencing relatively high interest rates, low inflation, a positive trade balance, and a strong economic forecast.

Trade Consulting

Using their expertise, banks can help companies assess both their prospects and risks in international commerce and help companies with the paperwork associated with international transactions. The international banking consultant may also work with and/or recommend other agencies that can be of help to a business wanting to branch into international markets.

U.S. Export-Import (Ex-Im) Bank Some banks work with the U.S. Export-Import (Ex-Im) Bank to help raise capital for companies that have the potential to produce goods or services for export but need funds to do so. Ex-Im offers a number of financing programs, as well as credit insurance programs, that cover the risks of nonpayment by foreign buyers. Ex-Im does not compete with commercial banks, but assumes higher risks than commercial banks can normally accept. Its goal is to increase U.S. exports.

Overseas Private Investment Corporation (OPIC) Overseas Private Investment Corporation's (OPIC's) goal is to assist U.S. companies in building their business in developing nations. OPIC's programs are beneficial for both the developing nations and for U.S. exports. OPIC will provide loans, loan guarantees, and political risk insurance to qualifying companies. OPIC will provide this assistance for ventures seen as too risky for commercial banks. In spite of the assumed risks, OPIC has made money every year since it was created in 1971.

Small Business Administration (SBA) While not specific to helping international business, the SBA provides financial, technical and management assistance to help Americans start, run, and grow their businesses of any type, including those involved in international trade. Services include business loans, loan guarantees, and low-interest, disaster-relief loans.

CHECK**POINT**

What is a letter of credit?

_____

_____

THINK CRITICALLY ••••••••••••••••••••••

1. What factors do you think contribute to increasing globalization of economies?

_____

_____

2. Name three organizations that specialize in helping U.S. firms engage in foreign trade, and describe types of payment methods used.

_____

_____

_____

3. Give two specific instances of events that might be part of country risk.

_____

_____

_____

_____

4. Why might banks dealing in international services be in a good position to offer trade consulting?

_____

_____

MAKE CONNECTIONS •••••••••••••••••••••••

5. SOCIAL STUDIES Although English is the language of business around the globe, it helps traders immensely to know the language of their business partners. Find out the top five languages in the world, as ranked by number of speakers. List them and the number of speakers for each below.

_____

_____

_____

_____

6. BANKING MATH In January 2002, eurodollars, or euros, became the currency of member nations of the European Union, a group of Western European nations banding together for economic purposes. Using the Internet, find the current value of a euro as compared to the U.S. dollar and convert the cost of U.S. goods valued at $40,000 to euros.

_____

_____

7. POLITICAL SCIENCE Locate information on countries with fluctuating currency exchange rates and analyze the causes for fluctuation.

_____

_____

_____

_____

Lesson 9.2
INSURANCE AND BROKERAGE ·············

GOALS

EXPLAIN the effects of the Gramm-Leach-Bliley Act of 1999

LIST typical insurance and brokerage products available from financial institutions

A NEW ERA

Banks are offering more products and services than ever before. The competitive nature of today's banking business, along with the mergers and acquisitions many banks have undertaken, have placed them in a position to diversify even further. As a result of ongoing changes in financial services industries and new legislation, banks may now offer financial services that they once were prohibited from selling. This "one-stop-shopping" approach can offer customers a way to combine their financial planning into a single package, with products and expertise available from a single source. In addition, the door swings two ways: insurance companies can acquire banks just as banks can enter the insurance business. The new rules do not simply open the door to unsupervised market chaos in the financial services industry. One sure result of the new era is that competition for consumers' financial business, whether in banking, insurance, or securities, will become even more keen.

As a small business owner, Amelia Lopez is considering offering a health insurance plan for her employees, but she is undecided as to which type is the best. She is surprised to learn that her bank now offers insurance policies. What types of plans are available to her? What are some of the choices she must make in addition to the type of plan to offer?

The Old World: Glass-Steagall Act

The Glass-Steagall Act of 1933 was a response to the Great Depression. Bank failures and investment losses at that time nearly destroyed the banking system and the national economy. Among other provisions, the law prohibited banks from owning brokerage firms and selling stock and from affiliating or sharing offices with businesses that did. The intention of the law was to create a "firewall" between speculative business and banking institutions. Enacted during our nation's darkest economic period, it was part of a set of legislative actions that stabilized the banking system.

The Glass-Steagall Act kept banks from competing with other financial service providers. As the economy modernized, banks and other financial institutions suffered and occasionally were at risk because they couldn't compete. Gradually, laws such as the Bank Holding Company Acts of 1956 and 1970 allowed some side roads into other financial businesses, but they still prohibited direct affiliation and limited the regions in which banks could do business. Even as banks became deregulated in the 1980s, the prohibition of direct securities trading and insurance underwriting remained.

The New World: Gramm-Leach-Bliley Act (GLBA)

The Gramm-Leach-Bliley Act of 1999 was the most dramatic change in banking regulation since the Great Depression. After years of involving themselves in insurance and securities businesses only by side paths, banks were at last free to pursue those businesses directly. The law also required financial services companies to have and provide to customers a written privacy policy. Furthermore, the law allowed the sharing of consumers' financial information among affiliated firms so long as the consumer was notified. The responsibility to prohibit sharing of information with third parties, called an "opt-out," rests with the consumer. Some proponents of the law oppose the privacy-policy portion of it. They feel that requiring companies to seek permission of every consumer to share information creates an unnecessary burden of compliance. They also believe that free sharing of information among affiliates allows for quicker, more efficient, and less costly service to customers with less duplication of effort. Some privacy advocates take a strongly opposite view, feeling that the law was structured to make it easier for companies to trade in private data with little restriction, and note that many of the uses of data in affiliated companies fall outside the third-party opt-out provisions.

Interview officers at three local banks. Find out what products each bank has added to its services as the result of the passage of the Gramm-Leach-Bliley Act. What are the most popular and least popular new services? Compile your answers from the banks and write a report that summarizes the information you obtained.

Limits and Regulation

The Gramm-Leach-Bliley Act effectively supersedes state law, although it acknowledges the interest of states in "reasonable" regulation of the financial service industries. State commissions on banking, insurance, and securities still have jurisdiction on some practices, but may not discriminate in licensing against affiliated firms. Other controls come from agencies directly involved in the businesses themselves, such as the Securities and Exchange Commission and the Federal Trade Commission.

Why did the Glass-Steagall Act limit the participation of banks in a wide range of financial businesses? What was the major result of the Gramm-Leach-Bliley Act?

_____

_____

_____

WORKSHOP

In groups, make a list of as many types of insurance as you can. Identify several possible providers of these policies by name.

INSURANCE AND BROKERAGE PRODUCTS

The GLBA essentially repealed the Glass-Steagall Act, sweeping away legal barriers that had separated the securities, insurance, and banking industries. Modernizing the financial services industry, the law allows for a new corporate structure, called the financial holding company (FHC), and allows banks, securities firms, and insurance companies to diversify and/or merge their businesses if they so choose. The stated purpose of the GLBA is to promote competition. Banks, therefore, can offer a complete range of insurance products for individuals and businesses.

The Workings of Insurance

The primary goal of insurance is to allocate the risks of loss from the individual to a great number of people, or to protect holders against financial disaster. Each individual pays a *premium* into a pool from which losses are paid. Whether the particular individual suffers the loss or not, the premium is not returnable. Thus, when a home is destroyed by fire, the loss is spread to the people contributing to the pool. In general, insurance companies are the safekeepers of the premiums. The government and the courts use a heavy hand in ensuring these companies are regulated and fair to the consumer.

Personal Insurance Products

Operating as full-service financial institutions, banks offer a full spectrum of insurance products.

- **Auto Insurance** Auto insurance protects the owner from the risk of injury to people and damage to vehicles or other property in the event of an accident. It can also protect the owner against loss or damage through theft, vandalism, or natural disasters.

- **Credit Insurance** This insurance, sometimes called *credit life*, is designed to repay the balance of a loan in the event the borrower dies before the insured loan is repaid.

- **Disability Insurance** Disability insurance pays benefits when the holder is unable to earn a living because of illness or injury. Most disability policies pay a benefit that replaces part of the disabled holder's earned income.

- **Life Insurance** Various types are available, as shown in the following table.

TYPES OF LIFE INSURANCE POLICIES

Policy Type	Characteristics	Suitable For
Decreasing Term	Level premium, decreasing coverage, no cash value	Financial obligations that reduce with time, such as as mortgages or other amortized loans
Annual Renewable Term	Increasing premium, level coverage, no cash value	Financial obligations that remain constant for a short or intermediate period, such as income during a minor's dependency
Whole Life	Level premium, level coverage, cash value that typically increases based on insurance company's general asset account portfolio performance	Long-term obligations, such as surviving spouse lifetime income needs, estate liquidity, death taxes, funding retirement needs
Universal Life	Level or adjustable premium, level or adjustable coverage, cash value that increases based on the performance of certain assets held in the company's general account	Long-term obligations, such as estate growth, estate liquidity, death taxes, funding retirement needs, and so forth
Variable Life and Variable Universal Life	Level or adjustable premium, level coverage (can be increased by positive investment performance), cash that are directed to a choice of investment accounts (bond, stock, money market, and so forth) by the policy owner	Long-term obligations, such as estate growth, estate liquidity, and death taxes, and so forth for the more active investor
Single-Premium Whole Life	Entire premium is paid at purchase, level coverage, cash values	Asset accumulation vehicle for long-term obligations, such as surviving spouse lifetime income needs, estate liquidity, death taxes, funding retirement needs

- **Health Insurance** The need for a comprehensive, high-quality health care program, equitably accessible to all residents of the United States, has been the topic of national debate for years, but no national policy has been legislated. Various health policies include the following.

    Traditional This type of policy allows holders to visit any doctor or hospital they want and receive coverage for any treatment covered under the policy. Premiums for traditional insurance tend to be higher than those for other plans.

HMO A health maintenance organization (HMO) is a health-care system that organizes doctors and hospitals in a network. An HMO's two basic features are that members must choose a primary care network physician who performs basic health checkups and approves visits to other specialized physicians, and members pay a set per-person fee that gives them access to the HMO's services.

PPO A preferred provider organization (PPO) is a collection of physicians and hospitals that agree to provide health-care at reduced cost to PPO members. PPOs limit health care costs without the restrictions of an HMO.

- **Homeowner's Insurance**
Homeowner's insurance is designed to protect against a wide range of potential disasters, such as fire, vandalism, and theft of property, as well as against lawsuits if someone is injured while on the owner's property.

- **Mortgage Disability Insurance**
Generally, if an illness or accidental injury renders an insured borrower disabled, mortgage disability insurance pays monthly home loan payments up to a specific amount.

- **Title Insurance** This policy type compensates the owner of real estate if his or her clear ownership of property is challenged.

Business Insurance

Whether for-profit or nonprofit, businesses need certain types of insurance, such as liability insurance, which is highly recommended for property and automobiles. Workers' Compensation is state-required insurance for any business with employees. The following briefly describes several types of business insurance.

- **Commercial Liability Insurance** Commercial liability insurance pays part or all of the damages for liability that the law applies to a business as well as the cost of defending the firm when a claim is made against it. Unprotected liability could cause financial hardship or bankruptcy.

- **Disability Insurance—Short-Term** Regular employees working 30 hours or more a week who become disabled are provided with a level of income protection for a short period of time, such as 90 days. Coverage is generally for a percentage of normal income, often as much as 90 percent.

- **Disability Insurance—Long-Term** This insurance is available to employees meeting short-term requirements but who have been disabled beyond short-term disability time limits. Coverage is for a percentage of income less than that normally covered by short-term disability, often 60 to 70 percent.

- **Health Insurance** Many firms allow employees to participate in group health insurance plans covering basic health care, sometimes including vision and dental care. The employer determines the plan's coverage and the portion of the cost, if any, that employees must pay for it.

TECH TALK

FIRST INTERNET BANK OF INDIANA

Based in Indianapolis, Indiana, First Internet Bank of Indiana (or First IB) is the first state-chartered Internet bank with accounts insured by the FDIC. It is the first "extended value online bank" to deliver a full range of real-time Internet banking products with personalized interactive services as well as offering competitive rates. "Real-time" means that transactions are reflected in the customer's accounts immediately. First IB's business model enables customers to facilitate Internet banking in a real-time environment and to empower users to better manage their own finances.

First Internet Bank was one of the earliest banks to allow customers to conduct bank-related business from their web-enabled cell phones. First IB customers can now check their account balances, transfer funds from one First IB account to another, view their last ten transactions, set up new electronic bill payments, change due dates, and alter amounts or cancel planned payments for the first time from their mobile phone or hand-held computer.

THINK CRITICALLY

How does the success of this bank reflect on changes in our society? Why might some people be hesitant to use a bank without an advertised address for a walk-in lobby? Would you use this bank? Why or why not?

- **Officers' Liability Insurance** This insurance protects the company from losses due to the company's directors' and officers' alleged or actual breach of duty, neglect, error, misstatement, misleading statement, omission, or act.

- **Property Insurance** Like individual policies, business insurance protects the policyholder against risk. Policies can be customized to meet the special risks the specific firm faces.

- **Workers' Compensation** This insurance pays for medical care and physical rehabilitation of workers injured in the performance of their job, and it helps to replace lost wages while they are unable to work.

Brokerage Services

Brokerage refers to bringing together parties interested in making a transaction, such as buying and selling shares of stock. A broker charges a fee to execute the transaction. Banks now offer full investment services.

What is an HMO?

_____

_____

_____

THINK CRITICALLY ●●●●●●●●●●●●●●●●●●●●●●●●

1. How did the Glass-Steagall Act restrict banking services?

_____

_____

_____

2. Why are banks now able to provide one-stop shopping to customers?

_____

_____

_____

3. Explain how insurance works.

_____

_____

_____

4. What is the difference between an HMO and a PPO?

_____

_____

_____

_____

MAKE CONNECTIONS ●●●●●●●●●●●●●●●●●●●●●●●

5. CONSUMER AFFAIRS Consumers can use the Internet to do comparison pricing. Identify four different brokerage firms that offer Internet purchases. What percentage of the sale is the company's brokerage fee?

_____

_____

_____

_____

_____

6. SOCIAL STUDIES The GLBA has brought dramatic changes to the banking industry. Some people contend that these changes make sharing private data among companies too easy. How did the public communicate this concern to government officials? What has the government done to prevent banks from sharing nonpublic personal information? Has this action been totally successful?

_____

_____

_____

_____

_____

_____

_____

LESSON 9.3
CASH MANAGEMENT ••••••••••••••••••••••••••••••

GOALS

EXPLAIN why banks are in a good position to offer cash management services

LIST several cash management services banks perform for businesses

SYSTEM IN PLACE FOR CASH MANAGEMENT

Every business, no matter how large or small, needs to disburse and collect cash to complete business transactions. Banks are in a good position to provide cash management services to businesses for a number of reasons.

• **Experience** Banks have decades of experience in managing cash.

• **Business Knowledge** In conducting their own operations, banks have experienced the same opportunities and challenges that all businesses face, and they understand the nature and implementation of practices and policies that apply to efficient cash management for all businesses.

• **Technology** Banks have experience in applying technology to their cash management practices. Banks can afford to invest in the applicable

Amelia Lopez recently attended a seminar on outsourcing. Since her business recently began to sell its products in South America, the firm is growing, and its needs have changed. She thinks that outsourcing her accounting services might be a wise thing to do. How could this help Amelia in managing her growing business? What advantages and disadvantages should she consider?

technology and develop expertise in its use that most individual firms cannot. Banks allow other companies to tap into these efficiencies through the bank's cash management services.

- **Industry Expertise** Through their dealings with specific companies over the years, individual banks have developed expert knowledge of the practices of various industries. They can offer this expertise to other companies with similar needs.

Businesses recognize that constant changes in the financial industry and the regulatory world have increased their need to proactively manage their cash, but with continuous changes so hard to keep up with, they find they no longer have the knowledge and experience to do so. It is not unusual for organizations that have had effective cash management systems to seek ways to improve them.

CHECK**POINT**

Why is a bank in a good position to offer cash management services?

_____

_____

CASH MANAGEMENT

Sara Lee, a well-known manufacturer and marketer of high-quality, brand name products, has taken the practice of outsourcing to the extreme. The company now contracts with outside suppliers, bakeries, and distributors to develop, prepare, and deliver its food products.

Firms' focus on the "bottom line" has caused them to evaluate all activities they perform and to identify those that do not add value to the product or service they offer. For many reasons, one company can make a product or provide a service less expensively than other firms can. *Outsourcing* refers to a firm's practice of having an outside party supply a product or service that the firm had been producing or performing itself. The firm can hire a business that specializes in human resources, for example, rather than directly hiring individuals knowledgeable in this field. Savings would include inside employees' salary packages, including paid vacation and sick days, benefits such as health insurance, and various payroll taxes. The firm can devote the savings obtained to the activities that differentiate it. For example, a greeting card company might hire a new artist.

Outsourcing may be a practical approach for companies with seasonal/fluctuating needs that make keeping full-time employees impractical for some tasks. The Sutter Consortium reports that firms outsource for the following reasons.

29% Difficulty hiring skilled professionals
20% Lack of in-house skills
14% Budget
12% Business changes
12% CIO/senior management mandate
 7% Reorganization
 2% Downsizing

Accounting Services

Frequently outsourced accounting services include the following.

- **Payroll** All functions related to paying wages to employees. These include calculating deductions, paying employees, filing payroll taxes, and all related record keeping.

- **Accounts Payable** Short-term debt from purchases on credit that must be paid to suppliers of goods or services typically within 60 days or less. The bank sees that these are paid for the client at the appropriate time and that the client's creditor account records are kept up to date.

- **Accounts Receivable** Money due for services performed or merchandise sold on credit. The bank collects these and maintains the customer account records for the client.

Bank Collection Services

Bank collection services expedite the collection of a company's receivables, enabling it to collect funds and integrate information easily and cost effectively. Various products, including the following, accomplish this objective.

- **Deposit Services** Service that allows customers to make deposits in various ways. The bank will maintain and manage deposit accounts for the client in a way to minimize balances in noninterest-bearing accounts and maximize balances in interest-bearing accounts.

- **Lockbox Service** Service that allows accounts receivable payments to be sent directly to the bank, accelerating the conversion of receivables into usable cash.

- **Zero-Balance Accounts (ZBAs)** Accounts that start each business day at zero balance and are related to a central account. Throughout the day, transactions are debited or credited as payments are made or received. At the end of the day they are reconciled with the central account and are returned once again to a zero balance. This type of program ensures that funds do not stand idle in multiple accounts and eliminates the need for the customer to monitor accounts and initiate account transfers.

- **Automated Clearing House (ACH) Network** This is a highly reliable and efficient nationwide batch-oriented electronic funds transfer system. It is governed by rules that provide for the interbank clearing of electronic payments for participating depository financial institutions. The American Clearing House Association, Federal Reserve, Electronic Payments Network, and Visa act as central clearing facilities through which financial institutions transmit or receive ACH entries. The bank's use of this network helps it provide cash collections and transfer services efficiently.

Information Services

Electronic Data Interchange (EDI) is generically defined as the computer-to-computer exchange of business information through standard interfaces. Today, more than 50,000 U.S. companies are estimated to have implemented EDI. Banks can advise companies concerning this interchange and provide the services to the firms.

Credit Card Services

Credit has changed significantly in the past two decades. Once the only way to "charge" a purchase at Sears was to use a Sears card to charge to a Sears account. Now customers can also use various credit cards, such as Visa, MasterCard, and Discover. More firms are outsourcing the management of their credit services, which includes taking applications for credit, checking applicants' credit ratings, processing point-of-sale credit transactions, and providing credit information. Using a bank credit card shifts the risk of collecting the payment from the business to the bank.

Credit card processing primarily occurs electronically, although some companies still use paper forms. A business processes a customer's purchase with a specific card using a purchased or rented point-of-sale terminal, which links the business to the bank. The bank credits the business's account for the amount of the sale. Banks charge for this service, ranging from two to ten percent of credit sales processed. In choosing a bank, the merchant considers the length of time the bank takes to credit its account, the bank's charge for the service, and the availability of the card to customers.

Stored-Value Card The *stored-value card* is often called an *electronic purse* because of how it functions. It is also called a *smart card* when it carries capabilities for data storage in a microchip within the card. Unlike the credit card and the ATM card, which derive their purchasing power from a computer at the bank, the stored-value card itself contains a reservoir of purchasing power. It works like a traveler's check in that the consumer pays up front, gets a card to authorize a certain amount of purchasing power, and spends down that value over time. Prepaid phone cards are an example of an early use of stored-value cards. They permit the user to prepay the charges for long-distance phone calls. Now stored-value cards are used for everything from public transportation to grocery shopping. The Congressional Budget Office has estimated the potential market for stored-value cards to be roughly $20 billion a year. Banks can be instrumental in helping businesses set up smart card programs. The same banking technology systems that

BANKING MATH CONNECTION

A small business was able to make a large sale only by accepting a note of $8,075 plus a $925 service fee to be paid in 12 months. Shortly afterward, the business unexpectedly had to replace an expensive machine four years ahead of schedule. The business was short of cash and arranged for a local bank to purchase the debt for a factoring fee of 3 percent. How much will the business receive from the bank?

SOLUTION

First calculate the factoring fee. The formula for calculating this is

(Principal + Service charge) × Factoring fee percent = Factoring fee
($8,075 + $925) × 0.03 = $270

Then subtract the fee from the total amount owed.

Amount owed − Factoring fee = Amount received from bank
$9,000 − $270 = $8,730

transfer balances from buyer accounts to seller accounts with the use of debit cards is used to transfer amounts from prepaid cards to client accounts.

Credit analysis is a cash management process frequently outsourced. Banks are skilled at determining the creditworthiness of loan applicants and can use these skills to evaluate potential client credit customers.

Capital Services

Businesses must often commit large sums of money (capital) to projects that will continue well into the future. Capital expenses usually involve the purchase of things that last more than a year. Examples of firms' capital purchases are large printing presses, equipment to implement environmental regulations, expansion into a new territory, and a fleet of new trucks. Many firms aren't able to perform the complex analyses necessary for making the decisions, so they turn to their bankers for help.

Capital Investments Capital investments differ from investments in stocks and bonds in one significant way. Stocks and bonds can be sold on an organized market for cash. A capital investment requires a much longer time to convert to cash during which time the firm might incur additional expenses, such as building or equipment maintenance. Making capital investment decisions requires the use of numerous analytical tools and techniques for evaluating if the investment will result in the desired profits for the company. Banks have the expertise to use these techniques in advising their clients. Establishing capital budgets is also part of the service.

Financing Once capital investment projects are decided, banks can advise their clients of the best ways to finance while keeping the company's debt-to-equity ratios at the desired level.

Factoring A capital service provided by banks, *factoring* is the practice of buying debt at a discount. A firm that needs cash immediately can sell a debt owed to it. The purchasing bank provides this service for a fee, often a percentage of the amount owed. In making its decision to provide this service, the bank evaluates the ability of the firm's customer to pay the debt. The customer pays the amount owed to the bank. Factoring dramatically improves a company's cash flow so it may meet current financial obligations.

Bank Outsourcing

Many businesses outsource cash management services to banks. Many banks, in turn, may outsources services as well. For example, ALLTELL Information Services, based in Little Rock, Arkansas, provides information processing management and professional consulting to many financial institutions, from community banks to mega banks and mortgage lenders to computer finance companies. ALLTELL's systems and supporting business processes are at the foundation of some of the world's most successful financial services organizations.

Working in small groups, choose a type of business and define its capital expenses in terms of capital investments your business might need to make. Assign dollar amounts to each possible investment.

Explain the use of a stored-value card.

_____

_____

THINK CRITICALLY ●●●●●●●●●●●●●●●●●●●●●●●●

1. Many firms now outsource activities that they once performed themselves. What are the advantages of this?

_____

_____

_____

_____

2. Explain how credit card sales are charged electronically.

_____

_____

_____

_____

_____

3. What puts banks in a position to offer cash management services?

_____

_____

_____

_____

4. What is the EDI service that banks offer?

_____

_____

_____

_____

MAKE CONNECTIONS ●●●●●●●●●●●●●●●●●●●●

5. **TECHNOLOGY** Many banking functions are offered over the Internet.
Choose one of the services discussed in this lesson and research its
availability over the Internet. Prepare a written, oral, or computer presentation that discusses how these services are purchased on the Internet,
describes the way the service is performed, and includes the fees
involved.

6. **COMMUNICATION** Contact several local businesses and find out
whether they outsource any of the accounting services discussed in this
lesson. Determine the reason(s) they do or do not outsource. Compile
your results as a class.

_____

_____

_____

_____

_____

_____

_____

LESSON 9.4
TRUSTS

GOALS

EXPLAIN what trust services are

IDENTIFY important types of trust services banks provide

WHAT ARE TRUST SERVICES?

The concept of trusts dates back some seven hundred years to Medieval England. At its simplest, a **trust** is an arrangement by which one party holds property on behalf of another party for certain defined purposes. Banks are well versed in providing trust services to their clients. Banks typically have trust departments whose staff understand all types of trusts and their advantages and disadvantages and have experience in setting up and administering trusts to meet their clients' needs. Banks advise clients on the various types of trusts, which are discussed in the next section.

Terminology related to trusts is somewhat specialized, and you should understand the terms on the next page.

BANKING Scene

Now that Amelia Lopez's business is successful, she thinks it's time to start planning for her family's financial future. Her two daughters plan to go to expensive colleges. She also wants to make sure that she and her husband will be comfortable during retirement. Amelia realizes that she will need to plan carefully to minimize the tax consequences on her estate when she dies. What are some of the options she should consider? Could IRAs meet her needs? What should Amelia know about estate planning?

- **Donor**, or *settlor*, is the person who creates a trust.
- **Beneficiary** is the person for whose benefit the property is held.
- **Corpus**, or *res*, refers to the property that is held. Sometimes a distinction is made as to the *principal*, which is the property that is held in trust, and the *income* that the principal produces.

What is a trust?

_____

_____

TRUST SERVICE PRODUCTS

In addition to assisting a client in planning how to provide for financial needs during that person's employment years, banks offer advice regarding client's retirement requirements and for passing on his or her assets upon death. The following are various types of trust products.

Retirement Planning

Various products are available to help individuals plan and save for their retirement. An **IRA** (individual retirement account) is a great way to save for retirement. There are two kinds of IRAs—traditional and Roth. Funds are invested in a traditional IRA on a before-tax basis, which allows the earnings on the investment to compound on a tax-deferred basis. This means that the money invested in a traditional IRA isn't taxed until it is withdrawn after age $59^1/2$. There are penalties for early withdrawal. You must begin withdrawals from a traditional IRA beginning at age $70^1/2$. Beginning January 1, 1998, the Roth IRA became available. This investment is made with after-tax dollars. As long as the assets have remained inside the account for five years, all earnings and principal can be withdrawn totally tax-free after age $59^1/2$. Unlike a traditional IRA, Roth IRA funds do not have to be withdrawn at age $70^1/2$. The Economic Growth and Tax Relief Reconciliation Act of 2001 made changes to the amounts that an individual can invest in either a traditional or a Roth IRA. In 2002, individuals can invest up to $3,000 a year, and, if age 50 or over, $3,500 a year.

Another retirement plan, the **401(k) plan**, allows employees to make tax-deferred contributions to a trust and direct their funds to be invested among a variety of choices, getting their money back at departure or retirement. Many companies match the employee investment, usually at between 25 and 75 cents per dollar, to a defined maximum (such as 6 percent of pay).

A **variable annuity** is an investment that offers an opportunity for tax-deferred growth. It combines the opportunity for tax-deferral with a choice of portfolios and the flexibility to vary annual contributions according to the investors' needs or market conditions. Many people find variable annuities to be a good complement to other tax-deferred retirement investments such as IRAs and 401(k)s.

A family can save tax free for its children's education through Coverdell Education Savings Accounts (ESAs), once called *Education IRAs*. Contributions to an ESA can be made on behalf of a child under age 18 for education expenses. As of 2002, the annual contribution increased from $500 to $2,000.

Estate Planning

Estate planning is the process by which an individual or family arranges the transfer of assets in anticipation of death. An **estate** is the total property, real (real estate) and personal (all other possessions, such as automobiles, jewelry, and bank accounts) that an individual owns. The cornerstone of any estate plan is a **will**, a document by which the individual gives instructions as to what is to happen upon his or her death in regard to property and remains. An estate plan seeks to preserve the maximum amount of wealth possible for the intended beneficiaries and to provide flexibility for the individual prior to death. Federal and state tax laws are major considerations in estate planning.

    Probate is a court proceeding that settles an estate's final debts and formally passes legal title to property from the decedent to his or her heirs. It is initiated in the county of the decedent's legal residence at death. Wills must undergo formal probate administration, which can last two years or more, depending on the size and complexity of the estate. Court permission is needed to buy and sell assets, and beneficiaries usually must wait until the probate is concluded to receive the bulk of their inheritance. There are measures that may be taken to avoid assets being tied up in probate, such as naming beneficiaries for retirement accounts and placing assets in a living trust.

Estate Settlement

Estate settlement generally involves the following.

- *Identifying and valuing the estate assets.* An **executor** or *fiduciary* (the person named in the will to administer the estate) must identify all assets in the estate, including securities, business interests, and retirement plans, and determine their value. The executor arranges for professional appraisals of such items as real estate, artwork, and jewelry. If there is no will, the court will appoint an executor.

- *Paying creditors, estate expenses, and taxes.* The executor must ensure that the estate has sufficient cash to pay legitimate creditors and related estate expenses, including taxes. In fulfilling this role, the executor may have to decide to sell securities or other assets to cover expenses.

- *Preparing and filing the necessary tax documents with Federal and/or state authorities.* Record keeping must be exemplary to ensure that all documents are present, accurate, and complete. The executor must file all documents with the appropriate courts and other agencies in accordance with specific requirements and deadlines.

- *Distributing assets to beneficiaries.* The executor must make timely decisions concerning the distribution of estate assets in a prudent and efficient manner.

Testamentary Trusts

Testamentary trusts are established by a will and take effect at the donor's death. They receive the assets of the estate to hold and manage for the benefit of the heirs.

ETHICS IN ACTION

Banks have the ethical responsibility to inform customers in a clear manner on subjects such as the customers' rights and obligations as well as any and all benefits and risks of the products and services provided to them.

THINK CRITICALLY

What are some things you believe a banker should tell a prospective customer about the risks related to retirement planning? What are some things customers should do to be sure they are making informed decisions?

As a class, make a list of national charitable organizations that you believe would be proper recipients of CRTs.

Charitable Remainder Trusts

A *charitable remainder trust (CRT)* is an irrevocable trust designed to convert the highly appreciated assets of a *trustor*—the person who sets up the trust—into a lifetime income stream without generating estate and capital gains taxes. CRTs have become very popular in recent years because they not only represent a valuable tax-advantaged investment but also enable the trustor to provide a gift to one or more charities. A CRT can potentially

- Eliminate immediate capital gains taxes on the sale of appreciated assets.
- Reduce estate taxes that heirs might have to pay upon the trustor's death by as much as 55 percent.
- Reduce current income taxes with an income tax deduction.
- Increase the trustor's spendable income during lifetime.
- Create a charitable gift.
- Avoid probate and maximize the assets the trustor's family will receive.

Living Trusts

In simple terms, a **living trust** is a legal document that provides an expedient way to transfer property at a person's death. Generally, living trusts are established during an individual's lifetime and can be modified or changed while that person is still alive. For this reason, a living trust is set up on a "revocable" basis. The *revocable trust provision* means that while the person lives, he or she still has control of all of the property that has been transferred into the trust and can sell it, spend it, or give it away. The trust does not transfer to the beneficiary until the trustor dies. Living trusts speed up the process by which property moves to designated beneficiaries upon the trustor's death. One of the advantages of a living trust is that it avoids probate, although it may not offer the tax benefits related to CRTs.

What are the responsibilities of an estate executor?

_____

_____

THINK CRITICALLY ●●●●●●●●●●●●●●●●●●●●●●●

1. Why would a person want to set up a trust?

_____

_____

_____

_____

_____

2. Why would a person want to avoid having his or her estate go through probate?

_____

_____

_____

3. What information would you need to know if you were interested in setting up a living trust?

_____

_____

_____

4. Why might people avoid deciding how to dispose of their assets at their death?

_____

_____

_____

_____

MAKE CONNECTIONS ●●●●●●●●●●●●●●●●●●●●

5. COMMUNICATION Talk to adult family members or friends about the type of retirement plan(s) that they have. Discuss at least four different retirement plans. Prepare a one-page report. Mention any concerns that your friends and family members have about the plans.

6. PROBLEM SOLVING Use your Internet search engine to find information on the topic of estate tax repeal. List the advantages and disadvantages of this legislation.

_____

_____

_____

_____

_____

_____

_____

_____

CHAPTER SUMMARY

LESSON 9.1 International Banking

A. Types of institutions engaged in international banking include branches and agencies of foreign banks operating within the United States, U.S. banks offering international services, edge corporations, and correspondent banks.

B. Banks offering international services help their customers negotiate, finance, ship, transfer, and collect their international accounts.

LESSON 9.2 Insurance and Brokerage

A. As a result of the Gramm-Leach-Bliley Act, banks have entered a new era in which they are able to provide financial services not previously allowed.

B. Personal insurance, business insurance, and brokerage services are now available through banks.

LESSON 9.3 Cash Management

A. Banks possess the experience, the knowledge of business and industry, and the technology to efficiently provide cash management services to clients.

B. Banks assist their clients in managing their cash by providing accounting, information, credit card, and capital services.

LESSON 9.4 Trusts

A. Trusts are financial planning vehicles that arrange for the transfer of property from one entity to another under specific circumstances.

B. Retirement planning, estate planning and settlement, and trust establishment and supervision are among the trust services clients seek from their banks.

VOCABULARY BUILDER

a. 401(k) plan
b. correspondent bank
c. country risk
d. currency risk
e. edge corporation
f. estate
g. executor
h. foreign exchange rate
i. IRA
j. letter of credit
k. living trust
l. probate
m. trust
n. variable annuity
o. will

Choose the term that best fits the definition. Write the letter of the answer in the space provided. Some terms may not be used.

_____ **1.** Political, legal, social, and economic conditions that affect international businesses

_____ **2.** Arrangement by which one party holds property on behalf of another party

_____ **3.** Court proceeding that settles estates

_____ **4.** The value of one currency in terms of another

_____ **5.** Federally chartered institution allowed to engage only in international banking

_____ **6.** Person named in a will to administer the estate

_____ **7.** Provides a way to transfer property at a person's death

_____ **8.** Degree of risk posed by variations in exchange rates between countries

_____ **9.** Act a as a point of contact for other banks that do not have a branch, agency, subsidiary, or corporation in the host country

REVIEW CONCEPTS

POINT YOUR BROWSER

banking.swep.com

10. List four ways that banks seek to meet their clients' international banking needs.

_____

_____

_____

11. Describe the functions of the World Bank and the International Finance Corporation.

_____

_____

_____

_____

12. How does a letter of credit work?

_____

_____

_____

_____

13. How did the Gramm-Leach-Bliley Act change banking institutions?

_____

_____

_____

14. Why might firms seek to outsource products or services that they may have been previously producing or performing within their own organizations?

_____

_____

_____

_____

15. List reasons why businesses seek expert help when making capital investment decisions.

_____

_____

_____

_____

_____

_____

16. Give three examples of retirement planning services.

_____

_____

_____

17. What is the probate process?

_____

_____

_____

_____

18. List four advantages that a charitable remainder trust provides.

_____

_____

_____

_____

APPLY WHAT YOU LEARNED

19. How does the USA Patriot Act of 2001 attempt to stop the financing of terrorist activities?

_____

_____

_____

20. How does the term "one-stop-shopping" apply to banks?

_____

_____

_____

21. How does a stored-value card work?

_____

_____

_____

_____

_____

22. Name four types of trust services.

_____

_____

_____

_____

23. Describe factors that impact foreign exchange rates.

_____

_____

MAKE CONNECTIONS ● ● ● ● ● ● ● ● ● ● ● ● ● ● ● ● ● ● ●

24. SOCIAL STUDIES Laws often result from what is happening in the society. Write a two-page report on how the banking industry was affected by the Glass-Steagall Act and the Gramm-Leach-Bliley Act. Discuss how each act was a reaction to current events of the time.

25. POLITICAL SCIENCE How did the Enron crisis affect current and former employees' retirement planning? Do research on the Internet to find out how the pensions of people other than Enron employees were affected.

_____

_____

_____

26. CURRENT EVENTS Discuss the economic environment in the twenty-first century in terms of what makes it important for banks to advise their customers in the international arena.

_____

_____

_____

_____

_____

27. COMMUNICATION Interview an executive of a local bank on the subject of a particular insurance product. Get detailed information about how the product protects the consumer. Present your findings to the class in an oral report. Jot down ideas for interview questions here.

_____

_____

28. BANKING MATH Find the current value of a Japanese yen (¥) as compared to a Chinese yuan. What is the cost of goods valued at 70,000 ¥ in yuan?

_____

_____

29. RESEARCH Using the Internet, find out more about The World Bank and the International Finance Corporation. List additional functions of both institutions.

_____

_____

_____

_____

_____

Photo Credits

Cover photo © Phil and Jim Bliss/SIS
4: © CORBIS
6: © CORBIS
36: (321581) Rob Bartee
40: © Bettmann/CORBIS
41: © CORBIS
44: ©CORBIS
46: (384439) Stock Montage
50: ©CORBIS
84: © CORBIS
94: © CORBIS
110: © CORBIS
116: © CORBIS
123: © CORBIS
128: © CORBIS
130: © CORBIS
134: © CORBIS
136: © CORBIS
154: © CORBIS
157: © EyeWire
160: © CORBIS
163: © EyeWire
All other photos © Getty Images/ PhotoDisc